Historically, the best barometer of the state of climbing has been alpinism. And the last stylistic climax in alpine climbing came in the mid- to late 1980s when many of the 8000-meter peaks were climbed in single-push style, often by new routes. Such climbing was termed "night-naked" by Voytek Kurtyka; he, Jean Troillet, Pierre-Allain Steiner, and Erhard Loretan were at the center of adapting this bivouac-less style to the peaks of the Himalaya.

—Steve House

NIGHT NAKED

• • • • • •

A CLIMBER'S AUTOBIOGRAPHY

ERHARD LORETAN

WITH JEAN AMMANN

Foreword by
DAVID ROBERTS

Translated from the French by
CORINNE MCKAY

LEGENDS AND LORE SERIES

**MOUNTAINEERS
BOOKS**

Mountaineers Books is the publishing division of The Mountaineers, an organization founded in 1906 and dedicated to the exploration, preservation, and enjoyment of outdoor and wilderness areas.

MOUNTAINEERS BOOKS

1001 SW Klickitat Way, Suite 201, Seattle, WA 98134
800.553.4453, www.mountaineersbooks.org

Original French-language edition *Les 8000 rugissants* first published by Editions La Sarine, Fribourg Suisse

Distributed in the United Kingdom by Cordee, www.cordee.co.uk
19 18 17 16   1 2 3 4 5

Layout: Jen Grable
Series design: Karen Schober
Cover photograph: © Yaniz Aramendia

Library of Congress Cataloging-in-Publication Data
Names: Loretan, Erhard, 1959-2011. | Ammann, Jean.
Title: Night naked : A climber's autobiography / by Erhard Loretan, with Jean Ammann ; foreword by David Roberts ; translated from the French by Corinne McKay.
Other titles: 8000 rugissants. English
Description: Seattle, WA : Mountaineers Books, [2016] | "Original French-language edition Les 8000 rugissants first published by Editions La Sarine Fribourg Suisse"--T.p. verso.
Identifiers: LCCN 2016019587| ISBN 9781680510065 (trade paper : Alk. paper) |
  ISBN 9781680510072 (ebook)
Subjects: LCSH: Loretan, Erhard, 1959-2011. |
  Mountaineers--Switzerland--Biography. | Mountaineering--Himalaya Mountains--History. |
Himalaya Mountains--Description and travel.
Classification: LCC GV199.92.L667 A3 2017 | DDC 796.522092 [B] --dc23
LC record available at https://lccn.loc.gov/2016019587

Mountaineers Books titles may be purchased for corporate, educational, or other promotional sales, and our authors are available for a wide range of events. For information on special discounts or booking an author, contact our customer service at 800-553-4453 or mbooks@mountaineersbooks.org.

♻ Printed on recycled paper

ISBN (paperback): 978-1-68051-006-5
ISBN (ebook): 978-1-68051-007-2

I am not talking about living dangerously.
Such words are meaningless to me.
The toreador does not stir me to enthusiasm.
It is not danger I love. I know what I love. It is life.

—from *Wind, Sand and Stars*
by Antoine de Saint-Exupéry

CONTENTS

FOREWORD

IN THE EARLY 1980S, TWO of the greatest mountaineers in the world went head-to-head in one of the fiercest competitions in climbing history. The only trouble was, neither man would admit there *was* such a competition.

The race was to be the first human being to reach the summits of the fourteen highest peaks in the world—all those above the "magical" line of 8000 meters (26,247 feet). The two men could not have been more different in temperament and background. By 1980, an Italian from the German-speaking South Tyrol, Reinhold Messner, was already the most famous climber in the world—thanks not only to such bold feats as the first ascent of Everest without bottled oxygen (with the Austrian Peter Habeler in 1978), but also to the numerous books he had written and the massive sponsorship he commanded.

In contrast, the Pole Jerzy Kukuczka climbed in relative obscurity, scraping together through such onerous jobs as painting church steeples the dough to finance each successive bare-bones expedition. As both men closed in on the prize, Messner bagged a number of 8000ers by their easiest routes, while Kukuczka's purism dictated such stunning ascents as K2 by a new route on the south face and Annapurna in winter.

Messner had begun his own campaign back in 1970 on Nanga Parbat, when, in a still-controversial summit thrust, he topped out with his brother Günther, who would lose his life in a desperate descent of the opposite side of the mountain. Kukuczka launched his campaign in 1979, on Lhotse. So intense was the Pole's pursuit of 8000ers, however, that he almost caught up to his rival. In October 1986, Messner closed out the race on Lhotse. Only a year later, Kukuczka would complete his own circuit on Shishapangma.

As different as the temperaments of the two men were the books they wrote about their campaigns on the 8000ers. Messner celebrated his own deeds in a somewhat mystical memoir called *All Fourteen 8000ers*, as well as in individual tomes devoted to specific expeditions. Kukuczka laconically narrated his astounding career in a 189-page book called *My Vertical World*. Seldom in the history of adventure has a great explorer recounted his exploits in so understated and elliptical a fashion.

After Lhotse, Messner turned away from the mountains and toward other kinds of adventure. Today he presides over the mountaineering world as its éminence grise and arbiter of all controversies.

Kukuczka's passion was undimmed after Shishapangma. In October 1989, he was killed in a fall when a rope broke near the summit of the south face of Lhotse, on his daring attempt on what was then being hailed as "the last great problem" of the Himalaya. He had completed his memoir only months before.

Nine years would pass before another climber got to the summit of all fourteen 8000ers. As the talented Swiss mountaineer Erhard Loretan contemplated becoming the third man to grasp that prize, he saw it as an almost meaningless goal. As he writes in this book, "I couldn't imagine that, more than eight years after Kukuczka and nine years after Messner, there could be anyone on earth, other than my brother and my mom, who would care about the third person to climb all of the 8000ers."

Yet in the autumn of 1995, a competition even keener than that waged between Kukuczka and Messner claimed the Himalayan stage, as the Frenchman Benoît Chamoux showed up on Kangchenjunga at the same time and on the same route as Loretan. Both men had thirteeen 8000ers under their belts, and both were determined to get to the summit first.

In his memoir, Loretan paints his rival as a heavily financed, media-driven climbing star, in contrast to his own more laid-back character, relatively indifferent to fame. Ancient enmities between the French and the Swiss may have played their part here—in 1950, a number of Swiss commentators argued that the French under Mauruce Herzog had never reached the summit of Annapurna. There is little reason, however, to doubt Loretan's take on the Kangchenjunga duel. In one of the most riveting chapters, Loretan unrolls this mounting drama of tentative cooperation and bitter one-upmanship in all its sordid and ultimately tragic particulars.

Loretan's book about his own campaign, published by a small Swiss press in 1996 and for a long time out of print even in Switzerland, here appears in its first English-language edition. I got hold of a copy of the original—how, I forget—years ago, but only skimmed a few passages. It was not until Ed Viesturs and I collaborated on books about Annapurna (*The Will to Climb*) and Everest (*The Mountain*) that I sat down to read Loretan's chapters about his amazing climbs on those two Himalayan giants.

It did not take long for me to realize that I was reading one of the finest memoirs ever written by a mountaineer. And that, even more startlingly, the book was unique. Loretan's vision of life and climbing springs from some deep, Samuel Beckett–like sense of the absurd, invigorated all the same by a driving quest for joy and transcendence. I know of no other writing by an explorer that bears any resemblance to this high-wire performance.

Loretan's claim to lasting fame far outstrips his feat in becoming the third man to bag the fourteen 8000ers. His approaches to the great Himalayan mountains bespeak a blazing creativity, a willingness to embrace the Stygian depths of extreme risk, that virtually no climbers before him had exhibited. On Annapurna in 1984, with teammate Norbert Joos, Loretan solved the fiendishly long and complex east ridge, passing over three major subsummits before attaining the highest point. Cut off from all hope of reversing their route, Loretan and Joos plunged off the north side of Annapurna, with only a pocket postcard to indicate route lines, as they desperately sought the top of the Dutch Rib.

Theirs was a genuine survival epic. Yet Loretan narrates it as a voyage through a hallucinatory psychic landscape. A line from a song by the Nigerian-born British singer Sade, cycles and recycles through Loretan's scalded brain. He riffs:

It was a good question: Tell me why we're here, at 8020 meters, in
this cold that our bodies are trying to shake off the way a dog shakes
off fleas. I took off my boots, stuffed my overboots into my sleeping
bag, removed my two pairs of socks and tucked them next to my
stomach. I put a pair of down mittens on my feet, then my honey-
comb socks, and my feet felt something like warmth. I thought to
myself that the snow cave would be comfortable were it not for the
northwest wind rushing in and the powder snow swirling in after
it. It was my first night at 8000 meters and I was afraid of what
might happen because of this bivouac. We were at the point where
the smallest error could turn into a disaster. I wished that the refrain
"Tell me why . . ." would stop kicking around in my head.

  Tell me why, on Wednesday, October 24, we got out of our
sleeping bags, which were covered with blown-in snow; why did
we brush foot-sized clumps of snow off our boots; and why did we
continue on to the main summit, when the wind was more violent
than the previous day, and surely less violent than the next.

After a series of nightmarish close calls, the two men reach the foot of
the Dutch Rib, only to stumble upon a macabre scene:

  We saw the remains of a camp, and went to investigate in the hope
  of finding something to eat—anything more substantial than our
  Ovo Sport bars. Instead, we found the corpse of a Sherpa that a
  team from the year before had abandoned, with no burial other than
  a straightjacket of frost and no tomb other than the dome of the skies.

Later even on the verge of salvation, Loretan perceives his quest as an
absurdist journey:

  Back on firm ground, we could once again think beyond the pres-
  ent moment. We no longer had to use the word "tomorrow" with
  "if"—"Tomorrow, if the seracs hold . . ." "Tomorrow, if we find the

right line . . ." "Tomorrow, if we can get past the bulge . . ."—and
we caught ourselves using the future tense unconditionally.

Two years later, with his compatriot Jean Troillet, in a feat still unmatched three decades later, Loretan blitzed his way up Everest via the dangerous Japanese and Hornbein couloirs in the astounding time of forty-three hours roundtrip. In doing so, the two Swiss experts invented a new style of alpinism, climbing without tent or sleeping bag, bivouacking during the relatively warm afternoon hours, and pushing unroped through the night.

Once again, Loretan narrates this unprecedented deed as absurdist folly. Shortly before launching on the route, Loretan had nearly killed himself crashing his hang glider on the Rongbuk Glacier. As he tells it:

As I unfolded my paraglider, the wind was whipping. Even better!
The fierce wind would make up for the lack of lift at these alti-
tudes. I spent another hour and a half messing around with takeoff
attempts; the wind crumpled the wing as soon as I launched it.
Finally, a rainbow appeared and the wing filled with air. I took
off! The only difference between flying and falling is how long the
experience lasts: If you fall for a long time, that's flying; if you fly
very briefly, it's a fall. Those who saw my flight unanimously termed
it a fall. The doc confirmed that opinion when he examined me: "A
serious ankle sprain, trauma to the heel, sharp blow to the tarsal
bones, and damage to the calcaneum. Hopefully nothing's broken or
cracked. Complete rest for eight to ten days, then you can try putting
shoes on and see how it goes."

Undaunted, Loretan heals and heads up Everest. Of one bivouac in a snow hole, he writes, "In order to enjoy it, you would have to also enjoy elevators, spacecraft, submersibles, squash courts, and any activity that takes place in a tin can."

Approaching the summit, Loretan is seized with the "third man" hallucination—the conviction that he and Troillet are climbing upward with a shadowy companion right beside them, whom they can never quite confront.

On top, Troillet has his own hallucination, as he sees an electric transformer take shape in a distant cloud. "I knew for sure that there was no electrical transformer near Everest. . . ." Loretan writes. "We needed to go down." The two men glissade the Hornbein and Japanese couloirs as if they are playing in a neighborhood park.

By 2010, as I knew from the climbing scuttlebutt, Loretan had retreated into reclusive anonymity in the small town of Crésuz, not far from where he had grown up. As Viesturs and I started work on our Annapurna book, however, electrified by the account of his first ascent of the east ridge and traverse down the north face in *Les 8000 rugissants*, I managed to find an email address for Loretan. In French, I wrote, "[Your memoir] is one of the finest mountain books I have ever read." I added that his Annapurna climb was one of the most beautiful and impressive ascents ever made of the mountain, and that "Ed is truly stunned by your exploit." Might I ask Loretan for all kinds of further details about that adventure?

I got a single, characteristically modest response (in English): "Thanks for your mail. I think you are a bit exaggerating about our climb and book!!??"

Before we could plunge into an e-mail correspondence, however, I got the terrible news. On April 28, 2011—his 52nd birthday—Loretan fell to his death when his girlfriend made a misstep on an easy guide's route on the Grünhorn in the Bernese Alps and pulled him off the ridge. Roped together, both fell some 700 feet. She survived with no memory of the event after the slip of her boot. Loretan did not.

Once again, a great mountaineer had survived all the epic ordeals of his glory years, only to die thanks to a tiny mistake on a route that was trivial for him. (Kurt Albert, Lionel Terray, Toni Kinshofer, Jim Madsen, Jim Baldwin . . . the list is too long.)

Fortunately, before his death Loretan was interviewed by the French climbing journalist Charlie Buffet. In 2013, the biography—*Erhard Loretan: Une vie suspendue* (éditions Guérin)—appeared. Buffet's deep and affecting portrait of Loretan makes a fitting complement to this English-language translation of *Les 8000 rugissants*, *Night Naked*, and one can only hope that it also soon finds light in an English translation.

Buffet analyzes the fatal accident as well as it can be reconstructed. The slip of a single boot was an error of mere inches—hard ice scraped to the surface through crusty snow. More importantly, Buffet tells, without sensationalism or overbearing moral judgment, the tale of the great tragedy of Loretan's life. Unthinkingly, Loretan shook his seven-month-old son in order to stop his crying; the baby died as a result. "Shaken baby syndrome" was at the time still a little-known phenomenon. Loretan was given a four-month suspended sentence by a Swiss court, but the man's grief was boundless, and he made the details of his case public in the hope of preventing future deaths.

Many in the climbing world attributed Loretan's reclusiveness to this doleful event, and to his shame. But those who knew him best, like Jean Troillet, reported that Loretan was by instinct a private and retiring man.

The great revelation of Buffet's biography—a contradiction I am still trying to wrap my head around—is that far from the blithe absurdist treating his adventures as Quixotic jeux d'esprit, Loretan went at his mountains full of a fretful, anxious, insecure malaise. No great climber, it seems, ever doubted himself more. How the writing of his memoir reconciled that fundamental paradox in the man's soul, we shall never know.

Meanwhile, let us rejoice in the publication of *Night Naked* in English. The shining example of Loretan's visionary climbs will last for a long time, as will the inimitable recounting of them in his memoir. But as for the man himself—we shall not look upon his like again.

—David Roberts
January, 2016

PREFACE

When I perceive
His quiet energy makes him move
I do not doubt —
The sense of life is in rising.
When I watch him climbing
I understand —
The essence of rising is equilibrium.
And soon I comprehend —
The essence of equilibrium is creation.
I remember his strong fingers
And I muse — what is creation
That which creates and that created?

Suddenly a worrying news arrives
from him
And I grasp it —
God created the man to his resemblance.

Notes in my diary on Erhard
—*Voy [Voytek Kurtyka]*

"The Gastlosen are still my favorites, above all."
—Erhard Loretan

Hello Climbing, Goodbye Life!

"All climbers know that luck plays a critical role in mountaineering success when you're young. Anyone who was never young can cast the first stone."

—Anderl Heckmair

How old was I? It was in the sixties. Maybe I was seven? Ten? As I remember it, I was hanging from the branches of a tree that had fortuitously taken root right next to our house. I recall distinctly that as I hung there, several feet above the street, I was determined to earn my nickname: Everyone called me "the monkey." With that name, they hoped to cut me down to size as I moved upward and added a new dimension to my life. Nearly thirty years later, I still remember the feeling of well-being I experienced during every one of my aerial escapes: All my life, I have never felt as happy on Earth as when I'm getting closer to the sky. From the top of a tree, you can see everything around you. And you realize that the tree rises above a fleeting, temporary world. Higher still were the mountains. Our neighbors, the Dousses, would take me mushroom picking. I loved mushrooms, because they grew in the mountains. In Bulle, near my house on Abbé-Bovet Street—named after the priest who wrote the

Swiss folk song "Le Vieux Chalet," with its enchanting lyrics, "Up there on the mountain. . . ."—lived another neighbor, Michel Guidotti.

I saw Michel head out every weekend with his pack on, his gear jingling as he walked by. For me, as a child, mountaineering had a name: Michel. When I think back now on how attracted I was to the heights, how fascinated I was by Michel Guidotti, I feel that this was my destiny.

I was seven or eight when I decided that I would become a mountain guide. Someone with a better sense of drama might have come up with a catchy slogan, like "I will be Bonatti, or nothing." But I was satisfied with my childlike conviction: I would be a mountain guide. My commitment held a touch of reality—it was Michel who set off all geared up to confront the abyss—and a great deal of imagination: The serialized adaptation of [the classic mountaineering novel] *First on the Rope* had just been broadcast. Some people never get over *Ivanhoe*; for me, it was *First on the Rope*. Walter Scott versus Frison-Roche: There was no contest, in my eyes.

One day, my hero—perhaps uncomfortable with so much admiration—suggested putting my dreams into action. Michel Guidotti was going to take me up the 1829-meter Dent de Broc, by its west ridge! I was in heaven. Or, more correctly, in the entryway to heaven, where I didn't sleep a wink, imagining and reimagining the ascent of the mountain that taunted me from the other side of my window.

Twenty-five years went by between that ascent of the Dent de Broc's west ridge and my ascent of Kangchenjunga. I've forgotten the details. I know that there were three of us; Michel went first, I was in the middle, and Fred Sottas was third. I remember the physical shock of that first climb: I was shaking. It was as if, after years of metamorphosis, I had found my element; I felt as drunk as a caterpillar that, one fine morning, discovers it has wings. It was 1970. I had eleven years of life behind me and an introduction to the *Assez Difficile* (AD) rating when I made my vow to be faithful to the mountains.

That was the spark. I had been a runner; now I felt claustrophobic in a stadium, and track running lost all its appeal. My meager pocket money went to fattening the profits of the local sporting goods stores, and my mother lamented over my report cards as she watched her son trying to keep his balance on the tightrope of academia. School bored me compared to the newfound thrill of climbing. I was happy with a passing grade—early proof of my desire to push boundaries. But there was a notable exception! During my neglected school career, one book awoke the student in me. It was written by a professor with a crew cut, who always wore a jacquard sweater. The professor was Gaston Rébuffat. The book was *On Ice and Snow and Rock*. In it, one learns the ABCs of mountaineering; between maxims such as "To be able to really see, one must not only open one's eyes. One must, above all, open one's heart," it advises the student to meditate on the bowline and the beautifully named guide's knot. And thanks to my tree, on which I placed gear with as much care as a Russian expedition to Kangchenjunga, I moved from theory to practice. So I learned this profession on my own, with—to be fair—Gaston Rébuffat.

The Loretans come from Loèche-les-Bains, in the Swiss canton of Valais, but some of our ancestors felt the urge to migrate; they crossed the Gemmi Pass and have now lived in Kandersteg for two generations. My cousin Fritz Loretan, a mountain guide, was asked to serve as the caretaker of the Fründen hut, in the Bernese Oberland. In 1970, he hired me as his helper. Two months at 2500 meters: My dream come true. But the two months were only for the first year, because the next year, my mother—the sole parental authority in our family—decided that I would go to summer camp with my brother, Daniel. So after one month, my spirits dragging, I left the high ground of the Fründen hut for Lagrune-sur-Mer in Normandy. Someday, someone will have to explain to me why people are so passionate about returning to Normandy . . .

That oceanside exile lasted only one year, and then, every summer until 1974, I spent the two-month summer vacation at the Fründen hut. I made memories and grew strong by carrying loads, weighed down with forty-five pounds on my back. When I had finished with the caretaker work, I still had a few hours a day to myself, to apply Professor Rébuffat's teachings. On the little rock face above the hut, I spent hours placing pitons and setting up bivouacs. Sixty-five feet above the hikers but even closer to the sky, I did everything in my power to be like the heroes in the books I had read. From time to time, Fritz said to me, "Tomorrow, we're going climbing." After that,

I stopped living, or sleeping. I came back to life at our departure time. It was with Fritz, my cousin who was like a brother, that I did my first big climbs: the north face of the Doldenhorn (3645 meters, rated *Très Difficile*, or TD), the southwest ridge of the Fründenhorn (3368 meters, rated *Difficile*, or D), the east ridge of the Doldenhorn (rated D+). And we always climbed fast: four hours for the north face of the Doldenhorn, for example.

I gained experience. So much and so well that, once I got back home to Gruyère, the student replaced the teacher after a few hours one day, when the teacher got a little beaten up on the crux of the Marti route in the Gastlosen, the range of limestone peaks closest to where I lived. Partly due to the difficulty of the climb, partly due to the army having assaulted it for three weeks, Michel Guidotti met his match on the infamous Red Wall. Its few grade 5 [5.8–5.9] moves terrify beginners and contribute to the route's reputation. I watched my leader flailing, and suggested to him that I take the sharp end. As I asked the question, I was sure that the wall wouldn't defeat me. It was my first time leading. The rope now stretched downward between my legs, and I understood the role reversal that had just taken place. The knots were still there, but the safe zone seemed farther away. The pins seemed twice as far from each other. I finished the climb on lead. From then on I led, and there was pride in that kind of trust. It was a memorable day, even more so because I also met Vincent Charrière and Pierre Morand, who would soon join me in all my endeavors. They were fourteen, the magic age that allowed them to join the youth section of the Swiss Alpine Club. I was only thirteen. Mom, why was I born a year too late?

The next year, in 1973, I was at the Gruyère secondary school when I saw two silhouettes approaching; I recognized them from the Gastlosen. Vincent Charrière and Pierre Morand asked me if I wanted to join their group. Along with Jean-Maurice Chappalley, they were a climbing team of three. But three was a hard number to divide in two without jeopardizing a person's health, so they thought that a group of four would be more practical. "Would you like to climb with us?" I felt as if I had been accepted by my peers; I was soaring with the angels. I agreed, without asking my mother. I would have to convince her. It wasn't easy, but I think she soon understood that the mountains would become the guiding force in my life.

From then on, I was pulled between two worlds—the high world and the low world, heaven and hell. My mother used this situation as an instructional tool: If I didn't fulfill my responsibilities during the week, I was sentenced to stay in the lowlands for the weekend. Hell! The weekend, shimmering at the end of five long days of school, had become my reason to live. And the five days of waiting only fanned my desire. If I had a half-day free, I went climbing; if I had an hour, I devoured a book about the mountains. I climbed everything in my path: the pillars of a railroad bridge, the brick walls of the buildings I passed in town, rock slabs. All these moments stolen from my daily routine fueled my passion. I would have done anything to go to the mountains.

And I did do whatever it took. I remember one outing with Pierre Morand (from now on I'll call him Pommel, for reasons of historical accuracy). Pommel and I really wanted to go climbing in the Gastlosen, twenty miles away. We had one wish, and one moped. One moped for two people wouldn't do; just a few ccs of engine capacity shared between riders and gear simply wasn't enough! So I took the bus to Bellegarde while Pommel took off on his moped, backfiring all the way. When we met up in Bellegarde, we still had a few miles to go. We agreed on a three-step plan: First, Pommel would head off with the moped and the two packs while I ran behind; second, after whatever distance Pommel decided was appropriate, he would leave the moped and the packs by the side of the road and start running; third, when I reached the moped, I would hop onto it and catch up to Pommel. Then we would start again at step one. Maybe the quality of our warmup was beneficial: That day we climbed Dünnefluh, via the hardest route in the area at the time. It was rated TD+, which meant that everyone flailed on the first pitch. At the top of Dünnefluh, buoyed by being fifteen years old and having conquered a few "extremely difficult" moves, we had become unstoppable.

Our parents were lucky to have unstoppable children; it's a hard-earned privilege. For example, you have to get up early, maybe four in the morning, when a pair of unstoppable teenage boys has decided to conquer "Emile's Route" on the south face of the Grand-Pouce (TD), intending to be back by noon.

By 1975, we had trodden all the beaten paths, and we thought it was time to make our own mark. With Vincent Charrière, I planned to put up my first new route, on the south face of the Dent de Broc. I was back where I had begun. But this time, I was determined to (as the phrase says) go where no hand of man had set foot before. Knowing that we were the first to climb there thrilled me. And I had an ever-present feeling that I was living a great story from the annals of alpine literature. I had read Bonatti, and now I was doing the same as he had. Did Bonatti drink coffee when he was doing a first ascent? I turned the question over and over in my mind. Vincent's mother had made us thermoses of coffee that we sipped all day long. And now, suspended at our bivouac, we could confirm the stimulating qualities of caffeine. "At 11:00 p.m., the moon appeared. At 12:15 a.m., I started climbing, looking for handholds illuminated by the full moon," I wrote in my climbing journal. Right from the start, I made a habit of writing about my experiences. Why was I obsessed with writing, whereas at school I only wrote when I was forced to? Maybe because in the mountains, life seems more ephemeral than it usually does and the urgency of youth creates the desire to bear witness. In any case, we continued our ascent under the benevolent eye of the moon; by morning, we had put up our first new route. It was a tricky thing rated TD, and the line was in the spirit of our common mentor, Emile Sonney, who recommended placing only a few pitons. And I still won't stand for people adding pitons to my routes! The mere mention of it brings homicidal thoughts to mind. On our way home, the sky anointed us with drops of rain that fell like stones; thankfully, our helmets protected our brains that day (or whatever served as our brains!).

And if the brain is indeed the seat of reason, how can you explain the fact that it allowed my sudden wild behavior? I was sixteen when, finding no physical limits to my climbing, I decided to probe my psychological limits. I was able to climb anything, so I had to find something new. I started roped soloing. When I came back from my first solo climb, on Gross Turm (TD+), I wrote in my journal, "This adventure was my first big alpine, and big emotional, experience. I learned a lot about the technique, and also about myself." Of course, in the heat of the action, I didn't understand what was happening inside me, but I had just crossed the fragile boundary between courage and recklessness. Now, I can see that I yielded to my fascination with pure risk. In soloing, I enjoyed flirting with death and telling myself that the smallest mistake would be fatal. And not only a human error, which would be my fault, but also a technical failure; if a piton pulled out, I would be taking the big plunge. I wanted to explore my psychological limits, and I was about to get more than I wanted, which would cure me of the urge.

The other climbers in our group were skeptical about soloing, but I threw myself into it. One day, I set off to Grand Pfad (Pfadflue, 2064 meters), on a climb where I would shortly be saying what I thought, for a few seconds, were my final goodbyes to life. My friend Jean-Claude Sonnenwyl had warned me, but I was already in the zone and didn't hear him. This is what I wrote in my journal:

At 7:00 a.m. I started up. The first several feet were strenuous and soaking wet. I roped up using my usual method: I was focusing on my climbing as much as possible. On the fifth pitch, I used my hammer on a few in-situ pitons that seemed dodgy. My arms were straining, and I started cramping up. After a short bolted traverse to the right, I arrived at a grassy ledge. The belay station had only one bolt; I attached a sling and continued up for thirty-five feet. I then secured myself to a piton and clipped a cordelette to the bolt below me. I retied myself to the rope, removed the twenty-foot cordelette, and hoisted myself up on the piton. Suddenly everything exploded and I tumbled backward. This time, I was done for. I landed with my shoulder on the ledge, felt the rope shudder, and then I was in free fall again. Shit! (Excuse my language.) My self-belay had failed. Goodbye, life. After a moment that felt like an eternity, I felt a harsh impact and found myself hanging eighty feet below the anchor. What had just happened? How was I still alive? It was impossible, a miracle. I went to pieces, and for the first time in the mountains, I sobbed. What was I supposed to do now? Continue up, descend, or wait? For the next ten minutes, I did nothing. Fortunately, Nicole couldn't see me. Wait for what? Come on, pull yourself together! Go up to the anchor. Using prusiks, I gingerly climbed back up to the ledge, fearing that the whole system would fail. I pulled the rope through again and decided to go down. I was only three pitches from the top. It was noon, and the long descent started with a series of sixteen-foot rappels. Soon I heard voices, and that comforted me. It was Nicole, Françoise, and their mother. I did one last 260-foot rappel, and finally my feet were back on the ground. After resting for ten minutes, I could barely walk. I was covered in bruises. Was I lucky, or unlucky?

From a strictly physics point of view, let's say that I fell 115 feet onto a bolt and a sling, with the rope doubled. Experts on gravity will be impressed. I will never forget the yellow piton that let me down; it was as yellow as a dandelion, and I almost ended up pushing up dandelions because of it. At the time, the mountaineering set considered me reckless and was convinced that I wouldn't reach old age. This kind of story did little to dispel that notion.

Some of my friends called this period my crazy time; I also did some big climbs back then. In 1975, from July 27 to August 3, we went to explore Chamonix. In my mind, the town was more Armand Charlet than René Desmaison. I envisioned a little village with a main street running through it; at the end of the street would be the famous mountain guides' office. But I found that the mountains had birthed a large town. Jean-Maurice, Vincent, Pierre, and I, the four of us like the three musketeers, set off for the ridge of the Aiguille des Pélerins, then for the Aiguilles du Diable ["needles of the devil"] traverse. The devil did everything possible to make his presence known in the area. First came a storm, then a second, more violent one. Our ice axes were arcing off, and the air was alive with electricity. We were sixteen years old and didn't know where the descent route went. All of a sudden, we heard voices. We came across a rope party: Mont Blanc du Tacul had two other clueless people on it. At around 9:00 p.m, we made it to the Cosmiques hut; the caretaker, a kind old man who must have been older than the four of us put together, took one look at us and asked, "Did you see the devil?"

In 1976, I had the opportunity to explore another mountaineering masterpiece: the Cima Ovest di Lavaredo. On the morning of July 15, I set off with Pommel as my second. I had decided not to let myself be overawed by the topo. It seemed to have been created so that no one would ever follow in Riccardo Cassin's footsteps. I had never attempted such a long route that absolutely had to be finished in one day. The historical significance of the Cima Ovest intimidated Pommel. He moved with a clumsiness that was unusual for him. Then we arrived at the infamous Cassin Traverse. With one pin every three feet, it's certainly not going to fly away. It ends on a ledge that's so wide, you could ride it on a bicycle. When we came out on the summit shoulder, we had put in eight hours of arm-sapping work, eaten half an apple each, and swallowed a few mouthfuls of water that had already evaporated from our throats.

In *On Snow and Rock*, Rébuffat had written, "Climbing is also the pleasure of communicating with the mountain as a craftsman communicates with the wood, rock or iron that he works." I took this definition of climbing literally: Along with my mountaineering studies, I enrolled in a cabinet-making apprenticeship with a small-scale craftsman in Bulle. The wood was the only thing exuding warmth in that shop. For me, mountaineering time started on Friday evening; for my boss, work finished on Saturday morning. So the two activities competed for those hours. The boss didn't take kindly to that, and in order to shackle me more firmly to the workbench, he assigned me chores to do. For two years, I lined up the dovetails; I made an astronomical quantity of them. I liked wood, I liked the craft, and yet I burned out on it as a career because I no longer felt anything but hatred for that man. One fine day, I laid down my apron for good. The issue wasn't how I managed to quit, but rather how I managed to survive for two years in that situation. I found another job at a furniture company, and I completed my apprenticeship.

In any case, I had in no way given up on my previous commitment: I would become a mountain guide. In 1978, I wasn't yet twenty, but I could see how important the mountains had become in my life. I had already done everything that an alpinist, at least an alpinist in the Alps, could do: rock climbs, on limestone in the Gastlosen and the Dolomites, and on granite on the Aiguille du Midi; mixed routes in the Oberland and the Mont Blanc massif; winter climbs in the Gastlosen; first ascents rated *Extrêmement*

Difficile (ED); classic climbs like the *Major* route, on the Brenva face; routes that had rarely been repeated like the *Supercouloir* on Mont Blanc du Tacul. I quickly understood that the mountains are a game and that every game has its own rules. I was almost buried by an avalanche on the Dent de Broc; I saw one of my climbing partners get carried away by a rock slide; on the Aiguilles du Diable, I heard the sound that a mountain makes when it's about to close in on top of you: The trap is set, and then it rumbles like thunder. I learned the value of friendships that are forged in motion. In my friends' gazes, in the beauty of their gestures, in the purity of the landscape, in the light on certain mornings, and in the twilight on certain evenings, I learned the meaning of the word "happiness." Between age ten and age twenty, I experienced what some people take a lifetime to accumulate, because for me, life and the mountains were rolled into one. I never asked myself why I climbed, because I never asked myself why I lived.

ERHARD—MY SON, MY WORRY

Mountaineering and the maternal instinct aren't a great mix. Erhard's mother, Renata Loretan, understood this as soon as her son started leaving home to go climbing. She lived with this anxiety right from when he was eleven years old; it was a manifestation of a mother's love. Beginning on that day in 1970 when Erhard first went exploring in the mountains, soon to fall into their clutches, Renata Loretan didn't want to know what he would be doing up there. She wanted nothing to do with his acrobatic activities. Tolerating his calling, that was one thing, but it was quite another to expect the trapeze artist's mother to applaud her offspring's exploits!

"My mother doesn't want to know what I'm doing. So much the better! If I put myself in her place, it would terrify me to see my son take off for the Himalaya," Erhard Loretan acknowledged. He made a valiant effort to introduce his mother to the joys of mountaineering. He talked her into—in his words—"a stroll in the mountains," and she found herself at the foot of Eggturm, on a 4+ [5.7] route, a beginner's route that had one 5 [5.8–5.9] move. It was a test piece for all of the aspiring climbers in the area. "At the top," she recalled, "I was proud of myself. I was able to understand what Erhard felt." She also went on a trek led by Erhard to the Annapurna Sanctuary: thirteen days of walking to "see what was so appealing to my son."

She certainly made an effort to keep him in the nest as soon as he started testing his wings. But how can you hold back a migratory bird that dreams of touching the sky? "When I realized what he was doing, I was horrified. I called Pierre Morand's mother. I understood that we shared the same fears, but she told me that it was no use forbidding them from going to the mountains; we would only make them unhappy . . ." So, because he absolutely wanted to reach for the heavens, she turned to the heavens for help. She prayed to Our Lady of Bourguillon and Notre Dame des Marches. She sewed a medal of the Virgin Mary into Erhard's shirt. He accepted this divine protection and attributed his longevity to it, having been spared at the age of sixteen by a miracle. "When he fell on one of his solo climbs, he came home and said that the medal had saved him," noted Renata. Learning that her son has been chosen by God, that's what a mother finds reassuring. It must be said that in the Holy Family, as everyone knows, bringing up the eldest son was no easy matter, and that Mary has always stood in solidarity with the suffering of all mothers. In the sporting goods store owned by Renata Loretan, the Virgin Mary kept watch from among the postcards that had arrived from all over the world. She opened her merciful hands between the west buttress of Makalu and the north face of Everest—an amusing collection of chapels.

Renata Loretan didn't wait for Erhard to pursue his career as an alpinist before she called on divine intervention. She found herself a single mother of two boys after her divorce; Erhard was eight and Daniel was five.

It was a struggle to make ends meet. She worked all day in a chocolate factory or in a sewing workshop. Erhard was the oldest, and the weight of responsibility was on him while other boys were out playing. When Renata came home in the evening, she often found him scraped up; sometimes it was a knee, sometimes his head. "He always loved being in motion," she recalled. "When he was less than two years old, I had to walk him around all day long. He was a daredevil right from the beginning. And once he was a little older, he barely went a day without having an accident." After spending too much time in waiting rooms, she decided it was better to call on God than on doctors: She had Erhard blessed by a Capuchin monk. "Go ahead and laugh, but there were fewer problems after that." Fewer problems didn't mean none. When Erhard was about ten, he had a gymnastics accident: An elbow injury nearly left him disabled for life. Were it not for the work of a well-known orthopedist, Erhard would have been left with a paralyzed elbow.

As he moved into his late thirties, Erhard was rabid about the Himalaya, and a year never went by without an expedition. By that time, Renata Loretan was resigned to it. He talked about "difficult goodbyes." She talked about "a day she does nothing but cry." When they said their goodbyes before every expedition, they both knew that it might be for good. "I know that a lot of his friends haven't come back," she remarked. At the outset, she thought that these accidents would turn her son away from the mountains, that he would curse this sacrificial idol. And then she had to face reality: The funerals came one after the other, but the passion didn't die. During each of Erhard's expeditions, Renata would cut herself off from the world. No radio, no newspapers, nothing that could notify her of a tragic event. Nothing that might seem like the cry of Job, the unanimous protest of every unfortunate person: "My fears have come true." Besides, Renata didn't need the media to follow her son to the ends of the earth. He visited her in her dreams. Like the time she saw him getting beaten up. It was in 1993, and when he came back, he admitted to Renata that he had gotten into a fight with the porters. "A mother senses these kinds of things," she said. One day, she received a letter from Erhard, who was normally a very secretive young man. "It was a wonderful letter. I thought that he must have been awfully shaken up to write such beautiful things. He must have been twenty-five." And he had just survived the traverse of Annapurna.

Erhard always came back, thank God! And that was the only thing that mattered to his mother. "I couldn't care less whether he reaches the summit or not!" People said that Erhard was the greatest Himalayan climber of his time. What did his mother think? "Of course, I feel a certain sense of pride. But at what price? It's hard to be the mother of a child who does such dangerous things."

The journey of Renata Loretan (née Brancale) was certainly an unusual one. Who could have foreseen, when she left the rice fields of Lombardy, that she would become the mother of a world-class Himalayan climber?

IN THE ANDES, LISTEN TO THE TAXI DRIVERS

"In that type of situation, getting out of an avalanche is possible only if everyone can jump off the moving snow onto the snow that isn't moving."

—Albert F. Mummery

IT WAS OUR DESIRE TO climb Nanga Parbat that led us to summit five peaks in the Cordillera Blanca; our dreams of the Karakoram propelled us to three first ascents in the Andes: Caras I (6025 meters), Pallcaraju (6247 meters), and Ranrapalca (6253 meters).

In 1976, I was seventeen. I was the kind of teenager who had a hard time detaching myself from what I read. In the great works on mountaineering, I found absolute heroes. Hermann Buhl was one of them. This man's story blew me away: In 1953, he climbed Nanga Parbat (6900 meters) alone, conquering it after seventeen hours of effort; along the way, he had jettisoned everything that might slow his climb, and he returned just in time to hear people crying over his presumed death. He could scarcely believe his own accomplishment, which was so much ahead of its time. I could have easily seen myself in the title role of a work that would be called, I don't know, something like *Loretan of Nanga Parbat*. Our first experience outside the Alps would therefore be Nanga Parbat. We needed a few tips. We were able to convince Vincent that, out of all of us—because of his natural ability with people, his education, and his good manners—he was the best choice to ask Yannick Seigneur, *the* Mr. Yannick Seigneur, for a meeting.

Yannick Seigneur had just come back from Nanga Parbat, and surely he wouldn't refuse to drop a few crumbs of wisdom to a few philistines who knew nothing about high altitude. He granted us an audience at his home in Chamonix. Jean-Claude Sonnenwyl, Pierre Morand, Vincent Charrière, and I arrived trembling at his door. No one home. Mr. Yannick, like the lord he was [*seigneur* means "lord" in French], had stood us up. Second appointment. Yannick Seigneur honored us with his presence, but made sure we understood that this was a privilege with limits. "I have thirty minutes for you; ask your questions!" This kind of benevolent tone was so encouraging that, all of a sudden, we couldn't think of the slightest question. Twenty years later, I don't know what we learned from that meeting, but I know what I think of Yannick Seigneur.

The door to Nanga Parbat closed with a bitter click. We hadn't really lost our desire for far-off horizons, but we (literally) lowered our ambitions. We decided on Peru, and the Andes cordillera, where a few alpinists from our region had already gone.

Our first expedition required funding our first-ever budget by weaving various threads together. At that time, sponsors were called patrons, but the term didn't change the process at all. We had to swallow our pride in the hope of soon swallowing something more substantial; we visited all of the local pharmacists in order to collect packets of baby food. Armed with the packets, on Wednesday, June 11, 1980, we took off from Zurich for Lima, the capital of Peru. Only three of us made the flight, because Vincent had been all too happy to kick a ball around. In Switzerland, soccer is the most accident-ridden of all sports: 25,770 incidents in 1979 alone. During the years he played soccer, Vincent did everything in his power to keep it at the top of the accident statistics published by the Swiss National Accident Insurance Fund, and to make sure that he played a major role in the 38,772,061 francs that the sport cost the other people paying into the insurance. Anyway, surely now you understand that we disapproved of his soccer habits . . . So the three of us—Jean-Claude Sonnenwyl, Pierre Morand, and I—landed in Lima. From there, we took a bus to Huaraz. There was another gringo on the bus: René Desmaison. You can believe me or not, but he didn't recognize us.

Huaraz is like the Chamonix of the Andes, perched at an altitude of 3200 meters. Despite the season—it being winter in the southern hemisphere—it was surprisingly hot. Before leaving for the summits that towered above the city, we decided to do a short acclimatization trip. Disdaining superstition and the superstitious, we left the city by taxi on Friday the 13th. At 5:00 p.m., we set up camp at about 4000 meters; our heads were pounding with a heretofore unknown drumbeat. I had never had such a bad headache as that one in the Cordillera Blanca. The hammer blows made sleep impossible. At around 7:00 a.m., we packed up and continued on to a col rising to 5100 meters. The pain wasn't subsiding, quite the opposite; and every step rattled my brain. It wasn't until we had descended to 3700 meters that I felt any improvement. What had happened? For the first time in my life as an alpinist, I had met the one enemy that, later on, I would never let out of my sight: altitude sickness. Back then, I knew absolutely nothing about cerebral edema. Fortunately, we emerged unscathed from that first battle.

It's normal to rhapsodize about a trip, and about the associated culture shock. For us, the shock was more health-related than cultural. The morning after our oh-so-beneficial acclimatization hike, Pommel and I confirmed that traveling doesn't mold you as a person so much as it molds your digestive system. For many travelers, exotic horizons end up being limited to the exotic environment of a latrine. A dog has never been as sick as we were for the two days that we alternated between our beds and the toilet. Gathering what remained of our strength, we went looking for a doctor. We found one in the back of an office that, elsewhere, would have made an excellent garage. He examined us behind a pile of tires, grabbed a syringe, and injected us one after the other, without getting a new syringe or disinfecting the old one! I don't know what he could have injected us with—to be precise, I don't know because he jabbed us in the ass—but two days later we were seated in front of a steak and French fries, and on Friday, June 20, we set off in the direction of Ranrapalca.

Geographers will eagerly tell you that the Andes, and in particular the Cordillera Blanca, are exceptional mountains due to being located close to the equator. We were able to confirm that assessment: These are exceptionally strange mountains. They have their own laws, which they enforce with the severity of a tyrant. They are perpetually in motion; their ridges are made of compacted sugar, and their cornices have a morbid tendency to break loose. And there, more than in other places, one's assessment of the objective hazards is subjective.

Ranrapalca (6253 meters) was a good example of these distinctive conditions. Once we had climbed the west ridge of the peak over two days via a new route—as direct as possible given the gigantic flutings—we had to plan our descent carefully. We had the choice between the melting snow of the north face, and three-foot-deep powder on the south face. Our tent was at about 5400 meters, at the bottom of a slope that was just waiting for our weight to set it loose. It tolerated us that time. But once I was back near our camp, I felt that my body had been brutally tested. The action of planting my ice hammer in the soft ice and pulling it out again, over and over, had given me chest pains; on the descent, I had some violent palpitations.

The next day, we still had to cross the bergschrund. Jean-Claude was the first to go at it. He later wrote in his journal, "We were tense, listening to the concerto of the seracs threatening our descent. A 130-foot rappel to cross the bergschrund at the col. Lower down, going through a narrow spot above a large serac wall, I was placing my ice ax when there was a horrible cracking sound. My friends were belaying me from fifty feet above, and they felt something collapse ahead of me. The serac band fractured, blocks detached underneath me, and fear gripped me by the throat." The slope that was supporting us shook. When my turn came, I thought about each movement and held my breath. I avoided planting my ice ax, as if the slightest pressure might make this crystal wall explode. I clearly felt that my presence irritated the mountain: It cracked in all directions, it groaned and scolded. I was about to jump across the final bergschrund and thought that I had finished walking on eggshells for that day—walking on eggshells is even more complicated when you're wearing crampons—when, just to finish in style, the serac wall collapsed. I saw the magnitude of the avalanche and ran to get out of the line of fire. Pierre and Jean-Claude were powerless 100 feet below me. I thrashed about, but I had no illusions: I was going to be suffocated by the cloud, and I protected myself as best I could. After a few seconds the ground stopped moving, and, miraculously, we were still alive. We had no time to celebrate that fact, as we galloped off like a shot through the enormous blocks that had momentarily come to rest. At around noon, after eight hours of effort, we reached the hut. We ran into four French climbers who were planning to ascend Ranrapalca via our route; I could only wish them good luck. As for us, shivering in a cold sweat, we warmed ourselves up in the sunshine of those mountainous tropics.

Huaraz: bistros and dancing. For four days we recuperated after what Ranrapalca had done to us. On the evening of June 28, Pierre Perroud, a friend of Romont's, met up with us. He had a Chilean woman with him. We realized that nothing had changed since Ulysses: From time immemorial, men have been torn between women and adventure. Without us, it's certainly possible that at that point in time, Pierre Perroud would have chosen the woman. But friendship is a solid guardrail for lost souls, and we were able to get him back on the right path. Half an hour later, the four of us set off for the east face of Artesonraju (6025 meters). Pierre Perroud was the filmmaker of the bunch, and he was there to make a movie about our expedition. The filmmaker wanted the expedition to adapt its pace to the film crew's. At around mid-morning, he informed me of his corporatist demands: "We've been walking nonstop since three in the morning. I insist on at least a thirty-minute break, and after that I'll see how it's going." After the thirty minutes had gone by, the film crew talked it over and agreed to keep climbing. Two hours later, we were on the summit of Artesonraju. The descent was via the *direttissima*, on forty-five- to fifty-degree slopes covered with unreliable snow. At 7:00 p.m., we were back at the tent.

Friday, July 4, was a day of transitions—we moved from Artesonraju to the Caras base camp—and meditation. Since we knew that the exit on Caras I was blocked by a huge serac band, that Pierre Perroud had already had his fill of excitement on Artesonraju, and that the conditions were treacherous, was it really reasonable to attempt the south face? Often, in this kind of undertaking, the only courage needed is the one to make the decision. Once the decision is made, action takes over from doubts and questions. I let my thoughts wander. An image came to me of the people I held dear—Nicole and my mother—thanks to whom I could say that I was happy and that, surely, absence makes the heart grow fonder. I had spent 200 francs in a month of travel . . . Sleep interrupted my philosophico-materialistic musings.

The sun rose and so did I. Jean-Claude, Pommel, and I left to investigate the south face of Caras. Upon closer inspection, it lost a bit of its menace: The exit was not a serac band, but a snow slope that led to a rock wall. It was as if the mountain had just let down its guard, and we decided to hit it quickly with an uppercut. On Sunday, July 6, we set out for the face. It was a unique approach hike: more of a climb than a hike. In some sections we had to take off our packs in order to move more easily. In the end, we had to bivy at the bottom of the face. We didn't wait for the night to go by. At 10:00 p.m. the alarm went off; we each gobbled down three packets of baby food, and at 11:30 we started across the glacier. It took us three hours to make our way through that labyrinth and start the actual climb of the face. At noon, we were at the beginning of the difficult section. There were ice slopes of up to eighty degrees, and the ice was so thin that I had to hammer in a pin. Despite the altitude, I felt in great shape. After three pitches, I was at the base of the last rock band.

In the grand scheme of things, what is sixty-five feet? Less than the length of a swimming pool, less than the world record for the shot put, less than the word record for spitting a cherry pit . . . But it was more than enough to dishearten me. First I tried right in the middle, but the veneer of ice covering the rock was too thin for any decent protection. Pommel, convinced that advice is always cheap, told me to try going left. I went along with the idea, and got the first piton in. The more I progressed, the more the outcome seemed uncertain. Geology had changed its mind many times here, wavering between rock and sand; in the end, it decided on sand. The rock was disintegrating everywhere. I tried on the right. Same situation. Despair made an appearance, and I knew that my existence in this world now depended only on forces that would be negligible in a physics problem—the forces of friction. It would have taken nothing at all for me to slip and go crashing down to the bottom of this headwall, because you can't rely on the purely psychological benefits of a piton. I unroped, and Jean-Claude sent up a set of pins. I hammered one in. But I couldn't fool myself; I knew that it wasn't enough for me to go for it. I trended right and hammered a V piton into the ground. I put a sling on it and got another pin in. This was no longer mountaineering, it was carpentry. I topped out dripping with sweat. Jean-Claude cleaned the gear, and Pommel ascended the rope. Those last sixty-five feet had taken me two hours!

We continued along the ridge, and it was 5:00 p.m. when we got to the summit. The fading light cut short our celebration: We had an hour of daylight left, at the most. We hurtled down toward the glacier, but soon we were surrounded by darkness, and our headlamps kept it only slightly at bay. The inevitable bivouac was required. We set up a fifteen-foot rappel using an avalanche shovel. Once down, we retrieved both the rope and the anchor by pulling all three of us together on the whole setup. We had no gear: no sleeping bags, no tent, no stove, nothing to soften the rigors of the Andean night. So we decided to dig a snow cave. A snow cave? That's a fancy name for a hole dug into a mountain. Pommel begged off the snow-scaping duties because he's claustrophobic. So there were only two volunteers left to do the work. Keeping in mind the old mountain adage that the longer you take to set up your bivy site, the shorter the bivy you have to endure, we ended up taking two hours to dig the snow cave. Pommel got over his phobia in just one night. The three of us shared this rodent burrow and a frozen orange; we had nothing left to drink. It was a long night. It must have been on a night like this that the Swiss writer Ramuz wondered, "What *If the sun were never to return?*" [The title of one of his books.] Against all odds, the sun did return, and we absorbed as much warmth as possible before plunging back into the descent. We slalomed between the seracs and the scree, and when we looked back up at the ridge, we congratulated ourselves on waiting for daybreak before descending it. Rejoicing over one's own decisions is a source of happiness for mere mortals. At our high camp, we had a bite to eat. At base camp, some mountaineers from Spain and Geneva studied our route; they decided that it was a first ascent, and we decided that we had no problem with that.

On Wednesday, July 16, 1980, the four of us (including Pierre Perroud) set off for the south face of Pallcaraju, which had never been climbed. And, frankly, in light of our adventures, our nonexistent predecessors shouldn't be blamed for that. Pommel was the only one to lose interest in the face, having been reminded of his human condition by intestinal problems. We reached a col at about 5:00 p.m.; it was really just a cornice that was lower than the others. We bivied in the wind, to the sound of a burping stove. The next day, we encountered some cornices that we didn't dare to cross. We set up a rappel on the face, dropped our packs, and headed unloaded toward the summit. Once we were on the shoulder, a huge ice mushroom appeared, just waiting to kill someone. In the face of all this adversity, we abandoned the summit push and returned to our packs. We were in the process of tackling a slope of sun-warmed snow, when, all of a sudden, we heard a noise, then I felt a bizarre sensation under my feet. I realized that we were on a wind slab—an enormous wind slab. The entire slope was releasing!

As luck would have it, the fracture had occurred three feet above where we stood. We ran, and jumped off the slab, which was easily five feet thick. We anchored our axes into the ice and heard the mountainside crash down into the couloir below us. A slab that was just under half a mile long and over a third of a mile wide had just let loose . . . The four of us were all roped together, attached to a peak in the Andes cordillera, thanking Providence for having put us in the right place at a wrong time: A few feet lower, and we would have ridden the elevator into the abyss. Providence had spared us, but Providence wouldn't return our packs. All of our gear had been left on an adjacent slab that was just waiting to take off. It had already cracked, to get the process going. Jean-Claude agreed to be lowered across the slab. The 260-foot rope was too short for him to reach the packs. He untied. One step at a time, he crossed the remaining 130 feet to our gear. We watched him moving without a net. He came back with two packs and collapsed into the snow. It was my turn. Any sense of safety evaporated at the end of the rope. I descended as gingerly as possible. I picked up the packs. And then I climbed back up, cursing the weight that slowed my every movement and made each second on the slab feel like an eternity. Finally I was at the rope, then at the belay. I was drained. Drained as if I had left everything inside me back on the cracked slab. We tore down toward base camp. In the evening, I wrote that everyone was going to bed "with his soul at peace." The difference between our souls at peace and (may God grant) peace to our souls, is only a matter of word order when it comes to language; when it comes to life, it is sometimes only a matter of luck. That evening, I fully appreciated our lucky word order.

Luck is like a shoelace: Pull on it too much, and it breaks. We opted for a more moderate route on Huascaran (6770 meters)—the standard route. We finished it in two days, despite the fact that I had wanted to make the ascent in one. On July 26 at 10:00 a.m., we stood on the summit.

On August 2, 1980, a small item appeared in the Peruvian newspapers with the heading *Suizos escalan bellas paredes de 4 nevados.* This seemed to mean "Swiss ascend the impressive walls of four peaks." For our climbs to deserve the description of *sensacionales escaladas virgenes,* we had needed to escape the thousand perils that await every alpinist who seeks to become an Andean climber, on those *vertiginosas paredes de la Cordillera blanca.*

And to think that the taxi driver who drove us to the start of Pallcaraju had warned us, "Don't go there, it's full of avalanches!" You should always listen to taxi drivers. And to your mother.

NICOLE NIQUILLE: HEROIC LOVE

What would adventurers be without women? Would Ulysses have blinded the man-eating cyclops, would he have escaped from the monstrous Scylla and the divine Charybdis, if he hadn't pined for Penelope? Would Jason have conquered the Golden Fleece without Medea's love? And didn't Lancelot triumph over the horrible Meleagant just to impress Queen Guinevere? Nicole Niquille and Erhard Loretan spent twelve years side by side and one in front of the other—he in front of her would be more accurate.

It all began with love at first sight. Preceded by his reputation, Erhard had arrived at a rock-climbing camp. She was "immediately attracted to this little guy," and, as the old Philippe Chatel song goes, he was seduced by her lively eyes that radiated the pure air, and by her flowing blond hair. She was twenty and had a tiny two-horse-power car; he was seventeen and had a moped. From then on, the little car was left waiting by the curb: Let the moped roll on to new adventures! Together, they climbed the best of the Gastlosen, opening new and extremely difficult routes. They succeeded on some of the great classics in the Alps; they set off for the world's highest mountains: K2 in 1985, Everest in 1986. It was a heroic love story. In 1986, Nicole became the first Swiss woman to be certified as a guide. "I've always been a woman. Becoming a guide made me happy; becoming the first woman guide was just chance," she told everyone who expressed surprise that a guide could be a member of the so-called weaker sex. At around this time, Nicole and Erhard cut the rope that had united them: "I was going to make a living from the mountains, and Erhard must have thought that I was going to live without him. I had my clients and he had his. Instead of bringing us closer, this profession drove us apart."

For twelve years, Erhard had a name for the blues: Nicole. When anticipation turned to fear in Peru, he thought of Nicole; when, on the Dent de Broc, an avalanche took him for a ride, Nicole kept him warm; when, during a solo climb, he envisioned himself plunging to his death, life carried Nicole's warmth. Nicole and her reassurance. She had to have the patience of a sailor's wife. She spent hours hanging at the belays, watching Erhard's progress on routes he was putting up or finding challenging, with only two monosyllables for conversation: "slack" and "take." Nicole was his belay. But Erhard had the gift of easing the discomfort of the etriers and transforming the narrow ledges into comfortable terraces. Nicole was starry-eyed for him, and she would have cultivated any illusion: "Our first big route was Mont Blanc via the Brenva face," she recalled. "I had never been above 4000 meters; I had never worn crampons. But I couldn't have cared less, because it was with Erhard. I would have gone anywhere, as long as Erhard was on the other end of the rope. I was right to trust him, because nothing bad ever happened to us." For two alpinists, love means looking together in the same direction: toward the summit. "When two people feel the same danger, they become closer," said Nicole Niquille. She never felt such a feeling of strength and security with any other Himalayan climber, not even Jean Troillet or Pierre Béghin.

This was a love story, but also an adventure story. Feelings never dampened the mountaineer's dreams. In 1982, Norbert Joos asked Erhard to go to Nanga Parbat. The "Queen of the Mountains" is a modern-day cyclops—a man-eater that had already devoured forty people. "It would never have occurred to me to make him choose between me and the mountains. I loved Erhard, the man, and the mountain man inside him." She helped him prepare for the Nanga Parbat expedition; she shared his joy, knowing that joy is a stronger sign of affection than is compassion. They had the same passion for the mountains, the same strength of character, the same notion of risk: "If he had been my brother . . . In fact, he should have been my brother," she blurted out in the course of the conversation.

Unlike blood ties, however, feelings can be retracted. By May 1993, the story they had written together was long finished. All that remained were a few flutters of the heart, when a simple outing turned tragic: While Nicole Niquille was picking mushrooms a few hundred yards from her house, a rock fell and hit her on the head. Her brain was injured. Three years after the accident, she was still in a wheelchair. She had come back safely from Everest and K2, and was felled on a Sunday stroll. As La Fontaine put it, "Again, great risks a man may clear, / Who by the smallest dies." Nicole said that this tragedy had robbed her of all that she was. She was convinced that there is no such thing as luck and that, on that disastrous Sunday, she was called to become someone else—to evolve. Erhard considered it the hand of destiny: Our fate is already determined; our time will come regardless of what we're doing and where we are. Did Erhard, the fatalist, know that Nicole saw no end point for him? "I feel as if Erhard is eternal. He can't die in the mountains. He will never make that fatal error."

| 3 |

DEATH OF A GUIDE ON NANGA PARBAT

*"Lack of oxygen also slows down and blurs the mental processes.
Beyond a certain point life itself is no longer possible."*

—Sir John Hunt

ONE SHOULD NEVER CRITICIZE THE army; it prepares you completely for the mountain guide course. While studying medicine with them for four months [military service is compulsory for men in Switzerland], I realized that surgeons are actually carpenters with gloves on, so I returned to my passions in the mountains. In four months, the Swiss army molds you into a medic, and most of all, it molds servile minds that will yield to any and all whims of their superiors without ever asking the slightest question. And that, as I mentioned, is really useful when your sights are set on the guide course, as mine were.

I was twenty when I enrolled in the apprentice-level guide course. I was following through on the commitment from my younger days, and it's always a nice surprise when the newly minted adult doesn't disown the child he once was. And maybe alpinists are some of those rare human beings who pursue their childhood dreams. On June 4,

1979, in Fieschertal, in the Haut-Valais, I answered to my name at the roll call, in the presence of the seventy-three other candidates. We glanced at each other out of the corners of our eyes, suspecting that a rival was masquerading as a friend, and a traitor as a climbing partner.

I hate examinations and the sound of knives being sharpened. The first day, at the foot of a cliff, we heard about climbing theory, and about the evils of climbing shoes and of guides who fall. Guides must not fall—and I don't dispute that. We then moved from theory to practice. I was roped up with the guide, who wasn't wearing climbing shoes. He was leading, and I watched his boots slip and skitter as the route became more difficult. The moment was near when his only movement would be immobility. At the moment of truth, my guide chose to have his route finding mocked, rather than his skill as a rock climber. "I'm on the wrong route, I'll come back down." I agreed with his decision, in accordance with rule number one of the guide regulations, which says that the guide is always right. Rule number two: In the event of a disagreement, see rule number one. My guide ran the rope behind a small shrub, I gave him some slack, and all of a sudden, he fell. The shrub bent, the rope popped off, and my guide took a soaring sixty-five-foot fall that left him hanging, bloodied, at the end of the rope. I lowered him to the base of the wall, where he was evacuated by helicopter to the hospital. It was the third injury that day! Would climbing shoes have saved the honor of the guide who fell?

I'm not going to criticize a system that accepted me, since I graduated first out of the aspirant guide class. During the actual [fully certifying] mountain guide course, luck was on my side. On the first day, I was told to lead a ski tour, using climbing skins. I had to go from Arolla to the Vignettes hut, via the Bertol hut, Tête-Blanche, Mont-Brûlé, and l'Evêque. In that kind of fog, even a radar instrument would have gotten lost! They gave me a compass. I had never used a compass. I led the group, looking curiously at the movements of a needle that, in other times and places, had allowed Magellan to navigate around the world. After hours of muddling through the fog, I came out exactly at the Vignettes hut. Didn't Mummery say, and I'm quoting here, that our best efforts must sometimes be seconded by the great goddess of Luck? Of those weeks spent climbing, downclimbing, putting crampons on, taking crampons off, under the eye of experts who were as likeable as elderly tax collectors, I remember one particular doctrine: The winner was the one who did the biggest climb in the worst weather. That mindset almost led us to disaster: During the course, twelve of us were caught in an avalanche on Tête-Blanche, in the Valais Alps.

In 1981, despite everything, twenty-eight of us had survived to receive our mountain guide certificates. I was happy to be able to make a profession out of my passion. I quickly realized that it is difficult to make a living solely from guiding. It's a profession that does an abominable job of providing for its men, including its "snow" men. And even when a guide is provided for, the profession still brings him trouble. Shortly after earning my certification, I was hired for three months by a mountaineering school in Thun. The school's profitability was put ahead of the clients' safety and, along with it, that of the guide. I found myself with five or six people on my rope, and when you set off for Mont Rose with that kind of party, you get tense. The pay was fair, but it was the only fair thing about that school. After having that sort of experience once, I never repeated it.

During the guide course, I met Norbert Joos, from Gris, and Peter Hiltbrand, from Bern, and they asked me if I was interested in an expedition to Nanga Parbat. At that time in my life, I would have been interested in any expedition whatsoever. And I was all the more so because it was Nanga Parbat, a peak I had been dreaming about for years. There was still one small detail to work out: the 10,000 to 12,000 francs it would cost for me to participate in this expedition. No problem . . . for a cabinetmaker who had quit his job to wander through the Peruvian Andes and was now working on the remodeling of a hotel in Kandersteg. So I swallowed my pride and decided to appeal to the members of the Gruyère Alpine Club. I wrote them a letter explaining that I was going to go on an expedition to Nanga Parbat and that, to be blunt, I needed cash. When I think back on it, I feel myself blushing with embarrassment.

Thanks to that plea, and to the generosity of an entire people, I set off for Rawalpindi on May 2. Seven climbers, including our leader, Stefan Wörner; 5000 pounds of equipment; and ninety porters assembled in view of the

Diamir Face of Nanga Parbat, a peak that (as of 1982) no Swiss expedition had summited. We experienced Pakistan for the first time: Pakistani roads and trails; the Muslim world and its love of long, idle conversations. It took us a day to select the porters and distribute the fifty-five-pound loads, then we walked for four days to reach base camp at 4250 meters. We had set an ambitious itinerary along the Diamir Glacier. But winter was still in evidence at base camp, and we had to clear away the snow in order to set up our tents. I was now at the foot of the Diamir Face: 13,000 feet that I would have to climb, one step at a time. It was as if I had been parachuted into a new world where the units of measurement no longer made sense. What did 3000 feet of climbing, or 300 feet, mean here? I was both intimidated and fascinated. Every alpinist, or everyone who calls him- or herself an alpinist, dreams of one day breaking the 8000-meter barrier. This is part of our never-ending quest: combining everything that is difficult about the Alps and adding one final element—the worst, the killer—which is altitude. In the Himalaya and the Karakoram, all of the 8000ers, even those that are less difficult technically, have a "death zone." I know that this term might seem bombastic, an expression that belongs only in adventure stories, but it reflects reality: Human beings don't belong above 7500 meters, and if they stay there, they die. It's that simple and cruel, and the history of mountaineering reminds us of that. How many people have met their end at those unbearable altitudes? The air holds 30 percent less oxygen; every element of human physiology changes; our reflexes are dulled and our brain works in slow motion. Up until our expedition, Nanga Parbat had seen forty deaths, and little did I know that we would add one more name to that epitaph.

After spending a night at base camp, we were eating breakfast when someone noticed that Peter Hiltbrand was missing. Our morning was unscheduled, so we respected his desire to sleep in. But after a while we began to worry, and when we opened the door to his tent, we found him comatose. Peter Hiltbrand, a solidly built 23-year-old woodsman with a respectable list of mountaineering accomplishments including summiting Huascaran, was developing cerebral edema. Being a traditional expedition, we had the advantage of a team physician, a portable hyperbaric chamber, and medical oxygen. We put Peter in the chamber and with the help of some porters descended to 2000 meters.

While Peter Hiltbrand was recovering, we began climbing the Diamir Face via the route Mummery had scouted in 1895. But the snow made that line too dangerous. Diamir is the home of giants; they groan, growl, and huff, sending down continuous avalanches. They have bad breath. On May 16 we had reached 6000 meters, and we decided to give up before we all died smothered in spindrift. Plan B: the Kinshofer route, which had already been climbed three times. We were a traditional-style expedition, with teams carrying loads to a series of high camps, but we were fairly light, having planned to fix only a few key sections, and so we were constantly coming and going on the mountain. On May 22, Norbert Joos and I were at Camp III at 6100 meters. On May 23, we arrived back at base camp after nine days of work. We planned on resting for two or three days before launching our final assault. But then the snow returned, and those two or three days turned into ten. Tension was rising. The expedition was like a boiling pot about to blow.

It wasn't until June 3 that Alex Berger, Martin Braun, Norbert Joos, and I left base camp, with the hope that we wouldn't return until we had bagged this 8000er, my first. Two hours later, we arrived at Camp I, at 5000 meters, where the results of the most recent snowfalls were fairly catastrophic. There was about six feet of powder snow, and the tents were completely covered. After digging them out, we saw that one of the center poles was bent; we straightened it by heating it over our stove. At altitude, it's critical to drink a huge amount of water—about a gallon per day—so we made tea straight through until bedtime.

Friday, June 4, 2:55 a.m. Hard time waking up—I had slept poorly. I didn't eat anything that morning. Starting the previous evening, my stomach had refused all food. Every future Himalayan summit would confirm this truth: At altitude, my body does penance and insists that I fast. I would be able to walk for days on just a few energy bars, with a few forced mouthfuls of liquid passing as hydration. At daybreak, we left Camp I for Camp II. The snow was deep and the climbing was arduous: We had to free the ropes that were buried by the snow. At Camp II, the scene was as distressing as it had been lower down; but fortunately, the tents had held strong despite the thick blanket of snow.

Saturday, June 5. At 5:00 a.m. we strapped on our packs and crampons. We had one extra tent because Alex was sick and had decided to descend to base camp. The climbing was just as tough. Before the sun hit us, we ascended the Kinshofer Couloir. It was very cold, and our feet suffered. We were now at the expedition's previous high point—Norbert Joos and I had reached this elevation on May 22. The sun warmed us a little. From there, we headed diagonally toward the section that led to the Bazhin Gap. Suddenly we found ourselves on an enormous wind slab that abruptly cracked several feet above us. What terror . . . We felt as if, in an instant, we had become playthings for the giants that dwelled here. Luckily, the slab held, and shortly afterward we reached a rock island where we set up Camp III at 6950 meters. Preparing the camp was backbreaking work with shovels and ice axes; after all, ice axes are only pick axes that bare their teeth.

Sunday, June 6. We set off at around 5:00 a.m. to break trail up to 7200 meters. From there, we could see the summit ridge. It looked so close that we even thought about pushing on to the summit, but prudence, "the science of knowing what to do and what not to do," reminded us that it was already getting late and that without bivy gear, the risk was unfathomable. So we decided not to use Hermann Buhl's method, and we descended to Camp II as planned. On the way, we met the second group: Stefan Wörner, Hans Staub, and Peter Hiltbrand. They were ascending to Camp III. They intended to set up Camp IV the next day and even wanted to try for the summit the day after that. We advised them against it because we thought they were insufficiently acclimatized; it was their first time above 6100 meters. They kept climbing. Was that the moment when our adventure began to morph into a tragedy?

Monday, June 7. After the 5:00 a.m. radio check-in, Martin Braun, Norbert, and I climbed toward Camp III. Having the trail already broken made the climbing easier, but the cold did not let up. When we arrived at the tent, the other team had just left. We watched their progress, which seemed slow. At 2:00 p.m., Stefan and Hans alone reached the location of Camp IV, and they started setting it up. Peter Hiltbrand was still nowhere to be seen. Stefan and Hans later said that they had waited an hour for him and that they had tried to convince him to turn around. But Hiltbrand was one of those men who never gives up; he had a determination that bordered on pigheadedness. He finally arrived at Camp IV at around 7:00 p.m. He was complaining of digestive problems and had been vomiting all day. The rest of the expedition was advised via radio, and they started to panic. Someone yelled that Hiltbrand had to descend or he would be a dead man. But Hiltbrand did not descend. Norbert Joos, Martin Braun, and I were in Camp III, and thus weren't part of the drama. At around 2:00 a.m., Wörner came to our tent and asked us to climb higher, saying, "Hiltbrand is dying." We took off like a shot.

At 6:30 a.m., we were at Camp IV. Poor Peter was talking without making any sense, and answering every question like a robot.

"Peter, you're going down . . ."

"Yeah, yeah."

"So you need to put on your boots."

"Yeah, yeah."

But he stayed there, passive, not caring what happened to him and not caring about his gurgling lungs. He was suffering from both cerebral and pulmonary edema. We wrapped him up in a canvas bag and started dragging him along the shelf at 7400 meters. The shelf continued for two to two and a half miles; after about fifty feet, we were exhausted. We had to face reality: At that altitude, we would need two days to reach Camp III. Peter kept saying, "It will be all right." But at around 8:00 a.m. or 8:15, as if he knew that what we were trying was pointless, he told us, "Leave me here to die!" and then he died. We closed his eyes, covered his face completely, and slid him into a crevasse. We were heartbroken. We cried. There are times when we wish we could revolt against the rules of this game, even though we've accepted them. We descended back to Camp III. What should we do: Give up, or keep going? Giving up would do no good; it would just be one more failure, and it wouldn't bring Peter back. No. We would continue on in Peter's memory.

Martin Braun was suffering from hemorrhoids and was forced to descend. Two days later, he would be sent back to Switzerland and hospitalized.

Wednesday, June 9. There were only three of us left to try for the summit: Norbert Joos, Hans Staub, and me. We climbed back up to Camp IV and couldn't stop thinking of our friend in his eternal rest not far away. In the afternoon, Norbert and I broke trail up to 7500 meters; that would help us the next day. When we got back to the tent, we drank as much as possible and ate very little—nothing stayed down. I had trouble falling asleep. I was nervous, as I had been the night before my first big routes: I was terrified of the unknown, terrified at my recklessness. I was afraid that my feet would freeze or that the weather would deteriorate. I was afraid.

Thursday, June 10. Woke up at 4:00 a.m. The weather was perfect and my pack was ready: a thermos, bivy gear, a backup pair of gloves and sunglasses. I took the recording device with me. We started for the summit ridge at about 5:00 a.m. After half an hour my feet were already cold. There's no getting around it: Humans are homeothermic animals, which means that we do best when our body temperature is close to 98.6 degrees Fahrenheit. And "close to" didn't exactly describe the conditions on Nanga Parbat at the time—minus thirty-one degrees Fahrenheit. I accidentally hit my boot shell with my ice ax; to my horror, it cracked into a diabolical smile. The front of the boot was shattered, and there I was, wearing a sandal on the "Queen of the Mountains." What now? Should I take the risk of continuing? My feet versus uncertain victory? I didn't know what to do. I kept going for a little bit and we made good progress. At 7600 meters, I halted the machine. I took off my boots and my socks and massaged my feet to get the circulation going again. Once I got some feeling back, I put on a pair of socks and my boots, gaiters, and crampons; the crampons helped prevent the boot from disintegrating any further. A bit like asking the skin of an onion to hold the onion together. Norbert rejoined me and broke trail for a bit. It was 8:00 a.m. and the sun was timidly casting a few rays. On the next section, we met with fairly bad conditions; there were wind slabs everywhere. But my feet were "holding it together." I was no longer cold, and I hoped that this feeling wasn't caused by frostbite! My face was well protected by a balaclava that had only three holes: two for my eyes and one for my mouth. That was enough for our most pressing vital functions—seeing and breathing. After another 650 feet, the couloir split into two branches. The plan had been to head right, toward the summit. But the avalanche hazard dissuaded us. We continued left, up a fairly steep couloir with two bulges that I would rate between IV+ and V. Without a rope, it was no picnic. That couloir took us to a fairly tricky arête that ended at the north summit, 8035 meters.

The wind was violent, but reassuring because it was an east wind and thus guaranteed good weather. It was 1:00 p.m. Hans was really lagging behind. Norbert and I continued on toward the main summit. I felt very good and had no trouble breathing. I wasn't walking for as long without stopping, of course, but my pace was good.

The traverse toward the summit was easy. And at 1:30 p.m., I reached Nanga Parbat's 8125-meter summit. I made a recording of my impressions. I looked all around me, and felt content. There were no tracks up the other side. We were the tenth group, and the first Swiss team, to make this summit. A little before 2:00, Norbert joined me. We took a few photos, but how can you immortalize a moment like that? I pulled a small metal box, a piece of paper, and a pen out of my pack. But the piece of paper—on which I had written "Nanga Parbat, Swiss exp 82, Diamir 6/10"; I had only to add our names—flew away. I had a second piece of paper, but the pen didn't work. The Diamir giants denied us this bit of vanity, so our victory would be anonymous.

We still could not see Hans. We surmised that he had been forced to settle for the north summit. At 2:00, we announced our success over the radio.

Was this "victory" really worth the price?

As of June 10, 1982, Nanga Parbat had claimed forty-two victims and seen ten victorious expeditions. The risks involved in this kind of undertaking are well-known, but passion prevails. I'm sure that if Peter came back, he would say, "Bravo, boys!" At least that's the kind of argument we use to explain our actions. Fourteen years after summiting my first 8000er, this quote from Hermann Buhl sticks with me: "My emotions of the previous day coursed through my mind like an impossible dream which had only for an instant come true."

STARVED FOR OXYGEN

In the Himalaya, there are crevasses, cornices, avalanches, wind slabs, rock slides, crumbling walls of rock . . . All of that is normal for mountaineers. But in those high mountains, there is an ever-present and insidious danger: altitude. The first explorers of the Third Pole would catch their breath, then try to explain—to those who never left the ground floor of the world—what was going on up there and what happened when their wings got too close to the sun. "At 8000 meters, there is three times less oxygen than at sea level. That means that you need your entire force of will to catch your breath. The entire being concentrates on just one goal: the next inhalation. And only after a few minutes, when breathing becomes regular, does one come back to life," explained Maurice Herzog, the conqueror of the first 8000er to be summited, Annapurna.

These lines, written in the fifties, are a little dated now. Since then, modern man, that shatterer of dreams, has triumphed on Everest without supplemental oxygen, enchained a number of 8000ers, and turned the stopwatch into the final foe in the Himalaya. Some climbers vaingloriously claim the title of "sprinter." In this demythologization process, altitude has lost some of its fearsome prestige. The Lilliputians thought that Gulliver was sleeping, and began to dance on the giant's stomach. Peter Hiltbrand's death on Nanga Parbat, and other, similar tragedies, remind us that very high altitude has kept every ounce of its virulence: It can snuff life out with a deadly embrace.

Altitude is a threat to the human organism. But how? What happens in the body of an alpinist who has clawed his or her way up to 8000 meters? Medical dictionaries teach us that oxygen is indispensable for breathing and for producing energy. Hemoglobin in our red blood cells circulates oxygen in our blood. We define the quantity of oxygen available in the body using a wordy term: the partial pressure of oxygen in the pulmonary alveoli—to scientists, PAO_2. Enough of the generalities. Now, let's look at the case of a mountaineer. At sea level, where barometric pressure is highest, the climber's PAO_2 is 90 to 100 millimeters of mercury. All is well, because this pressure ensures nearly complete hemoglobin saturation: 95–98 percent of hemoglobin molecules are loaded with oxygen. But alas, sea level is not a Himalayan climber's natural habitat. The higher the climber goes, the lower the barometric pressure and, consequently, the lower the PAO_2. A few figures to help you understand this complicated explanation: At sea level, PAO_2 is 100 millimeters of mercury, as mentioned above. At 5000 meters, a little higher than the summit of Mont Blanc, PAO_2 is 35 millimeters of mercury, which is the critical threshold; below that level, the organism has too little oxygen and problems begin to develop.

But those are data from the lab; humans, as do all other animals, adapt. Our brain has receptors that are sensitive to barometric pressure. When the ambient air pressure decreases, those receptors arouse the body, causing more rapid respiration. When respiration speeds up, the bone marrow produces more red blood cells to transport oxygen. This partially compensates for the decrease in PAO_2. So hyperventilation allows us to gain a considerable amount of altitude. A logical question might be: If the body adapts so well, then why do people die due to altitude? In fact, PAO_2 drops off dramatically, and it is required for hemoglobin to bind to oxygen. With a PAO_2 of 100 millimeters of mercury, the hemoglobin molecules are 100 percent saturated. With a PAO_2 of 40 millimeters, oxygen saturation falls to 75 percent. At the summit of Everest, PAO_2 varies between 24 and 29 millimeters of mercury; this means that hemoglobin saturation varies between 45 and 55 percent. In essence, the body is putting forth the same effort as at sea level, but with half the oxygen.

The faster respiration induced by higher altitude changes the human body's pH balance. The climber's pH is no longer at a normal level of 7.4; it falls a bit, and this decrease in pH further complicates the hemoglobin's oxygen uptake. To put it succinctly: Mountaineers must expend a colossal amount of effort when their hemoglobin refuses to transport oxygen.

Climbers enter a phase where they have nearly stopped drinking and urinating and their respiration has become the only method of regulating the body. If even one cog in the wheel seizes up, the system breaks down. Oxygen deprivation, or hypoxia, leads to dysfunctions in the cardiac system. The heart can no longer eliminate its waste products: It becomes saturated with calcium and then begins to fail. It cannot pump enough blood to the aorta or the pulmonary artery, resulting in weaker circulation. Fluid from the blood vessels stagnates first in the lungs, then in the alveoli. Only a tiny amount, but because the human body has 300 million alveoli, the infiltration quickly becomes a flood—pulmonary edema. Another possibility: The fluid can pool in the brain, causing it to swell. The brain then pushes against the unyielding interior of the skull, and its cells are damaged—cerebral edema. Whereas pulmonary edema can occur at fairly modest altitudes (beginning at 3000 meters), cerebral edema seems to be a disease of very high altitude. Experts say that it is frighteningly similar to a pre-mortem syndrome.

What does a physician friend think of extreme altitude? "For the body, it's catastrophic," he says categorically. But when this same physician remembers that he is also a mountaineer and that, in a moment of folly, he climbed as high as 7500 meters, he corrects himself: "Mountains definitely deserve the sacrifice of a few cells."

Thanks to Dr. Paul Robadey, who oversaw this description of altitude sickness.

| 4 |

8000ERS ARE LIKE PEANUTS

*"The perils that threaten the climber are very few,
and very rarely encountered."*

—Albert F. Mummery

ON APRIL 23, 1983, WHEN I took off for Rawalpindi, Pakistan, I
didn't know what danger I was headed for, but I knew that I had
just escaped cirrhosis. For weeks, in order to fund this expedition to
the Baltoro region, we had been selling cases of wine to people who
loved mountains and wine. In our region, that was a lot of people.
Jean-Claude Sonnenwyl, Pierre "Pommel" Morand, Gérard "Minet"
Spicher, and I made home deliveries of the wine. Our good manners required us to accept the buyers' hospitality; they were often
our friends, and we quenched our thirst as we chatted. Such was our
enthusiasm that we left these joyful gatherings mellower than the
case of wine we had just delivered. Finally, it was time for our team
of alcoholics to leave for our attempts on Broad Peak (8047 meters),
Hidden Peak (8068 meters), and Gasherbrum II (8035 meters).

On Nanga Parbat, I had realized that very high altitude wasn't
a handicap for me. That's a lucky break for someone who dreams
of climbing 8000ers, because mountaineering has no shortage of

talented people who simply cannot break the 7500-meter barrier. I think that it's a physiological predisposition and that there's no fighting it—either you can tolerate altitude or you can't.

I was just back from Nanga Parbat when I applied for a permit for Hidden Peak, also called Gasherbrum I. Jean-Claude Sonnenwyl, a twenty-five-year-old woodsman from Fribourg; Pierre Morand, age twenty-five; and Gérard Spicher, a twenty-seven-year-old auto mechanic, were willing and able. We were still in the planning stage when I got a call from Stefan Wörner, who had been the leader of the Nanga Parbat expedition. He said, "I'm on the Gasherbrum II permit and you're on Hidden Peak. Why don't we request Broad Peak as well?" The year before, the great Reinhold Messner had enchained Gasherbrum II and Broad Peak; there was definitely a temptation to add a third 8000er to our expedition. At that time, Pakistan was more flexible than it is today, and we received the third permit. As the only French-speaking Swiss person (in German: *Welsche*) on Nanga Parbat, I had been the symbol of the multicultural Switzerland that people read about in history books. In the Baltoro region, I was a gangway tossed out between the linguistic communities, because there were nine Swiss climbers: five German-speakers and four French-speakers. This expedition upheld the stereotype of the Swiss as disliking everything that the other part of Switzerland likes, such as type of food or music, but getting along all the same because they can't understand each other and they observe the other group with the amused curiosity of an ethnologist. Such is the miracle of the 700-year-old Swiss puzzle.

On Wednesday, May 4, we left for Skardu via the Karakoram Highway, which links Pakistan to China. It's a road that humans have inflicted on the mountains and that the Karakoram finds intolerable; it has only one desire—to send the road hurtling down into the waters of the Indus—and from time to time, it succeeds. Drivers on the Karakoram Highway are the unrecognized heroes of motor sports: Every day, they brave this racecourse, never making it into the sports papers. Sometimes the road gets the upper hand or something mechanical fails them, and they tumble to their eternal rest in the unmade bed of the river.

Our expedition was a light one, but on Saturday, May 7, it took on an appearance that would have pleased the Duke of the Abruzzi: Four tons of supplies were divided between 145 porters who snaked along the Braldo River to Concordia. From Dassu, it took us twelve days of walking to reach base camp. This approach trek was an adventure in itself: The rivers had sudden mood changes that made the fording unpredictable; the bridges held up only through force of habit; and the thirty-six-mile-long Baltoro Glacier was hiding a few traps. Minet was carried away by the current but rescued himself by grabbing a log. Pommel nearly bit the dust while descending a moraine. But it's no coincidence that this approach march has become a popular trek: We were moving through spectacular mountains—the Trango Towers, Mustagh Tower, Masherbrum . . . And our arrival at Concordia was marvelous. Suddenly, the trekker is surrounded by some of the highest peaks in the world: In the distance are K2, the Gasherbrum cirque, and Broad Peak. It's one of those places where the earth has unleashed its full power.

As a contrast to this geological majesty, this kind of approach march makes you aware of the pettiness of certain people and lets you realize that a medical diploma can be incompatible with doing daily chores, as well as confirming that biscuits are to be rationed and that whiskey was invented to smooth out interpersonal conflicts in the Swiss community. On Wednesday the 18th, we arrived at base camp, at the confluence of the Abruzzi Glacier and the South Gasherbrum Glacier, at 5300 meters.

For seventeen days, the mountain did its best to interrupt our card games. We made six attempts to establish a cache on Gasherbrum II, but it was snowing almost continuously, increasing the avalanche danger. While we were returning to base camp after one of those attempts, Marcel Rüedi disappeared into a crevasse. There was thirty feet of slack in the rope between Marcel and Fredy Graf, and Fredy was yanked toward the opening. Jean-Claude, Pommel, and I barely had enough time to tackle Fredy and keep him from plunging into the abyss. We returned to base camp after saving Marcel from that bad situation. It was May 23, and we wouldn't be reaching the summit anytime soon. I learned how to do nothing, and joyfully abandoned myself to idleness. "It's crazy to be alone in the tent, doing nothing,"

I wrote in my trip journal. I realized that humans are frustrated loafers. The days passed, the snowdrifts rose, and so did the tensions. When the time came to decide on the teams, I was picked for the first rope party. I was flattered. The three other French-speaking Swiss climbers saw me as a traitor to the francophone cause: I was Judas, stoning the eleven irreproachable apostles on Good Friday. I knew that ill will is stoked by disloyalty and that twenty-year friendships can fall apart in two days of forced togetherness. Then I went through my mountaineering accomplishments to justify my situation. On Tuesday, May 31, I wrote in my journal, "I don't mean to boast, but I think that we'll be on an equal footing once everyone has climbed to 8000 meters without oxygen." So, there you have it!

We spent another ten days in base camp, progressing from false hopes to true disillusionment. Soon we stopped being fooled by the brief breaks in the weather, and our morale tumbled along with the avalanches. And then, on Sunday, June 12, the German-speaking Swiss contingent took advantage of a lull in the weather to raise their sails. They set off in the direction of Gasherbrum II while we prepared ourselves for battle. I took a bath in the melted ice of a creek and did laundry. In the evening, I tried to sleep while mulling over the question: Will the good weather hold for another six days?

At 1:45 a.m., I woke up and looked at my altimeter. It had fallen even farther, meaning that the good weather was sticking around. I sounded a wakeup call, and at around 3:30 a.m. we left camp. The temperature was not so bad, and we moved at a good pace. At 7:00 a.m. we arrived at Camp I, at around 6000 meters. Above us, Stefan Wörner and the lead group were battling with the Gasherbrum II buttress. They looked as if they were fighting hard. When I say "they," I'm mostly thinking of Marcel Rüedi, who tackled 90 percent of the lead work. At around noon they were at the cache, at 6900 meters, and they set up the tents. We ran into Dölf Fröhlich. He informed us that he was giving up. I knew that if he didn't come back up with us the next day, he would have to abandon his higher ambitions. His summit dreams died that day, on June 13. In our tent, in the middle of this icy world, the temperature was practically tropical: Pierre and I were down to our underwear.

On June 14, I left camp at 2:30 a.m. It was pitch-black, and I realized that I should have brought a headlamp—a good thing to have when it's completely dark! I could more or less make out the route, and I felt great. At 5:00 a.m., I surprised everyone in Camp II; they were still in their sleeping bags. Marcel Rüedi and Fredy Graf were soon ready. I handed out the medications and cigarettes that various climbers had requested. I put on my crampons, unloaded one tent from my pack, and set off again. I found a route through a wall of seracs. The snow was neither powdery nor crusty, and I sank up to my knees. That section was fairly easy, but exposed. When I got to the top of the seracs, I allowed myself a break. I took out my water bottle and, just to prove that I'm a glutton for extra work, dropped it. It stopped at the edge of a depression about 150 feet below me. But when you're climbing an 8000er, 150 feet isn't anything to be afraid of; I went down and got it, and climbed back up with a joyful heart. Fredy and Marcel had caught up to me. From there, I could see Camp II and the three other French-speaking Swiss members, who communicated that they weren't going to climb any higher that day. I was sorry to hear that, because the more miners in the mine, the better. Breaking trail is exhausting work, and Marcel and I took turns. We pressed on to the big shoulder where Messner had established his last camp the year before. I was still in front and having a rough time of it. I came across a tent and an ice ax that belonged to two Austrians who had never come back from Gasherbrum II. They must have ended up somewhere close to the summit—cryogenically preserved, as they say in science fiction novels.

It was noon and we decided to continue upward. The more we pushed our way through the quicksand, the more we felt anger welling up inside us. And since we couldn't get angry at the natural world, we directed our anger at the three men behind us—Stefan Wörner, Fredy Graf, and Alfred Meyer—who still hadn't broken a single foot of trail! We climbed up along the buttress and realized that we would have to keep going if we wanted to find a spot for our camp. We stopped at about 7400 meters. It was 5:00 p.m. and I had been on the move for more than fourteen hours. I was tired, but less tired than the others, who collapsed into the snow so emphatically that I was drafted to set up the bivouac. I ate a bit of cured pork and some gingerbread, but I drank very little. Sleep eclipsed all of my other physiological needs. In my torpor, I saw a few questions float by: I had not yet slept above

6000 meters on this expedition, and I wondered how I was going to respond to spending the night at altitude.

At two in the morning on June 16, Stefan started heating water. I drank two cups and got ready. At 4:00 a.m., we all left camp together. The cold immediately sank its claws into us. My jacket cruelly informed me that from now on, it was powerless against what was happening, and I felt the cold nipping at my heels. I was wearing only underwear under my pants, and with all due respect to my sensitive regions, it wasn't enough. After a few yards, Marcel and I pulled ahead of the group even though this meant that we had to break trail. We both understood that the others would be of absolutely no help to us. Now I know why cyclists riding in pelotons hate "wheel suckers"—parasites who come buzzing in your nostrils. Anyway . . . A traverse would lead us to the col; it was a dangerous section across some wind slabs. At around 9:00 a.m. we were on the col, at 7600 meters. I looked for some evidence of the Austrians' bodies, but I saw nothing. The summit looked so close, the snow was firm, and our spirits were high. But after 700 feet, we hit the same type of snow again; it trapped our feet, and we had to wrestle them away from the mountain. At around 10:00 a.m., I got on the horn to our sirdar, Riffat, and told him my plans: I would call back at 11:00, and by that time I very much hoped to be on the summit. The climbing became so arduous that we took turns being out in front every thirty feet. A sudden pain behind my shoulder blade was my only distraction—just what I needed!

The last 1300 feet were interminable. At noon, we were on a gentle depression at 8015 meters. Stefan and the two Fredys (Alfred Meyer and Fredy Graf) caught up to us. They were ready to collapse. Much lower, near the col, I saw a sixth person coming up; it could be none other than Jean-Claude Sonnenwyl, who had sensed the bad weather and gotten ahead of it. I was torn: I was at 8015 meters and was tempted to be satisfied with that success. And I was also thinking of Vincent Charrière, my friend and mountain partner, who had died in an avalanche just a few months before. His memory stuck with me. So I decided to launch into the final traverse. Marcel went ahead of me; I followed him while leaning on a ski pole—a method that the old-style guides would have disapproved of. We reached the top, and it was shrouded in clouds. The weather was poor. I placed Vincent's dog tag on the summit; his name was engraved on it. I took a few photos, including one of Marcel Rüedi as he basked in his 8000-meter fantasy, brandishing a large photo of Nastassja Kinski. She—it seemed—wanted to climb an 8000-meter peak as well. Finally, three of us in total reached the true summit, and we began to make our way back down.

I was following the ridge when something broke loose under my foot. The cornice had just released, but because my body weight was on my other foot, I stayed on firm ground and only the cornice took the plunge! We met up with Jean-Claude Sonnenwyl. I told him that I would wait for him a little lower down. At around 3:30 p.m., an unsteady shape staggered toward me. It was Jean-Claude, coming down from the summit. He had gained almost 5000 feet of elevation in eight hours. I looked at him; he vomited, and I said to myself that in such a state of exhaustion, one is close to having one foot in the grave. At around 4:30 p.m., we got to Camp III, where everyone had gathered. Pommel and Minet would try for the summit the next day. The whole group was tired. Marcel and I decided to continue down, and we insisted that Jean-Claude come with us because I was afraid that another night at altitude would be one night too much for him.

We got to Camp II at 7:30. I remembered the images from Camp III—all those bone-tired bodies—and I thought that everyone should have come down. The problem is that most of them were not physically capable of descending. I got into a Dunlop tent by myself, and Marcel and Jean-Claude shared a tent. I didn't eat or drink anything. My throat was burning and sleep eluded me. I sucked on a lozenge for my throat and took half a tranquilizer to get to sleep.

The next morning, Pierre and Minet radioed to tell me that they were unsure about coming down and that they might wait a little bit and try for the summit. At 8:30 a.m., we set off for Camp I. At 10:00, there was another radio call; everyone had decided to descend. I was relieved, because the sky hung like a lid, low and gray over Gasherbrum II. The snow fell harder. I went first to break trail, and started to reacquaint myself with the feeling of hunger. I had a craving for dal, a local lentil-based dish. At 2:30 p.m., we arrived at base camp. There are no words for the feeling that comes over you at a time like that; I can only say that I would give anything for that moment when I'm back, when I'm once again a social being, when I forget that dry feeling swelling in my throat—the taste of danger.

At 4:00 p.m., a radio call transported us 6500 feet back up the mountain, into the eye of the storm. We were stunned to learn that the entire team was preparing to spend the night at 7100 meters, in a spot that made no sense given the snowfall. I was very concerned. The radio waves carried my heated words, but the air dispersed my anger to the four winds. I begged them: "Try. Try to at least descend to Camp II!" I threatened them: "Otherwise, something bad is going to happen!" I brandished the radio like a useless remote control while, high on the mountain, they prepared to spend the night. All I could do was pray for the avalanches to stop making a racket.

At 7:02 a.m., my heart had been pounding for two minutes; we had planned a radio call for 7:00. Two minutes are enough for the imagination to run wild. But Pierre's voice soon calmed the gallop of my dark thoughts. I was relieved, but not reassured. The night had been a hard one for everyone, and, I quote, "The Totos are in tatters." ("Toto" is our slightly pejorative nickname for our German-speaking countrymen, used when we forget about 700 years of peaceful coexistence). They arrived at Camp II at around 11:00 a.m., and I learned that the expedition doctor's fingers were already turning black—a sign of third-degree frostbite. I advised Pierre to belay him on the descent, even if it took all day.

At 6:30 p.m., Pierre told me that they had arrived at Camp I. At 7:30 the radio crackled to life again, with a new contact person. It was Stefan Wörner, calling to chat and play the tough guy. It should never be forgotten, and we have to remind them if necessary, that without Pommel and Minet, they would all be starting a long hibernation, and only returning to the valley floor in several tens of thousands of years—as frozen shells!

Saturday, June 18. At 5:00 p.m., after spending seven days on the mountain, the survivors of Gasherbrum II arrived. Pierre was the first one to base camp; he made for the tent and tried to relax despite his tension. He had never experienced an adventure like that: He told me that it was a miracle no one had died on the descent. The expedition doctor, Alfred Meyer, had let go of the rope when they were climbing back over the buttress. Pierre had caught him by the leg! I was following the story of their misadventures when I heard the bragging and boasting coming from the neighboring tents. People can be divided into two unequal groups: the blabbermouths and the brave.

The other climbers were watching the altimeter as if it were the entrails of a chicken and could predict the future. It was Tuesday, June 21, the summer solstice, and we definitely intended to make an attempt on Hidden Peak (Gasherbrum I). Marcel Rüedi and I had been walking for half an hour when we heard someone shouting. I didn't even need to turn around in order to figure out the content of the message: Jean-Claude, Pierre, and Minet weren't coming. The result was a small math problem: Five mountaineers set off through a thick blanket of snow toward a summit. After half an hour, three of them give up. Figure out how many are left to break trail. At the bottom of the large slope, I stepped aside to let Marcel go first. The gods were smiling upon him: A huge avalanche had just swept down the face, and only a hard layer remained, similar to linoleum. At 2:30 p.m. we reached Camp I, at 6500 meters. The next section of the route wasn't immediately obvious to us. The couloir was not in condition, the Sturm route petered off somewhere on the buttress, and the Messner route was bright blue with bare ice. At 6:00 p.m., we made a radio call, but reception quickly died. We heard no response, and left those useless two pounds of weight right there.

The next day, we battled with some slopes that I would call "weaselly." In our jargon, that means that they were giving us the heebie-jeebies, the shivers, a scare, a terror, a fright. Then we found a frayed fixed rope. Was it more fixed, or more frayed? We took the risk of hoisting ourselves up on it, and it held. After climbing on rock up the arête, we came out on a huge, steep snow slope. I ventured out on it, and after 160 feet, I sank into deep powder. I couldn't continue. So I headed toward the rocks alongside the slope, and there I found some holds. My first thought was about the rope between us: We had no pitons, so the protection was only symbolic. I untied but still tried to belay Marcel. Maybe tension stimulates the mind, because I couldn't avoid thinking about the slope possibly releasing and Marcel being carried away. Could I use just this fat piece of string to hold a whole Karakoram mountainside? No, definitely not. So if he got swept away by the mountain, it would be better to let him go and to pray that he would land intact, 2000 feet down the couloir. Fortunately, Marcel's arrival interrupted this charitable soliloquy.

Marcel took the lead; he preferred snow to rock and took an hour to go 130 feet. On the other side, the southwest face, the team of Kurtyka and Kukuczka, whom we had encountered over the previous few days, were at the same altitude as we were, even though they had left two hours later! I noticed the three other French-speaking Swiss climbers at the col. "They're not roped up, the fools!" I thought. But this was a high-altitude version of the pot calling the kettle black, because the gymnastics we were doing on these unstable slopes definitely didn't reassure me about my own mental health. Marcel shouted that he had found a good belay. I was thrilled, until he pulled the rock out of the snow and I watched the "good belay" go speeding away down the slope. I caught up to him and kept going, struggling on slabs covered with a foot of snow. Twice I risked falling. I shouted, I talked about giving up, I loudly expressed my powerlessness. Finally I pulled myself together: I was fifteen feet from the cornice; I had to keep trying. I forged ahead, straight up, and it worked—just barely, but it worked! Another few hundred feet of inhaling powder snow, and we set up camp. We must have been at 7100 meters, near the remains of a German expedition. We went to bed, rocked to sleep by the storm.

Thursday, June 23. Our tent was transformed into a spinnaker flying from the mast of Gasherbrum I. At 5:00 a.m., we set off for the summit. It was a long distance and the snow was deep. The sun caught up to us at about 7300 meters, at the Messner bivouac. I went first and outpaced Marcel, who was having a low-energy moment. At around 10:00 a.m., I stopped for a snack and to wait for my partner. In reality, I just drank a bit and we kept climbing. We agreed that we would be on the summit within two hours. We pressed on, Marcel via the snow slopes and I via the rocks. Finally I came to the summit ridge, which was protected by a cornice. I knew that once I had negotiated the cornice, I would be within 160 feet of the summit. I looked to the left and to the right; I spun my head around like an owl terrified of the light. I shouted to Marcel that without ice axes, we couldn't make the summit. But I refused to give up so close to the goal. In desperation, I tried on the right up a large, steep, hard slope. Success. A topo would have called that section exposed, but now I was on the ridge and it was only a matter of minutes to the summit. It was 1:30 p.m. and I was on top of Hidden Peak. To live happily, let us live hidden! I even went shopping at 8068 meters—I collected a Simond ice ax, a carabiner, and a piton. Between taking pictures, I worried about what had happened to Marcel. I stood up, and my Rollei camera fell and took off down the slope! I know that we shouldn't take God's name in vain, but I couldn't help myself. At 2:30 p.m., Marcel joined me on the summit. He had two exposures left on his camera: one for him and one for me. We charged back down.

I arrived at camp at 4:30 p.m. Pommel, Jean-Claude, and Minet were there too. They had just arrived. They were in for a night under the stars because they had no tent, but they dug some nice snug cocoons in the snow.

At 5:30 p.m., Marcel Rüedi joined us. All five of us ate in a Dunlop tent that would have been a tight squeeze for two. Outside, the storm roared. After our feast, Pommel wished us good night and went back to his cozy pit. A few minutes later he was back, having nearly suffocated! And to think that any old Greenland malamute and Siberian husky cross can spend the night outside at minus fifty-eight degrees Fahrenheit in sixty-mile-per-hour winds, in its thick fur with its nose in the air. But mountaineers aren't sled dogs, which meant that all five of us spent the night in that tent, already described as a tight squeeze for two. The night was more like a nightmare; actually that's a lie, because a nightmare would require that one be asleep!

The next morning, at 5:00, Jean-Claude and Pommel vacated the bunk, or more correctly the tent floor. That afforded us an hour of sleep. Minet refused to leave. He was going to descend with us. I discovered that the other climbers had stripped the rope from the rock section on their way up, so I started downclimbing that dangerous ("weaselly" would work as well) wall.

At 9:00 a.m. I was on the col: two and a half hours down after twelve hours up! At around 10:30, we started descending a crevassed slope below the col. Minet had dropped the rope, so we had to grope our way along; in that kind of situation, the lightest person always goes first. At 128 pounds, I am often the one to go first! I made my way across the invisible void without incident, arriving at Camp I at 11:45. Then we continued down to base camp. On June 24, Pierre and Jean-Claude reached the summit of Hidden Peak.

And for us, that made two 8000ers in eight days.

For Broad Peak, the third-highest of the four Baltoro 8000ers, we had to move our base camp. We set up a bare-bones camp at 4900 meters, to the west of the mountain. I intended to go directly up to Camp III—an elevation gain of 7200 feet in one day—because I knew it was outfitted with tents. Marcel Rüedi thought that we should take a tent with us; I disagreed so feebly that he persuaded me to carry it and the stove that went with it. So in this story, I am both the mule and pigeon. On June 29, I set off on my scouting mission, inching my way through the labyrinth of the glacier. I was almost there; I just needed to cross a small couloir. I traversed it, and kept going on soft snow. Suddenly the crust broke and I fell through: Both of my legs plunged into water, because the snow had concealed a creek. I probed with my pole but couldn't touch the bottom. My heart raced as I quickly took stock of the situation: Both of my legs were in the water, both of my hands were stuck in the snow. If the snow layer collapsed, I was a dead man, and the Indus would chalk up another piece of flotsam. I wanted to scream for help, but I needed to conserve my breath to get out of this mess. I managed to reach the bank by crawling, and I was soaked to the knees. Perfect for climbing one of the fourteen highest peaks on the planet! If a route can be judged by how wet one's feet are, I had to say that Fredy Graf and Marcel Rüedi had found a better route than mine.

At 1:00 in the morning, the three of us continued on together. We got the camps in order, and Graf used the hot air balloonist's technique of tossing ballast in order to gain altitude. At Camp II, he abandoned his stove. His pack was only decorative at that point. Before attacking the final steep section below Camp III, we ran into Doug Scott himself. That year, the Karakoram was the ultimate salon where everyone was talking about mountaineering: After Voytek Kurtyka and Jerzy Kukuczka on Hidden Peak, now here was Doug Scott. I didn't abandon hope of running into Messner as I climbed over a cornice. The wind had covered everyone's tracks, so Marcel and I went to work clearing the route. At around noon, we arrived at Camp III at 7100 meters. A beer belly announced the imminent arrival of Don Whillans, the mountaineering legend, who was accompanied by a porter. An Australian arrived from Camp IV and told us that their expedition doctor had died that morning at 5:00.

On the mountain, camping consists of packing more people into the tents than there are spaces for. What would be the fun of it without your neighbor's elbow jabbing you in the ribs, without your nose pressing against the tent, and without the tent sticking to your nostrils? There were three of us in the two-man Dunlop. But, oh joy, then Stefan Wörner and Dölf Fröhlich arrived in camp. Mr. Graf immediately accepted the offer to spend the night with them. The storm raged throughout the night. From time to time, I got out of my sleeping bag to shovel out the tent. And, in a show of chivalry, I also shoveled out the tent of the two Polish women who were there, Anna Czerwinska and Krystyna Palmowska, two high-level climbers who had been with Wanda Rutkiewicz on the winter ascent of the north face of the Matterhorn in 1978. When I got back in the tent and let myself enjoy the warmth of my sleeping bag, I wondered whether the previous two weeks hadn't exhausted me, whether I wasn't making unreasonable demands of my body. But all of the indicators were on the rise: I was eating and drinking, and I had just devoured 7200 feet of altitude gain. So I allowed myself a euphoric moment—tomorrow, if the engine held steady, it would be a done deal.

Thursday, June 30. Stove, tea, get dressed. Routine ruled, even here at these deserted altitudes. At around 4:30 a.m., Marcel and I left camp. As I had predicted, Dölf was worn out from the climbing the day before, and he stayed there. Graf and Wörner followed. I started off with difficulty, feeling tired. And then the human machine surged into motion. As we ascended, my strength improved. I was alone at the front. I overcame the difficulties— rock bands and seracs—which had all been equipped by previous expeditions. But Broad Peak is a mountain as fleeting as happiness, slipping away just when you think you have it in your grasp. A series of "crab tracks" ran up the long ridge, all the way to the sky. I followed them, and at 11:30 a.m. I stood on top of my third 8000er of the trip. It was my third in exactly fifteen days. The descent was more like a glissade. As I slid by, I thought I recognized Marcel; he was about an hour from the summit with Wörner, Graf, and the two Polish women. At 8:30 p.m., I was at base camp. On July 2, Jean-Claude Sonnenwyl and Pierre Morand summited Broad Peak. So three of us had added three 8000ers to our tallies: Marcel Rüedi, Jean-Claude, and I.

It's odd: Even though Broad Peak marked the realization of a dream, I felt torn. My joy was dampened by the enormous shadow of K2. I was seized by a desire to climb K2 . . . on a whim, if I dare to admit it. A thirteen-thousand-foot whim! Would I never be satisfied? No, I would never be satisfied, because humans are insatiable animals. The Arabs say that "Only the dust of the tomb fills men's eyes." And I'll add that 8000ers are like salted peanuts: It's better never to start.

ACCLIMATIZATION: THE DOPING
BENEFITS OF ALTITUDE

Expeditions progress on a schedule: first, the approach march; second, setting up camp; third, reconnaissance; fourth, waiting; and fifth, the final ascent. Mountaineers are creative people if they're anything at all, and yet in this aspect they're about as imaginative as a senile sergeant-major. One might find this surprising. One might also say that they are obeying the inflexible laws of physiology.

The first mountaineers learned about acclimatization on their first expeditions. In 1938, the approach march to Everest required a full six weeks, which is the exact incubation period for an ostrich. As if that kind of journey were not enough for acclimatization, the expeditions used a system of camps. The rope teams took turns pushing their incursions on the mountain ever farther. The conquest of Annapurna, for example, occurred after a ten-day assault on the Faucille route. Those heavily laden expeditions gave everyone the time to adapt to the altitude. It was the time of forced acclimatization. Today, approach marches have shortened to a week or even a couple of days. Aviation has made the Himalaya smaller, just as it has made the planet smaller. On their 1994 Lhotse expedition, Erhard Loretan and Jean Troillet were in Kathmandu (1300 meters) on a Monday, and on the Friday they were setting up at Everest base camp (5300 meters). Five days to gain 13,000 feet! An elevator has no trouble with that kind of ascent, but it's different for humans, so we have to adapt progressively. Acclimatization happens through forays to higher altitudes with frequent returns to base camp. Experience is no substitute for acclimatization: On Cho Oyu in 1990, Jean Troillet suffered from altitude sickness and had to leave base camp to "recompress" a bit lower down. He had previously climbed three 8000ers, yet he had all of the symptoms of altitude sickness!

What is acclimatization hiding? What methods does the body use to cope with altitude?

In the section on altitude sickness, we learned that at higher altitudes the air contains less oxygen. However, the human body is sensitive to hypoxia, or lack of oxygen. The red blood cells, or erythrocytes, mainly perform the function of transporting oxygen and carbon dioxide from the lungs to the tissue (and vice versa). When oxygen is lacking, a hormonal mechanism kicks in: The kidneys and the liver produce greater quantities of the hormone erythropoietin. That hormone then stimulates the bone marrow to produce more red blood cells. The body is therefore able to increase its own supply of oxygen, which makes up for the decreased oxygen in the air. Side note: Erythropoietin is also the name of a doping agent used by endurance athletes. Now, let's close that unfortunate side note.

A study was carried out on subjects who had stayed at 4450 meters for several weeks. Using a centrifuge, one can easily measure the quantity of red blood cells in a liter of blood: for men, 0.46 liters; for women, 0.41 liters. This can also be expressed as a percentage of hematocrit: 46 percent for men, 41 percent for women. To get back to our study, the subjects' hematocrit was 45 percent at the beginning of their stay at 4450 meters. It remained stable for the first two weeks, then it began to rise, ultimately reaching 55 percent after six weeks. The ratio of fluid to blood cells had by that point reversed. Beyond that amount of time, hematocrit remains stable and doesn't increase; the blood seems saturated with red blood cells. Their concentration at sea level had been 15 percent, and now it was 20 percent! A person's red blood cell count has therefore increased from five million per milliliter of blood to six and a half million. This is a considerable leap; those 30 percent more red blood cells ensure the improved transport of oxygen.

But alas, this increased oxygenating capacity is accompanied by a major drawback: The blood contains less plasma (fluid) than red blood cells, so it becomes thicker. Its viscosity increases, it doesn't circulate as well, and thrombosis becomes a risk. It is thus not uncommon—as we saw in the Nanga Parbat story—for well-acclimatized mountaineers to suffer from hemorrhoids, which are a form of circulatory thrombosis. These ill-placed varicose veins are there to remind us that, however high we're seated, whether in Versailles or at 5000 meters, we're still sitting on our asses.

| 5 |

"Tell Me Why," the Song Says

"One must no doubt have lost all hope in order
to be completely brave."

—Alain Émile Chartier

Manaslu is the proof that we remember what we want to remember from a story and that we stack up our memories in a specific order: roses on top, ready to be picked; the dark memories below, near the void of forgetfulness. This selective memory allows us to keep at it, to strap our packs on one more time, to set off again— even if, in a forgetful or lucid moment, we have promised to never go back to those cannibalistic mountains. For those of us intoxicated by the heights, that is like the pledge of a drunkard, quickly forgotten once safety sobers us up.

When anyone asks me to summarize my ascent of Manaslu, whose 8163-meter summit we reached on April 30, 1984, I can only think of generalities: "This peak didn't really affect me in any particular way; the standard route, even on skis, isn't at all extraordinary." And then these few words of summary remind me of others that are more precise, and I tell myself that Manaslu deserves a longer story.

This expedition to Manaslu was like a reunion: Marcel Rüedi, with whom I had climbed my three Baltoro 8000ers, was there, and so was Norbert Joos, who had stood with me on the summit of Nanga Parbat. On March 29, 1984, we were at base camp. Then came a month of bad weather, and the snow destroyed every one of our attempts. When we climbed up to the camps, we found them buried under three feet of snow and we had to dig everything out. And when the problem wasn't the weather, it was our physical condition: On April 14, we climbed to Camp II, a Sherpa slid 130 feet on a wind slab, we found him and kept going, and then, after spending the night at 6300 meters, we descended because we all had headaches. During those approaches, the avalanches' steam only whistled in our ears. Finally, on April 29, the day after my twenty-fifth birthday, Werner Burgener, Norbert Joos, Marcel Rüedi, and I met up at Camp IV, at 7500 meters, on the immense summit plateau. We had planned to ascend Manaslu on skis, but once we got to 7200 meters, it quickly became apparent that that would be impossible: The winds had blown the snow away and exposed the ice. We spent the night holding down the tent with all of our weight, terrified that it would blow away. The winds were gusty, and the tent blew out of shape. In that kind of following wind, any sailor would have taken in the sails. Our only hope was that the poles wouldn't break.

The next morning, at around 5:00 a.m., we started heating water on the stoves. I looked at my companions, and from their moods I deduced that only Marcel and I were still thinking about the summit. Above the clouds, we could see hints of good weather. Norbert and Werner finally let us convince them, and they geared up as well. I got out of the tent. It was as if the mountain gods had waited for this moment to draw me out: Visibility quickly closed in. At 10:00, Werner turned around, and Norbert didn't require much convincing to go with him. Marcel and I kept going. Once in a while, we caught a glimpse of the summit. We made progress, leaning into the wind. We were no longer two men in action, with our weaknesses and our intelligence, but two machines programmed to keep spinning their axles. At 2:00 p.m., we took turns standing on the summit just long enough to take a photo, but not so long as to take flight, nevermind the gravity of the moment. I don't want to flaunt my knowledge, but . . . how does a solid fly? A solid (in this case, us) flies when it has removed enough energy from a fluid (in this case, air) to transform that energy into lifting capacity. And at that precise moment on the summit of Manaslu, I felt very close to being lifted. In other words, I almost flew away.

At around 5:00 p.m., we got back to the tents. We had found them just by chance, because the plateau is huge, visibility was zero, and the routefinding was in God's hands according to some of us, and up to luck according to others. Norbert and Werner were still in the tent. They were reluctant to give up their summit hopes. I was past the point of hesitation, and I decided to keep going down and escape those hostile skies. Marcel was no longer as keen. The wind had strengthened, and it was becoming difficult to walk standing up. There was no doubt: We had to get down, and away from this hell! Finally, Marcel followed me. Just a few yards from the tent, I lost a crampon. On that glassy black ice with only an overboot on one foot, I found it impossible to move without slipping. I slid about fifteen feet down to a crack, where I was able to wedge myself. Marcel came down to me. It was so noisy that we couldn't talk, but I could see the terror in his eyes. He held out his ski pole to me so that I could regain my balance and get my crampon back on. The wind lashed us and blasted granular snow in our eyes; we could barely keep them open. We each retreated into our own interior world.

I kept descending. It was beyond precarious. We had to anticipate the wind gusts and cling to our ice axes so that Aeolus wouldn't immediately clear us for takeoff. After several hundred feet, I dared to glance upward. A shot of adrenaline ran through my body: There was no one there! Marcel? It couldn't be! To my right, a serac band hung over a huge void. Could Marcel, blinded, have fallen over the precipice? I had to get down lower, to the foot of the seracs, to see. I descended, gripped with anxiety—what was I going to find down there? At the base of the ice cliff, the winds seemed to have forgotten the reason for their anger: It was flat calm. I felt as if I had just opened my parachute after hours of free fall; I had been suffocating, and now I could breathe at my lungs' natural rhythm. There was no sign of Marcel. Hope returned: So he hadn't taken the big plunge. I couldn't do anything more that evening. Going back up to the tents would have been crazy. I headed for Camp III, located below a small serac band. The tent was nothing but a bump that stuck out a bit above the others. I dug it out and spent a sleepless night, haunted by the specter of Marcel Rüedi.

The next morning, I continued down to Camp II. It was only there that my anxiety was relieved; the expedition leader, Hans Eitel, told me that Marcel had turned around during the storm and climbed back up to Camp IV. He had spent the night there with Norbert and Werner. That day, I descended happily to base camp: What would a success be if it had cost a life? But my peace was short-lived. At Camp II, Werner Burgener was missing. Norbert and Marcel had seen him getting ready; Norbert had even heard him give the go-ahead for the descent. But we had to face reality—Werner hadn't followed the others, and he must have stayed at 7500 meters. At that moment, no one could be sure that he would ever come down.

It turned out, however, that our expedition was marked by good luck: We could have all disappeared in an avalanche; we could have all been blown away by the maelstrom that swept down on us, literally disintegrating our camps. But instead, we all ended up gathering safe and sound at base camp. On Wednesday, May 2, a rescue team made up of two Sherpas and two of the European mountaineers had found Werner; he was weak but alive. Edema had begun to sap his strength, but he was able to make it to base camp. On May 11, Norbert Joos reached the summit of his second 8000er.

Annapurna was the first 8000er for some, but it was nearly my last. Some authors and journalists who have summarized my Himalayan accomplishments have focused on only two or three events: Often they mention Shishapangma, Cho Oyu, or Everest—three direct and fast ascents. The general public understands numbers better than anything else, so if you tell them that Everest took forty hours, Cho Oyu took thirty, and Shisha took twenty, they're amazed. Annapurna is never, or rarely, highlighted, as if someone has decided that the 110-meter hurdles are less important than the 100-meter dash because they last three seconds longer. Come on! I've never pushed my limits as far as on the traverse of Annapurna. I've never felt so far from the living and so close to the dead. During those days spent between heaven and earth, I realized that being at very high altitude means putting a foot in the next world. I understood that when we were descending to base camp and life showed its stubbornness through the first few timid plants and the joyful flights of the mournful crows, we were ghosts, in the true sense of the word.

This is how we envisioned our ascent of Annapurna via the east ridge: first, a very technical section between 5500 and 6500 meters; then a very long ridge extending for four and a half miles between 7000 and 8091 meters, with a final technical section at around 8000 meters. This wonderful line had already been attempted by a Swedish team, but it had never been successfully climbed; it was Jöri Bardill's idea, before he unfortunately died during the guide course. Some mountaineers from the canton of Grisons then picked up the idea. Norbert Joos was in on it and asked me to join them. Thanks to the atmosphere throughout those two months, it was the kind of expedition that restores your faith in humanity.

On September 11, we started our approach march through the landscape that forms the backdrop to the famous Annapurna Sanctuary trek. Two porters fell into the water on the first day. Once they had dried off, they confirmed that it's hard to swim with sixty-five pounds on your back. Our doctor, Bruno Durrer, played Albert Schweitzer: One by one, the porters came for medical treatment, followed by nearly everyone from the villages. In that region, the lack of hygiene contributes to infections. Germs love Nepal at least as much as tourists do. Bruno added a medical specialty to his repertoire: One evening, using only a pair of pliers from the tool kit, he became a dentist and pulled someone's tooth. On the fifth and sixth days, the team crossed through a veritable jungle. The leeches were overjoyed that the trekking season was beginning a little early, and they descended on us. I ended up with the record—thirty-four bites. The fact that I walked in sandals may have played a role in that.

On September 17, we set up our base camp on the moraine. We were in the heart of the Sanctuary, one of the most beautiful places in the Himalaya. It's so beautiful that the Nepalis are sure the gods live there. We each had our own tent, and I appreciated the luxury. Along with music, it's the only indulgence I allow myself. If the taste for luxury increases with age, then I'm aging a bit every day. And besides, the right to be messy is a precious one: Aren't neat people just too lazy to go looking for their things?

On September 20, I made a second attempt to get to Camp I. The buttress involved rock climbing that could become tricky in bad weather. I set up almost 1000 feet of fixed rope before reaching the top of the feature. From there, it would probably take an hour to reach Camp I. On September 23, we attacked what would be the crux of the ascent: I fixed 1300 feet of rope to the base of a vertical ice wall. I then armed myself with two ice hammers, and for two hours I battled with 230 feet of mediocre ice. The lock had opened: From a technical point of view, nothing should stop us now! I was euphoric; I didn't see what could prevent us from succeeding, other than the weather and our physical condition. Details.

But isn't history all about details? The weather deteriorated and we hunkered down in base camp. On October 9, Norbert and I crossed the glacier to get some news from the outside world. When the Annapurna Hotel, which consists of two bamboo huts, came into view, we realized that trekking season was in full swing. We even found a few girls; after six weeks, we feared that the "species," meaning the female gender, had completely disappeared. The sight of them reassured us as to the survival of humankind. We went back to base camp in the rain. Fritz Hobi, Ueli Bühler, and Bruno Durrer were at Camp II, and it was snowing there. Our optimism sank, then rose again, according to the fluctuations of the barometer. We climbed six times to Camp II, at 6500 meters. One morning, I set off with Norbert Joos on what we hoped would be a summit attempt. After less than 1000 feet, we had triggered three avalanches! Mountaineers often subscribe to this theory: Each person has a quota of luck, and you're alive as long as it hasn't run out. Three avalanches for two people in an hour must have made a big dent in the quota. We decided to cut our losses and turn around. We were in the tent at Camp II. A candle lit the interior, we were listening to soft music, and outside a storm raged. The atmosphere was magical, yet at the same time it frustrated me. The peacefulness was almost unbearable. My mind was tormented; I even wondered if there was any purpose to what we were doing—to all this effort and ado. When I think this way, it's because of inactivity. I told myself that climbing an 8000er is worse than a turbulent romance. Failure or happiness hangs by a thread, and I'm not sure if we can choose that thread, or if we know how to. I took a sleeping pill and smothered my dark thoughts.

On October 16, I was back at base camp. I did laundry and took a shower. I was relearning how to function in civilization, because I would soon be returning to it. On October 17, the weather was perfect; it was perfect again on October 18! This time, the weather would hold. It had to. Ueli Bühler and Bruno Durrer started out. They would break trail to Camp III; Norbert and I would follow them in a few days. We reacquainted ourselves with optimism—we didn't even understand how we could have doubted our chances of success for an instant.

On October 20, the news from up high was good: Ueli and Bruno were at Camp III, at 6900 meters. So we were sure of reaching the ridge. On October 21, I lay awake for three hours before my alarm sounded the official wake-up call. Outside, the air was strange—the weather was beautiful and surprisingly hot. The wind carried grains of sand. The moraines were being scattered into the valley, and on the peaks, clouds of snow were being blown almost a mile from the ridges. I had never seen such strange conditions. At Camp III, they were surely stuck in the tent. We arrived at Camp I with the sun; it was 8:00 a.m. We loaded our packs with the sleeping bags and a little food, then we attacked the next section. We knew it by heart, and we climbed through sheer force of habit. Our pace was good despite how tired we were. At the ice wall, the fixed ropes were already stuck in the ice. At times I had to unclip my Jumar and climb several feet without protection to find the ropes again. We finally reached Camp II at around noon. We made a better base for the tent, which had been transformed into a bathtub. On the 5:00 p.m. radio call, we found out that Bruno and Ueli had tried to make it to Camp III but that the wind had quickly turned them back. When they returned to the tent, they were nearly suffocating. After gaining 7900 feet, we were tired, but we still took a sleeping pill since we absolutely had to sleep.

October 22, 4:30 a.m. I told Norbert Joos about my plan. It involved a blitzkrieg, to make up for the days that we had lost; we would climb directly to Camp IV, at about 7500 meters. Norbert was surprised, but he agreed. At around 6:00 a.m. we set out, motivated by the size of our goal. At 8:30, we were already at Camp III. We put on our high-altitude suits and kept going. Ueli, Norbert, and I took turns breaking trail.

At 1:30 p.m., we reached the 7490-meter summit of Roc Noir for the second time. It was then that Bruno Durrer remembered his professional responsibilities: He had to be back at work in Switzerland on November 4, and if everyone wasted their energy climbing peaks that would then have to be descended in any case, Switzerland's gross national product wouldn't be what it is. So we said goodbye there, at 7490 meters. We had spent fifty-two days together. I took a photo of him while the other two continued up the ridge. I started up again and passed Ueli. He muttered something surprising. I turned around and saw a green head on top of a high-altitude climbing suit. He was green! That didn't make me happy—not at all. I still remembered Peter Hiltbrand on Nanga Parbat, and I didn't want to relive that kind of tragedy for anything. Ueli was still lucid, which meant that he had lost none of his strong will: He would hear nothing of descending and wanted to continue to Camp IV, which was 330 feet above us. His stubborn head understood nothing of psychology. Finally we threatened him: "If you insist on sleeping here, we'll have to take you down in the middle of the night, the expedition will be a failure, and who knows how you'll end up!" He allowed himself to be convinced, and set out in Bruno Durrer's tracks.

We arrived at the snow cave and improved its living space. My feet were wet, which made me afraid of setting off the next day for a ridge that ended at 8000 meters, battered by perpetual winds. So I tried to dry them over the stove. I had more luck with Fritz's sleeping bag, and succeeded in setting it on fire on the first try. The snow cave now resembled a chicken coop. We tried to repair the damaged bag with small bandages, because they're so well-known for their insulating properties. The snow cave was as comfortable as one of those little thatched cottages that are better than a king's palace: The candles gave off some heat and flickers of light, and we enjoyed a gourmet meal—mashed potatoes and cheese. We went to bed building castles in the air: We would set off with all of the equipment we needed to complete the traverse, but reaching the east summit of Annapurna I would be a great success on its own. We hoped that the next day would be our lucky one!

October 23, 4:30 a.m. The weather was beautiful and the wind had died down. We didn't cook anything. At around 5:30, we left the snow cave and headed for the east summit. After half an hour, we came to a wall. It wasn't very steep, but I didn't like the looks of it. I started up it, avoiding the south side, which was to the right. So I was taking a line that was tremendously exposed. But after a few steps on the slab, I became afraid, and I slowly descended; it was too risky and I didn't feel like ascending to the heavens with a rope carefully coiled in my pack. I then did my best to belay Norbert, who set out across the slab. I followed. The slope eased off, and at 8:30 we were on the col, at the foot of the east summit. It looked close, but we were sure that it would take us four hours to arrive at the end of that optical illusion. We still had to gain 1600 feet to get there—1600 feet that would be magnified by the weight of our packs: thirty-three pounds that were crushing us and upsetting the fragile alignment of our vertebrae. I had terrible back pain, and the slope was endless. Fortunately, the snow was hard, which saved us from breaking trail. I thought of Frank and Fritz, watching us from Camp III. I imagined that they were quivering with the idea that we would soon be on the east summit. Norbert and I each had our own climbing style: He climbed fast and then rested, whereas I walked slowly and stopped as little as possible. Norbert the hare and Erhard the tortoise. There was no use running; we had to progress wisely, and in the end our speed was the same. But I felt myself growing weaker: My raging hunger reminded me that we had been walking for nine hours on empty stomachs. Just below the summit, we roped up because it was a tricky section. Norbert stayed in the lead; I had never suffered that much. At last, at around 2:00 p.m., we were on the east summit. The wind had come up and was blowing violently, as it always does at those altitudes.

Then something incredible happened: As if we had never doubted what to do, we plunged toward the col that separated the east and middle summits; as if both our energies had been programmed to conquer the main summit, we continued that unbelievable traverse. We hadn't said a word to each other, because our thoughts were in complete unison. The descent was much less difficult than we had expected, but the wind would have loved to send us waltzing over the edge. In an hour, we were at the col. We decided that the day had been long enough already. After one last radio call to announce our plan to descend via the north face after reaching the main summit, we got ready for the night. We dug into the surface, which looked oddly like a wind slab, and worked at carving enough space for two mountaineers out of the ice. Finally, at around 6:00 p.m., we had a place to lie down. We were at around 8020 meters, it was cold, and every fiber of our bodies was shivering. Who knows why we couldn't get that phrase from Sade's song "Why Can't We Live Together" out of our heads. It was a good question: Tell me why we're here, at 8020 meters, in this cold that our bodies are trying to shake off the way a dog shakes off fleas. I took off my boots, stuffed my overboots into my sleeping bag, removed my two pairs of socks and tucked them next to my stomach. I put a pair of down mittens on my feet, then my honeycomb socks, and my feet felt something like warmth. I thought to myself that the snow cave would be comfortable were it not for the northwest wind rushing in and the powder snow swirling in after it. It was my first night at 8000 meters, and I was afraid of what might happen because of this bivouac. We were at the point where the smallest error could turn into a disaster. I wished that the refrain would stop kicking around in my head.

Tell me why, on Wednesday, October 24, we got out of our sleeping bags, which were covered with blown-in snow; why did we brush foot-sized clumps of snow off our boots; and why did we continue on to the main summit, when the wind was more violent than the previous day, and surely less violent than the next. At around 10:00 a.m., the middle summit was behind us. We began descending toward the final col, which was just before the main summit. And what a surprise: We found ourselves above a 300-foot-high rock band, more than enough to break our bones! I thanked the heavens for encouraging me to bring two pitons—two sad pitons; two invaluable pitons. We set up some rappels and landed at the final gap. After leaving our packs there, we set off much lighter for the final few hundred feet of climbing. I felt as if I had wings. In an hour, we were on top of the 8091 meters that make Annapurna the tenth-highest peak on earth. It was 1:30 p.m., and we fell into each other's arms. A great feeling of happiness flowed through me. The statistician in me thought that we might have accomplished a new route over Glacier

Dome (7190 meters) that day, the third ascent of Roc Noir (7490 meters), the first ascent of the east ridge of Annapurna and its three summits (east, middle, and main), and maybe the first traverse of an 8000er in Nepal. You'll notice that I said "maybe." That's a wise linguistic precaution, because in order to celebrate this first traverse of a Nepali summit, you have to arrive at the north face base camp alive, and that, as the fishermen say, is another kettle of fish.

We had just done something amazing, and yet I felt strongly that the adventure had only begun. Why didn't we just retrace our route? Because the rock band eliminated that option. We stayed on the summit for ten minutes, then descended to the col, where we shouldered our packs before venturing down the north face. We progressed carefully, as if we were fording a river and each step might be our last, as if the torrential emptiness of this wall were going to carry us away. During the entire two-and-a-half-hour descent, there would be three of us: Norbert, me, and fear. Our only description of this gigantic north face was a postcard that I had brought in the pocket of my pack. The little that we could make out showed a face that was a heap of seracs, divided by vertical rocks. It would be an exaggeration to say that we faced certain death, but it would be false to say that our survival was assured. In fact, we would have to navigate through the zone between death and life; that, I think, is the very definition of survival. I knew that there were two routes on that north side: the historic Sickle route, which cost Herzog and Lachenal a good part of their hands and feet, and the Dutch route, which is more direct and therefore faster. We opted for the Dutch route. Now all we had to do was find it.

At around 6800 meters, we began setting up a fourth bivouac. We got out the tent, and one of the poles slipped out of our hands. It stopped 300 feet below us, in an inaccessible spot. Modern tents are well engineered: Every single pole is critical for stability. We secured the tent with a section of rope. It was 6:00 p.m. when the makeshift camp was set up. I made two liters of tea and broth. For thirty-six hours, we had drunk practically nothing, and we were fueling ourselves on two Ovo Sport bars per day. The tent shuddered in the violent wind while I summarized our situation: We were perched precariously above an icefall, our only equipment being an ice ax each, 165 feet of five-millimeter rope, and an ice screw. It wasn't exactly Medusa's raft, but it wasn't the *Clemenceau* aircraft carrier either.

The next day, on October 25, we waited for the sun, which didn't come out. At around 8:30 a.m. we resumed our descent. We absolutely had to find the start of the Dutch route—on the postcard, a tiny spur that was our life raft. We found the spur and realized that the life raft was full of holes: Menacing seracs hung above. I kept going and noticed a fixed rope 300 feet below us. Proof that someone had already attempted this line and that humanity wasn't completely unfamiliar with the area! But how would we get to it? Everywhere I turned lay horror. What I saw filled me with fear: Everything was vertical; we were prisoners of the vertical. What could we do? Go back up and take the French route? In our state of fatigue, that would take an entire day. It was unthinkable. So we decided to risk the descent.

Norbert passed me his ice ax and took the only ice screw from our meager gear rack; I started lowering him for what we thought would be 165 feet. But after about twenty feet, he shouted to me that the wall was overhanging. He then started doing a big pendulum—with the rope tied around his waist, and wearing a thirty-five-pound pack—and he was able to land on a ledge. Now he only needed to anchor himself; but without an ice ax, that was impossible. So I descended several feet and slid him an ice ax. He secured himself and passed the tool back up to me; then it was my turn to play this stomach-turning game. I spotted an ice block that looked more solid than the others, so I passed the rope around it to use it as a top-rope anchor and descended with Norbert belaying. In every game of Russian roulette, there's a moment when you have to pull the trigger: I came to the overhang and then I had to continue, despite my paralyzing fear. I jumped into the void and landed fifteen feet lower. Because the rope was too short, I unroped in order to carve an ice bollard as an anchor. It took us four rappels to reach the base of the pillar.

Contrary to our hopes, the next section wasn't very appealing, either. The ice was bare and we decided to unrope, because if you're going to slip and fall to your death, better to do that alone and cut the number of victims in half. This wasn't egoism, it was altruism. We descended sixty-five-degree slopes in terror; we would have laughed at them had we had two ice axes each. We found some old fixed ropes and followed them, and at around 4:00 p.m., we arrived on the big plateau. But this wasn't the end of our worries, because that was the runout for all of the avalanches that come off Annapurna. And to think that there are expeditions that climb the peak via that face! Those must be climbers who are tired of being alive. We saw the remains of a camp, and went to investigate in the hope of finding something to eat—anything more substantial than our Ovo Sport bars. Instead, we found the corpse of a Sherpa that a team from the year before had abandoned, with no burial other than a straightjacket of frost and no tomb other than the dome of the skies. When night fell, we collapsed near a rock, quenched our thirst at a puddle, got out our sleeping bags, and slid into them fully clothed. We were at the point where, as long as our primary needs were met, our souls were satisfied.

On Friday, October 26, we had been awake for an hour, waiting for the sun to hit us, when the mountain echoed with a sound that we knew well: the swelling roar of a serac avalanche. At first, we gazed at it like high-altitude aesthetes; it was a grandiose sight. But soon, one thought gained ground along with the cataclysm: Instead of spectators, we were becoming players in the drama. It was now clear that the avalanche was going to bury us, and I felt the hair rising on the back of my neck. We wormed our way into our sleeping bags and clung to our ice axes. Despite the distance, the air blast shook us. We were left dusted with powder and shaken, but alive and well under a couple of inches of snow—instead of six feet of dirt as we had feared.

At 1:00 p.m., we stepped onto the moraine. The gates of hell had closed behind us, and they held our doubts, fears, and anxieties captive. Back on firm ground, we could once again think beyond the present moment. We no longer had to use the word "tomorrow" with "if"—"Tomorrow, if the seracs hold. . . ." "Tomorrow, if we find the right line. . . ." "Tomorrow, if we can get past the bulge. . . ."—and we caught ourselves using the future tense unconditionally. We walked for an hour and arrived, like starving zombies, at a Japanese and Czech expedition's base camp. The climbers offered us something to eat and drink and congratulated us. In ten days, we would meet back up with our fellow expedition members in Kathmandu; but right there, right then, we were in heaven on Earth.

SISYPHUS THE MOUNTAINEER

There is a fundamental difference between alpinists and everyone else on Earth, between people of action and thinkers, and between the brave and the braggers: One group lives and the other philosophizes. Inevitably, there is a moment when the question of "Why?" arises. This is a summons to appear before the court of rational people: "Why, or in the name of what fallacious ideal, are you risking your neck?" asks the prosecutor, cloaked in his drape of virtue. The crowd approves, because "Once it has classified these feats as useless, it thinks that it has said it all. 'Senseless risk . . . You have no right . . .'; because everything in our society is perfectly regulated, even the risk of death," wrote Samivel. In a civilization of wage slaves, where people seek to survive more than to live, mountaineering is an enigma. And the contradiction has been apparent ever since the earliest ascents: After the Matterhorn tragedy in 1865, Queen Victoria became concerned about her subjects' longevity and briefly considered prohibiting mountaineering; Mallory answered awkwardly that he climbed mountains "because they were there." And a half century later, Warren Harding added a codicil: He climbed mountains "because they were there, and because [he was] crazy." By saying that, the conqueror of El Capitan hoped to escape the torment of the question, because by definition, a crazy person is one who is no longer responsible for his actions. Madness erases the need for any justification.

When Erhard Loretan began gaining media attention, the debate wasn't over. He was the third person to climb all fourteen 8000ers. Reinhold Messner had explained himself at length in his writing; through his books *The Seventh Grade* and *Free Spirit*, he secured his place as one of the great adventure theorists. "When I look for practical explanations, I find only pretexts, but no meaning. By walking, climbing, and action, I resolve the question of meaning." He believes that the answer lies in action. Jerzy Kukuczka, the second player in the 8000er trio, is no longer here to make his case, but he left a posthumous statement that is still being interpreted: "Up there, you live through more things in a month than in long years of the daily grind." Erhard Loretan admitted that he had no response. He saw that some individuals will never be satisfied with the limitations on human existence; he called these people "conquerors" and modestly included himself among them. Whether we're talking about Erhard Loretan or Reinhold Messner, Neil Armstrong or Vasco da Gama, their destinies have elevated all of humanity. Not everyone buys this argument. In January 1996, Erhard Loretan and two other alpinists were interviewed on German-speaking Swiss television. He was questioned by a theologian and by a woman whose husband had just died in the Himalaya. "When I saw you, I thought I was seeing death," the woman declared. "The general public doesn't understand why we climb the 8000ers and demands a response. How are you going to explain what happens up there, to people who've never even climbed a hill?" asked Erhard Loretan the next day. The interview had left him speechless.

These few words from Lionel Terray are enough to silence the critics: "the conquerors of the useless." It's a wonderful phrase, and the title of a wonderful book that contains this passage: "What we sought was the unbounded and essential joy that boils in the heart and penetrates every fibre of our being when, after long hours skirting the borders of death, we can again hug life to us with all our strength. Nietzsche defined it thus: 'The secret of knowing the most fertile experiences and the greatest joys in life is to live dangerously.'" And besides, maybe we need to see mountaineers as a symbol of humankind caught up in its existential quest, an eternal victim of the absurd? "Going to the summit, or at least to the limits of endurance, is enough to fill the soul and free the spirit," wrote the famous Doug Scott. His statement is reminiscent of Camus: "The struggle itself toward the heights is enough to fill a man's heart. One must imagine Sisyphus happy."

When the winds blew all around him and the mountains struck back against the humans sticking to them like spines, when the elements played furioso the score of a demented conductor, when danger frayed the thread of life, one must imagine Erhard happy.

| 6 |

NOTHING IS IMPOSSIBLE

"The cold is heavy. Contrary to what people think, a −50-degree cold weighs much more than a −40-degree cold. It's as if you had ten extra kilos on your shoulders."

—Jean-Louis Etienne

IN 1983, I WAS BARELY back down from Broad Peak when I became focused on one dream: trying to climb K2. I had just strung together three 8000ers in seventeen days, including the fastest-ever ascent of Broad Peak and a new variation on Hidden Peak, but I wasn't satisfied. "The worst thing in all this is that I really want to go to K2 with the English expedition," I confided to my trip journal. I remember going around to all of the base camps. The English expedition welcomed me warmly, invited me for a meal, and honored me with the opportunity to speak with Doug Scott, Don Whillans, Alan Rouse, Roger Baxter-Jones, and Jean Afanassieff, but I was waiting for an offer that didn't come: to go to K2 with them. The Spaniards offered me some tea and bread, the Italians (including Renato Casarotto) gave me fruit salad, yet no one invited me to join an expedition. However, after stuffing myself all day, I would have been out of place to complain. I left the Baltoro region with a full stomach, but frustrated. This is proof that man cannot live by bread alone.

K2 is unforgettable, a dazzling sight that stays forever in your eyes. In 1985, I decided to mount a Swiss expedition to K2. I brought together some climbers from my area: Nicole Niquille, who at the time was the first female aspirant guide in Switzerland; Pierre Morand, who already had two 8000ers on his résumé (Broad Peak and Gasherbrum I); and Jacques Grandjean, a mountain guide. I invited Norbert Joos, who had been with me on Nanga Parbat and Annapurna; and Marcel Rüedi, who had accompanied me on the three Baltoro 8000ers, as well as on Manaslu in 1984. Jean Troillet, from the Valais, who had been on Annapurna that same year, also joined us. That made for seven climbers and an ambitious goal: a new route on the south face. In 1983, Doug Scott had led an international expedition on the same face, and it had failed badly. If I remember correctly, at the outset we were all in agreement, with no misunderstandings: We would leave for the Baltoro region with the intention of trying a new route on the south face. When we arrived at base camp, ambition had waned, and every day our resolve weakened. In the shadow of K2, some of us thought that opting for the standard route up the Abruzzi Spur wouldn't be at all dishonorable, and even that it would be an honor to be the first successful Swiss expedition. Marcel Rüedi, who had already done six 8000ers and had set his sights on the race for all fourteen, was among that group, along with Norbert Joos.

The approach march was supposed to take us from Dassu to base camp. On May 6, the day before our departure, Pierre "Pommel" Morand made scientific progress toward using renewable energy. While he was trying to modify our stoves to use Pakistani gas, a huge fireball blew up in his face. The beard that he had been cultivating for ten days wasn't spared. Jacques Grandjean had the presence of mind to turn off the gas line, but in a fraction of a second, Pommel's cowboy look had gone up in smoke. We felt reassured with regard to our energy self-sufficiency and set off for the Baltoro with our minds at ease.

On May 23, our team split into two groups. Norbert, Marcel, Jacques, and Nicole focused on the Abruzzi Spur. Pommel, Jean Troillet, and I headed for the formidable south face. Concave and rugged, this 11,500-foot-high face gives K2 its characteristic pyramid shape. K2, like Ama Dablam and the Matterhorn, looks like the perfect mountain.

In fact, K2 is like forty-one Matterhorns stacked on top of each other in a remote part of Pakistan! If we were successful on our climb of the south face, we would dedicate it to Vincent Charrière and Jean-Claude Sonnenwyl. Vincent had died in an avalanche in March 1983, and Jean-Claude had died in April 1984 while attempting a ski descent of the north face of Mont Dolent. Their deaths had taken away our naïveté. On the 23rd, Jean, Pommel, and I climbed up the north ridge of Broad Peak to acclimatize and to photograph the south face of K2. On the 24th we were all back in camp.

Norbert and Marcel kept making attempts up the Abruzzi Spur, despite the heavy snow. We started for the south face. At midnight on May 29, we attacked. At about 5:45 a.m., we reached 6000 meters. We were moving quickly, but we had to admit that the snow conditions were dangerous. In addition, Pierre had an ear infection that we thought had healed but that had returned at altitude. After ascending 4300 feet, we turned around. Up on the spur, Nicole was alone at Camp I. Norbert, Marcel, and Jacques were in Camp II and told her that there was no room for her there. I don't know where I've read a story like that: In the dark, a woman was knocking on hotel doors asking for a room, and everywhere she was told that they were full. I even wondered if, in that story, the woman wasn't pregnant and didn't have her husband with her. Finally she found shelter in a crèche, between a bull and a gray donkey.

On June 4, we made another attempt on the south face. On June 6, we made it to 7000 meters. It was bitter cold, and although we were firmly heterosexual, Pierre and I zipped our sleeping bags together. I radioed Nicole to apologize for being unfaithful due to extenuating circumstances. But once again I was worried about the conditions: I had no confidence in the seracs that lined the south face like wrinkles. I had a bad feeling about things, so I convinced Pierre and Jean to go down. I've read that Chris Bonington made fun of these premonitions that we congratulate ourselves on: "I don't trust premonitions," he said. "You decide that an intuition was correct if you're still alive in the evening, and wrong if you're dead." But still I didn't come to regret our decision: A few days after we descended, the whole serac band that stood at about 8300 meters sheared off. In fifteen seconds it had ravaged the south face and was unleashing its rumbling crest on the God-win-Austen Glacier. The powder blast reached base camp, and you don't have to be a snow scientist to figure out what this tidal wave would have done to us on the face. Today, our three names would be engraved on a stone at the base of K2 for trekkers to pay their respects.

On June 12, Norbert and Marcel were tired of waiting. They had decided to take K2, as one would a fortress. On the 15th they were stuck in Camp II, at around 6700 meters, because of the wind. On the 16th, they tried again and made it to Camp III, at 7350 meters. The radio batteries were more depleted than the climbers, whom we struggled to understand. No news on the 17th or the 18th, so we thought that they must have given up. We assumed that within a few hours, their two silhouettes would come trudging down the glacier to put an end to our worries. The 18th came and went, with no sign of either Marcel or Norbert. On the 19th, we used binoculars to look for them, thinking that every shadow was a human form, but each one was hopelessly still. At around 6:00 p.m. the radio crackled, and we made out some words in the static: Marcel and Norbert had summited! They had just wiped out six years of failure on the Abruzzi Spur; Messner and Dacher had made the last successful ascent. This news lit a fire under the entire team—the next morning, at 4:00, all five of us would set off with a week's worth of food and fuel.

When we arrived at Camp I, at about 6000 meters, we met Norbert and Marcel. They had spent nine days on the mountain and three nights above 8000 meters, including a bivouac at 8350 meters; they were a sight to behold. They weren't in grave condition, but both of them had frostbitten feet. Norbert's case was the most severe: All of his toes hurt, and he was having trouble seeing. He would end up glissading on his rear end most of the way down, in order to spare his feet. But the damage was done: Jacques Grandjean, who accompanied them to base camp, later told us that poor Norbert's toes turned white, then purple, then black. At first they were swollen, then they became shriveled, then his feet swelled and his skin cracked. At base camp, Jacques followed the Broad Peak expedition doctor's advice and gave Norbert up to six injections of anticoagulants and morphine every day.

No one bivouacs at 8350 meters without a sleeping bag in extreme conditions with impunity. Norbert would have to have all of his toes amputated when he returned to Switzerland. Marcel escaped with second-degree frostbite.

I didn't intend to pay that kind of price to climb a mountain, even K2—the dream factory, as climbers refer to it. On June 26, we were at 8000 meters on the Abruzzi Spur, but it had been rough going through deep snow. We had spent two frigid nights and we were tired. Tired, but rational: We took advantage of a break in the weather to go back to base camp before the effects of our burst of energy became irreversible. No one wanted to freeze to death on that ridge or to die of exhaustion. When we arrived back in base camp, Jacques, Norbert, and Marcel had just been evacuated by helicopter. Now there were only four of us. The expedition had been enjoyable, but it was starting to drag out; we had spent almost two months at the foot of this "spike." That was too long, and every attempt chipped away at our motivation. Our desire to go home was prevailing over our spirit of adventure. Why go up yet again, to "freeze them off" up there? Together, we decided to make one last attempt on the summit and then go home, whether in victory or in defeat. On Thursday, July 4, the weather cooperated just as despair was moving in. Nicole, Jean, Pierre, and I left base camp at around 3:00 in the morning. A French team of four climbers followed close behind us; we recognized Eric Escoffier. It was a clear night and we climbed without headlamps. The snow conditions were much better than on our last attempt. We climbed straight to Camp II, at 6800 meters. We were perfectly acclimatized—not surprising in light of the time we had spent on the mountain. Our pace was twice as fast as before, to the extent that by 10:00 we were already setting up more tents for the crowd that was pushing its way onto the Abruzzi. On July 4 there were twelve of us on the ridge: climbers from France, Switzerland, and Japan.

At sunrise on July 5, we left the tents and continued upward. The first steps at dawn are always difficult, until you reach cruising speed—or what passes for cruising speed when you're hauling yourself up fixed ropes and ascending rock bands 7000 meters above sea level. That was the hardest day. At around 10:00 a.m. the sky was already clouding over and there were snow flurries. About 300 yards from Camp III, the snow became so deep that it was virtually impossible to continue. I was sinking up to my hips. Every movement took me back to where I had started; I had to set down my pack and dig a trench with my ice ax in order to move my feet up a few inches. The whole exercise would have been much less stressful if I hadn't been continuously worrying that the entire slope might slide! We were too close to camp to give up, so we pressed on. At 11:00 we arrived at the spot for Camp III, at 7400 meters. We set up two additional tents and immediately made hot drinks.

It was snowing harder and harder. We had counted on making it to the summit in one push by leaving that night from Camp III, but that plan was a nonstarter. Like Thomson and Thompson in the *Tintin* comics, I would say even more: Our chances of conquering K2 were compromised. No need for a lengthy discussion—I only had to look at my companions' long faces to assess our chances of success. The mood was morose.

At 6:00 p.m., to our great relief, the sky forgot its threats for a moment and some blue patches appeared. We prepared meticulously for what we assumed would be the most difficult hours of our lives. Out of the eight who had started that morning, there were only five of us left to try for the summit: Nicole, Pierre, Jean, Eric Escoffier, and me. We left camp at around 9:00 p.m. The night was thick, and the wind was strong. We didn't carry packs. I had only a half-liter water bottle with me. Sharp minds will point out that a water bottle has never made a bivouac very comfortable and that it's hard to sleep in a half-liter bottle, but I'll respond that we truly hoped to avoid camping out on this summit push. At around 7600 meters, Nicole felt the beginnings of phlebitis in one leg. At that point she knew that, for her, victory meant returning safely to base camp, so she decided to rejoin the rest of the team at Camp III, then go down to base camp the next day.

It was a cold night: minus forty degrees Fahrenheit. To push into the wind, the snow, and the cold, you have to love a good battle. But our confidence was unshakable: In a few hours, it would be summit day. We were perfectly acclimatized, and this would save us from spending a night at 8000 meters at Camp IV. I knew that above 7000 meters, nothing regenerates, even during sleep. The simple fact of living at that altitude is a luxury that wolfs down one's energy. I thought that the summit was doable in one push starting at 6800 meters. And who wanted to bet on the good weather holding? For all of those reasons, the conclusion was simple: We had to go for it!

At around 1:00 a.m. on July 6, we were at Camp IV. We had planned on stopping to eat, but a serac had gotten there before us, mowing down everything in its path; the tents were destroyed. There was only one solution if we wanted to avoid frostbite: Keep going. At daybreak, we were climbing a fairly steep couloir that led to the crux of the standard route—the Bottleneck, located below a large serac band. These were some of the most impressive seracs that I had ever seen, and we were extremely tense. We had to pass below this Sword of Damocles as quickly as possible. If it hadn't been for the altitude, the lack of oxygen, the exposure, and everything that gives the Karakoram its appeal, we would have run in order to spend as little time as possible in the line of fire. At 8200 meters, all we could do was "slowly hurry." Above the seracs, the snow was again very deep and there were more and more wind slabs. We relayed each other out in front continually, but it still took more than five hours to cover the final 1300 feet.

It was 2:00 p.m. Pierre, Jean, Eric, and I stood at 8611 meters on top of K2, the second-highest mountain on earth! We were bursting with joy; all of our efforts were being rewarded. The months of waiting, the discouragement, the interpersonal tension, all of it melted away. This hour when we felt like the kings of the world justified our insanity. The weather was splendid. We took photos and soaked up this one-of-a-kind moment. This time there would be no frostbite. By late afternoon we were back at Camp III. The descent was tricky, and we had to focus our attention. Fatigue dulled our reflexes; in our condition, the smallest error could quickly become fatal. On July 7, we arrived safe and sound at base camp. But Chogori ("Great Mountain"), as the locals call it, would claim one victim. The day after our victory, Daniel Lacroix was seen for the last time, at about 8400 meters.

Four months later, on November 9, Pierre Morand, Jean Troillet, Pierre-Alain Steiner, and I set off for Dhaulagiri (8167 meters) in winter. Somebody was once shrewd enough to ask me, "Why go to Dhaulagiri in winter?" First, because that's the season with the most extreme conditions; there is nothing more difficult than spending the winter at 8000 meters, and mountaineers, who are not to be confused with masochists, love to push their personal limits. Second, because mountain conditions are never as good as in winter, after the wind has scrubbed the snow off the faces. My first winter expedition confirmed these two theories—the climbing conditions were excellent, and the weather was horrific. It was exactly what I had come for.

On November 15, we left from Jomsom, fifty miles northeast of Pokhara, for Dhaulagiri base camp. For me it was a dream expedition. In this part of Nepal, I was able to forget K2, with its bureaucratic hassles, its interpersonal conflict, and the endless stay it had required. After an initial reconnaissance of the east face of "Dhaula," Pierre Morand quit the expedition and we went back to our snow cave below the wall, at 5000 meters. At midnight on December 6, we attacked the face, which towered nearly 10,000 feet above us. On K2 we had opted to go light and had climbed the Abruzzi Spur in two days. Here, we continued the trend: Our packs hung sadly on our backs, containing only a shovel, a bivy bag, and a few other trinkets. It was bold, but when you remove the turtle from its shell, it becomes a hare. The face was in excellent condition; the snow was hard and we progressed quickly without belaying. After eighteen hours of nonstop climbing, we were at 7900 meters. We only had 950 feet of elevation to gain, but we were stymied by darkness and the horrible wind. We decided to stop there for the night. In fact, we should have arrived there in the morning so that we could continue our summit push. We had planned our attack badly, and we would have plenty of time to ponder that planning error. If anyone slipped where we were, the face could easily turn into a toboggan run. So we started chopping a ledge, but the shovel was useless against the hard snow. We clawed a few laughable inches out of the mountain and barely had room to sit down on the flat spot. We got out our paltry gear, and then the wind made sure to disperse it.

The night began: one of the longest nights of my life. Jean Troillet had gone to the trouble of hauling his sleeping bag up. At first we scoffed at this concern for comfort, but as the night wore on and the cold settled in, our scorn turned into a kind of jealousy. Pierre-Alain and I had only Gore-Tex bivy bags, which repel the wind but not the cold, and we cast the evil eye at Jean in his billowy cocoon. Being a prince and a gentleman, however, Jean appeased us by offering a bit of his warmth, covering us with his sleeping bag one at a time. But it was a long night. From time to time, we forced a bit of conversation before the cold quickly snuffed it out, or someone attempted a joke to break the chilled silence. We tried to doze off to make the time pass; our thoughts were our only diversion, and our bodies were completely given over to shivering. We could not stop shivering . . . But the cold was not the kind of foe to be impressed by our quaking, and it pugnaciously gripped our bodies. It was a deep cold—minus fifty-eight degrees Fahrenhheit, we estimated. All three of us were chained to Dhaulagiri, hanging from ice screws, waiting for dawn. And when the sun came to herald our emancipation, no one considered taking advantage of that freedom. We got ready, and as if none of us had even thought of retreating as we lay awake, as if the words "give up" had never been part of our nighttime vocabulary, we kept going. That was a revelation for me; the fact that in spite of it all, we kept going that morning, helped me understand that nothing can stop a determined person. To this day, I can't believe that none of us mentioned giving up. At that moment I said to myself, "Nothing is impossible."

At 1:30 p.m. on December 8, we stood on the summit of Dhaulagiri. We had just made the first successful winter ascent of the east face. We stayed on the summit for forty minutes despite the wind, and then we descended. Pierre-Alain Steiner was suffering from the altitude; he no longer exuded his usual sense of security. After he took a sliding fall that caused disaster to flash before our eyes, we decided to rope up for the descent.

My honor has never been determined by the few millimeters in diameter of a rope.

"BIG BROTHER," PIERRE MORAND

Over time, Pierre Morand withdrew from the game. He appeared in Erhard Loretan's first adventures as "Pommel," a shadow on a limestone spire, a rope partner with whom to defy the abyss, and a brother in arms who endured those first high-altitude battles with Erhard. But on Dhaulagiri in 1985, he decided that for the time being, he had had enough of flouting gravity and its laws. Earlier that year, Pierre and Erhard had finished the *Portes du chaos* route on the Eiger (ED+) in a single day. On the east face of Dhaulagiri, however, with three men in pursuit of their fourth 8000er, in mid-December in arctic temperatures (reportedly minus fifty-eight degrees Fahrenheit), Pierre felt that his personal thermostat was no longer up to the task. "Dhaula in winter was awful," he later admitted. "There was the cold, of course, and our method. On the face, Erhard was out front with the rope in his pack, and the three of us—Pierre-Alain Steiner, Jean Troillet, and I—were hanging from vertical walls. I thought that we were half-crazy." That would be Pierre's final attempt on an 8000-meter peak, after having conquered Hidden Peak, Broad Peak, and K2. He turned his back on the Himalaya, convinced that if he had tried to keep up with Erhard Loretan's diabolical pace, he would have ended up at the foot of a slope somewhere, frozen. Following this change of heart, "Pommel" became Pierre Morand and ran a family business using the strength he had forged on the world's greatest faces.

Yet he still remembered, as if it were the day before, the first time he saw Erhard Loretan climb. The wall in the Charmey quarry was used by all of the local boys who wanted to test their teenage skills on it. But it seemed to offer itself to Erhard, whereas the others appeared to be violating it. This was an example of instinct. Otherwise, how can you explain the pet cat that one day wakes up as a predator, or the energy that awakens in the lark on the fall equinox? Otherwise, how can you explain that with rock, Erhard found a warmth and a closeness that were thought to have disappeared with the troglodytes? And when he ventured onto ice for the first time, how can you explain that crampons, which would make even a ballerina stumble, seemed like retractable claws on his feet? And how was Erhard so sure with an ice ax, so sure in his motion that he always found a good placement on his first swing? What explained his routefinding ability, which allowed him to part the fog, climb ridgelines, and escape from crevassed labyrinths, only to arrive exactly at the camp or the hut? Interviewed when Loretan was still alive, Pierre Morand summarized this mystery in one word: "Instinct!" He continued, "Erhard has instinct. At age fifteen he was a mountain man, in the true sense of the word: The mountains were his natural environment. From his first climbs, he was in a class of his own; over the years, the difference became less apparent, but it always came surging back at the crucial moments. I have climbed with very, very strong men like Pierre-Alain Steiner, and in the Himalaya I met the Polish climbers. But no one ever made an impression on me like that. Erhard is one of a kind." To close this description, which has become a bit effusive, let's say that one day a flying saucer landed on our good old planet, and Erhard came out of it.

Talented enough to recognize genius, Pierre preferred to be Erhard's second rather than lead with someone else. As a result of bivouacking on ledges that made for very close quarters, and shivering together to warm up, a "noble" friendship, as Pierre called it, grew between the two men. A noble and true friendship, as is the case in every friendship between two loners. Pierre offered a minimalist description of their relationship: "We can go for two days without talking; that doesn't bother me. Better to say nothing than to talk bullshit."

New routes in the Gastlosen, a first ascent in the Droites, the Supercouloir, the Cima Ovest di Lavaredo . . . Pierre Morand doesn't dwell on his memories. He refuses to become nostalgic, because he is on the fringe of humanity, among those who live only in the present: the adventurers. But there were also Jean-Maurice, Jean-Claude, Freddy, Vincent, Erhard, Bernard, Nicole, Françoise—a handful of characters the mountain had adopted. And how many of them set off joyfully for faraway climbs, only to rest forever on that now-dim horizon? Death, like a rubber band waiting to snap, barged in on their youth: Avalanches, falls, illness, and accidents decimated the group. Vincent, Jean-Claude, Freddy, Bernard, to mention only those in the inner circle, are gone. "All those friends you did crazy things with . . . And you can no longer talk about them . . . It takes away a big part of who you are," said Pierre. In his youth, he stood on firm ground and watched Erhard's solo climbs on Gross Turm. Decades later, nothing had changed. He followed Erhard's Himalayan tribulations with the indulgence of an older brother who knows that unruliness runs in the family. But when, after months of silence, the phone rang and Pierre heard Erhard's voice, he also heard himself exhale.

7

ANDRÉ GEORGES INTRODUCES ME TO HIS GRANDMOTHER

*"Swim. That's what everyone says. If you are caught in
an avalanche, swim. . . . The instruction manual writers
must be bloody comedians."*

—Joe Simpson

"HELLO? HI, IT'S ANDRÉ GEORGES. So, I'm thinking about trying
the 4000ers again this winter. Are you interested?"

" . . . OK, why not?"

I thought for as long as that ellipsis took to read. At the end
of 1985, when this phone call took place, I barely knew André
Georges—really only through reading a few newspaper articles about
one of his winter solos in the Alps. I also knew that he demonstrated
a certain kind of stubbornness: You don't have to succeed in order
to persevere. With the guide Michel Siegenthaler, he had already
made two attempts on what would be called the "Imperial Crown,"
the enchainment of thirty-eight peaks, including thirty 4000ers in
the Valais Alps, in winter. In 1983 they were turned back by bad
weather after traversing the Mischabels. In 1984 the project ended

in an avalanche on the Adlerpass, and Michel Siegenthaler almost remained there for good. For his third attempt, André Georges had picked me; it was the kind of honor one doesn't refuse. In the amphitheater, would a gladiator turn down an invitation from one of his rivals? I had just agreed, but the idea had always seemed crazy to me. How could we get three weeks of good weather in the middle of winter? In the heat of the action, I would come to realize that good weather was a secondary concern; it was just a piece of the decor, a sliver of blue in the photographs. Of the nineteen days it took for the enchainment, only seven would have good weather!

Since this adventure, this alpine marathon, I've learned a little more about André Georges. Alone and in winter, he had devoured (sinfully, like a glutton) the north faces of Lyskamm (Nessi-Andreani route), Mont Collon, the Dent Blanche, and the Matterhorn (the Gogna route on the Nez de Zmutt). He had also left his crampon tracks on all four ridges of the Dent Blanche in one day. No problem . . . He saw the peak every morning from his bed, and with his hands folded on the pillow, he could gaze out at the venue of his exploits. But he had outgrown the Herens valley when he climbed Ama Dablam. From the bio he had sent to sponsors (a modern-day necessity), I knew that he was married to Agnès and had three children, that he was born in 1953, and that he carried 203 pounds on his six-foot three-inch frame. Just a kid! So I was game. At that time, when achievements were defined by speed, why wouldn't André and I want to make the enjoyment last? Three weeks of strolling through the hills—I was thirsty for adventure. Was it possible to stay at altitude for that long, and in winter, under dreadful conditions? Could we physically stand it? How about emotionally? Could we climb for ten to twenty hours a day for three weeks? And deal with a monotonous diet? All of these questions made André's proposal appealing. I wanted to go and see for myself.

We selected the exact day for our departure: the next stretch of good weather. On February 12, 1986, I waited for André in the cafeteria at the Sion train station, my eyelids drooping. Carnaval season in Gruyère had wrapped up the night before, and I had just shed my Indian costume. I still had peace pipe smoke stuck in my throat, firewater in my stomach, and bison galloping under my scalp. It was a cold and beautiful day—and I needed André to show up. What on earth was he doing? By late afternoon, I decided to walk up to see Agnès; did she know where her husband was? Together we found out that André was in lockup at the Sierre police station for a ridiculous issue to do with his military service. Serve the homeland, and your efforts won't be forgotten! He was being held for questioning. I was torn: Should I head off on a climb with a criminal? Imagine the drama that might unfold in the icy solitude . . . But fortunately, André wasn't the excitable type, and the next day he met up with me to buy food and resolve some problems with our sponsors. We brought our supplies to Zermatt, where Air Zermatt would handle the food drops.

On February 14, we set off from Grächen despite all the indications that we should stay in our pajamas. The wind was blowing at fifty miles an hour on the Klein Matterhorn, and the mountaineering experts told us that this didn't bode well for enchaining thirty-eight peaks. Nevertheless, we left at 9:30 a.m., a helicopter dropped us off on the Riedgletscher, and we climbed five 4000ers that day. André Georges and I got along perfectly. We climbed at the same pace, we felt safe without needing a rope. I won't give the details of those nineteen days in the mountains. Above all, I don't want to bore the reader. But be assured that when we returned to Zinal on March 4, we had followed every ridge from Grächen to Zinal without ever going below 3000 meters.

The traverse was beautiful, very beautiful. In spite of the three days when we were stuck in damp, dark bivouacs. In spite of the nights spent melting snow between our thighs. In spite of the crevasses, even the one that trapped André on the Signalkuppe. In spite of the eleven days of bad weather. In spite of the great risks we took. In spite of the endless traverse of the Crêtes-de-Moming. But really, are mountaineers looking for something other than "in spite of"?

In spite of the endless Crêtes-de-Moming, I said. André, do you remember? For two days, we had been slogging through snow; it was up to your stomach and up to my ears. The stages were already long, and we were getting a little sick of it. After the bivouac on the Rothorn ridge, I asked you what was coming up, because I didn't know where we were going the next day. "We follow the Crêtes-de-Moming and then we climb the Schalihorn.

It's super-easy, a recovery stroll; I ran it with my grandmother!" I fell asleep, trusting in André Georges' grandmother. For an exercise walk, it was an exercise walk! Instead of the five hours that André had predicted, we slogged nonstop for ten hours on dangerous, exposed ridges. Man! I really need to meet your grandmother!

But I will never forget the splendor of the Saint Catherine Ridge, on Nordend. That one day was equivalent to a major winter ascent. Despite the blinding storm and our fingers freezing on the holds, it was the most beautiful stage of our journey. The technical difficulty, the bad weather, our isolation, the thirteen summits under our belts, the altitude of Nordend (4609 meters), all of that combined for a devilish atmosphere.

I've said that the weather wasn't the most favorable, because we had seven days of good weather. Of the other twelve days, we spent three of them stuck in bivouacs during storms. At the Gallarate bivouac on the Jagerhorn, André spent the day sewing while I cooked and tasted delicious high-altitude dishes. At the customs house at Testa Grigia, we sharpened our crampons and drank a bottle or two of Italian wine; and at the Hörnli hut at the foot of the Matterhorn, we did the dishes that other mountaineers had left there: You can't scorn others at high altitude. We also took advantage of the hut to dry our clothes out. The day before, we had been initiated into a semiaquatic sport. It had snowed heavily for two days. It was difficult to walk, and we made little progress. Bruno Jelk, our contact in Zermatt, gave us an ancient pair of skis with indestructible Kandahar bindings that were only seen in a few mountaineering museums and on the Swiss army's skis. "Unfortunately," he said, "I have only one pair, but you can use them if you think they'll help." And they were useful, once we did some Christian sharing. André adjusted the left binding to his size ten and a half, while I battled with the cable on the right ski. We set off like flamingos on skis down the slope from the Klein Matterhorn, then we veered toward the Hörnli ridge. It was a fast and effective method of locomotion, but our boots were full of enough water to overflow our before-dinner cocktail glasses. In fact, after this mono-skiing demonstration, I think I can attest that the manufacturers designed skis in pairs because we have two legs and, for mundane reasons of balance, it's preferable to have a ski on each foot.

On Tuesday, March 4, the adventure ended. It resulted in a solid friendship, mutual understanding without useless chatting, and terrific motivation. At no time had we envisioned giving up; we simply kept climbing. Let's be honest: We were sponsored by the now-defunct daily paper *La Suisse* (may it rest in peace). The days passed and the sidebars crowed: first, "Attacking the 4000ers," then "On the run in the 4000ers," and "Full speed ahead," and later "The fantastic ride," and "On top of the conquest," and finally "They're holding up well." So how would we have dared to go back to the valley? In the end, weary of the gods who spent time on high, we descended to the plains to rejoin the ants who live there.

It goes without saying that this "Imperial Crown," lauded by the media nonstop for nineteen days, earned us more than friendship. The president of the local chapter of the Swiss Alpine Club spoke of "personal vanity." Purists cried that we had defiled the alpine altar. To me, one fact obscured all of these criticisms: On the rest day that we allowed ourselves in Testa Grigia, the oldest and best-known guide from Zermatt, Ulrich Inderbinen, born at the turn of the century (1900), drinking with the best of them, and still going strong, came to encourage us. The rest was merely idle chatter.

Everest took up a good part of 1986. When I returned, André Georges and I threw ourselves into a project that was dear to my heart and that the conquest of Everest hadn't overshadowed: thirteen north faces in the Bernese Oberland in twenty days, with 37,000 feet of elevation gain. It was like the story of the high jumper who breaks seven feet, six inches, then, thinking he has some more in him, has the bar set at seven feet, ten inches. In sum, this enchainment seemed harder, longer, and more technical than the "Imperial Crown." It meant doing in three weeks what most mountaineers would dream of doing in a lifetime: the north faces of the Eiger, the Gspaltenhorn, and the Morgenhorn, among others. Seven routes rated ED (*Extrêmement Difficile*), three rated TD (*Très Difficile*), and three rated D (*Difficile*). We would have to use the full force of our legs, our forearms, and especially our calves, which would be tortured by crampons. Once you've done a few ice faces, you understand why ballerinas have such ample calves and you sympathize with their pain.

On Monday, February 9, 1987, I met André Georges in Grindelwald. Quick gear check. He had forgotten the matches that I was supposed to carry, I had forgotten my balaclava and my gloves. The responsibility was shared. We attacked the 4000-foot north face of the Gross Fiescherhorn (4048 meters), and four hours later we emerged, having climbed at a pace of 1000 feet per hour. We were in good shape for it. That night, the ringing of the phone brought the Mönchsjoch hut back to civilization. Our respective partners, Nicole and Agnès, caught up on our news; the newspapers were clamoring for a story; and my cousin Fritz, who was serving as our liaison, inquired about our health. We were doing fine, until the moment when he told us that the helicopter hadn't been able to do our food drop.

The next day, the conditions made it impossible to set out. We decided to take the train down to Eigergletscher and see what happened. The weather backed off a bit and we hesitated: Should we do the north face of the Eiger, or the north face of the Mönch? The Mönch is less exposed, so that's what we chose. But we shouldn't have. As the saying goes, he who is in a rush to choose sometimes chooses incorrectly. One should always pay attention to proverbs. At midnight on February 12, we got out of bed and put on our skis to begin the long approach that leads to the north face of the Mönch. We worked our way between rock bands of various heights; at one point, my ski came off and I stopped to fix it. André was just above me, several feet to the left. I heard him shout "Watch out!" but I didn't have time to look up before I was swept away by a snow slab that tossed me into the void.

The fall was long, or it felt long to me. I felt an initial impact, but it wasn't too harsh. Everything was fine and the snow was slowing me down. I needed to try to get a pole up, to stay on top of the snow. Would I stop soon? No, I set off on a second flight, one that went forever, and I tensed my muscles to their limit. I prepared for the inevitable forced landing. The impact was so violent that I felt an immediate pain in my back and an intense heat. Then I was off again, still alive and conscious, but I couldn't control my fall in the avalanche, this freight train from hell. I was a marionette whose strings had just been cut: I was in free fall. My God! If I continued like this much longer, it would soon be my last flight. Only angels can fall from the sky. I knew that, lower down, there was a 650-foot wall and that my luck wouldn't last past that. Finally, everything stopped. My head and one arm stuck out of the snow, but I couldn't move and my legs weren't working. I called for André. Nothing. After a few minutes I shouted again and his voice responded. He came down to me and looked at the twelve-foot-high heap of snow in which I was enthroned like a one-armed, legless cripple. "Get me out of here!" I said.

André called my cousin Fritz Loretan, who notified search and rescue. The helicopters were grounded by the foehn, and finally one came from Lauterbrunnen an hour and a half later. I knew the pilot, Dölf Gisler, one of the best in the area; I knew the doctor, Bruno Durrer, who had been with me on Annapurna. The mountains are a small world. Bruno asked me the usual questions: I told him that the pain was bearable. He put in an IV and loaded me into the stretcher, facing the Eigergletscher. "Are you OK?" everyone kept asking. "Yeah, yeah, I'm OK." I'm actually quite well, Your Highness. I slid 1300 feet in an avalanche, hopped a 100-foot rock band and then a 130-foot one, my ribs are smashed, I can't feel my legs, but other than that, everything is great. Everything is great.

An ambulance took me to the Interlaken hospital, where they stuffed me with sedatives. It wasn't until about 11:00 a.m. that a nurse informed me that, because the spine specialist wasn't there, they needed to send me to the Hôpital de l'Ile, in Berne. At 3:00 p.m., I was seen by a team of specialists who were miracle workers. For hours, I was taken around to nearly every department in this university hospital, from radiology to imaging. A little later, the doctor came back to tell me that my case was serious: My second and third vertebrae were crushed and the disks were 90 percent destroyed. He didn't hide the fact that my chances of walking again were slim. But he assured me that he would do everything that he possibly could.

I listened without panicking. I knew that in my line of work, paralysis was an everyday possibility. Of course, the worst outcome for me would be giving up the mountains, which were my whole life. But I think that people can do extraordinary things, even if they can only move around in a wheel-chair. For the moment, however, there was some hope at the prognosis stage, and I clung to it.

I was operated on that very night. The surgery lasted seven hours, and I woke up in a tangle of tubes in intensive care. You could have gotten lost in that mess; through the vines I could make out my mother, Nicole, and André, and I was happy to see them. I was there, but my legs were somewhere else. No one could be sure that they would return. The news of my accident had already spread like wildfire in the press, but I was allowed no visitors and only limited phone calls. It was then that I found out that I had "fathers" all over Switzerland: Journalists called, and when the doctors hesitated, they pretended to be my father. I think I gained four fathers in one day—and my mother hadn't told me anything about it!

The next day, my doctor, Christian Etter, dared to be optimistic and stated that the neurological tests looked good and that I should regain motor function. Five days later, my legs woke up. I felt gentle pins and needles, minute pulses, as if my heart had rediscovered the path that my limbs had wandered onto for a moment. I left the hospital ten days later almost as good as new, and in any case able to walk pretty well for someone who had just fallen down a 100-foot and a 130-foot rock band. The doctors designed me a lovely corset ideal for mono-skiing, which I tried three or four days later. Was that really reasonable? Feeling that the mountains in the area might disturb my peaceful convalescence, I left Gruyère and went to Brazil. There, with my friend Ruedi Zingg, I climbed Sugarloaf Mountain. But I had a hard time finishing 1987 in one piece. In July, I broke two vertebrae while paragliding. I was once again in the hospital in Berne, where there is only one spine specialist—the one who had operated on me in February. He definitely wanted to treat me, but he had to lecture me first: If I didn't follow the restrictions that would ensure a speedy recovery, he was going to put me in a cast from my head to my toes, and then there would be no more gallivanting. I promised to be good, and to wear my corset for three months. A quick mental calculation helped me understand the seriousness of the situation; if I continued breaking four vertebrae per year, in eight years I would have only one intact bone left. I would be as flexible as Erich von Stroheim in *La grande illusion*, which would bode well for some fabulous climbs.

Dreams don't die; they dry up, harden and turn to dust, but all they need is to be watered with a bit of enthusiasm in order to regain their scope and passion. On January 13, 1989, I accompanied André Georges on a new attempt to enchain thirteen north faces in the Bernese Oberland. André Georges, or the return of the living dead: On September 15, 1988, a mysterious Nepali correspondent had proclaimed him dead, but the news was then refuted. André was back with me, thumbing his nose at the maggots. We climbed up to the Mönchsjoch hut, and when we looked at the surrounding faces, a buzz of uncertainty ran through us. The walls were black, austere, and inhospitable.

On January 14, the situation repeated itself. We were at the foot of the north face of the Gross Fiescherhorn, just as we had been two years before. We reached the summit after four hours of climbing, just as we had done two years before. We skied back to the base, alone. This time we wanted to minimize the media hype: There were no journalists to ask how we felt and what we had planned, or to measure the decibel levels of our snoring, record the details of what we ate, and inquire about our digestive problems. The ski descent was fast and calm. We still had time to reconnoiter the approach to the Jungfrau. The slope leading to the big plateau was a sheet of blue ice; by the next day, the downclimb would be risky. We returned to the train station, where an employee bought us a coffee. While I was walking around the staging area, I saw a box full of nails: They were seven inches long—carpenter's nails! An idea came to me and I mulled it over all night. It could later be called a premeditated crime: The next day I went back to the train station and stuck a good-sized handful of nails in my pocket. I overcame my scruples by telling myself that a handful of nails had never put a serious dent in a rail company's budget. When the time came to start the descent, I took the fruits of my larceny out of my pocket and carefully hammered a nail into the ice. I passed the rope behind the nail head and gave André's 200 pounds the honor of testing this revolutionary anchor system. Nature smiled upon us and held him strong! In a few rappels, we quickly reached the base of our second objective: the north face of the Jungfrau.

We didn't usually read topos. We took off up the first couloir that seemed appealing. Of all of the faces, this was the most rotten, and the climbing on the headwall proved to be very tricky. Later, we would learn that we had just summited the Jungfrau via a new route in less than four hours.

The next day, I had an appointment with my old demons. I knew that they were waiting for me in their homespun robes on the Mönch. I took advantage of a TV helicopter to circumvent them. We got dropped off directly at the foot of the face. By avoiding the approach, I wouldn't have to go through the area where my accident had happened, and I felt relieved. There are places that hold dark memories; that slope streaked with rocks is one of them. But the bergschrund brought me back to the present: It was tricky, just like the chute that followed. The ice was fine and glassy. To liven things up, we had left our ice screws in the trunk of the car three days before. That was unfortunate, because a car has less of a need for ice screws than do two mountaineers on the north face of the Mönch on a winter morning. We unroped and continued side by side. The helicopter rose along with us, circling like a fly hypnotized by a lightbulb. We took an alternate route that led us directly below the summit: Three and a half hours to gain 3000 feet—we were in good shape!

The next day, January 17, we allowed ourselves a day to transition to the Eigergletscher in preparation for the north face of the Eiger, the largest face in the Alps. My cousin Fritz Loretan and our friend Simone met up with us. We seized the chance to place an order for fifteen carpenter's nails; they would be useful on Ebnefluh. At 5:00 a.m., we were at the foot of the Eiger. The conditions were excellent, and we didn't take out our rope until the Death Bivouac. There, we took a short break. We climbed the Ramp with the rope tight and without taking off our crampons. The leader would protect the pitch, and when he ran out of gear, the second would go ahead. We felt comfortable enough to take off the rope at the top of the Ramp even though the Traverse of the Gods is tricky. At 3:00 p.m. we stood on the summit. An hour and a half later, we were drinking beer at the Eigergletscher Restaurant. The Eiger is no longer what it was, and the major difficulty these days is routefinding. There are pins everywhere, which can easily mislead the indecisive climber.

On January 19, the ascent of Ebnefluh via its north ridge took us two and a half hours, and on January 20 we set off up the central couloir on the Gletscherhorn. After 300 feet I heard a strange noise. It was far away at first, then closer and closer, until it was on top of me. I dove into a hole, and already there were huge blocks of ice whistling in our ears. They were followed by a torrent of snow. Down below in the couloir, André was right in the firing line. I let the hail of bullets pass, which took almost ten minutes. I poked my head out and glanced below me; there was nothing but a smooth chute that a neat and tidy giant had just swept clean. I shivered. Where was he? On the unmoving mountain, I saw a wiggling mass of snow: André had managed to protect himself behind his pack, and he emerged without a scratch! Four and a half hours later, we were off this front line and no longer being bombarded by blind artillerymen.

On January 24, ten days after the Gross Fiescherhorn, we enchained three faces in one day: Weisse Frau, the Blüemlisalphorn, and the Fründenhorn via a route that I had opened in my younger years. And on January 26, we paraglided off the summit of the Doldenhorn, completing thirteen days of lofty adventures.

More than seven years after this "tour of the north faces" (thirteen faces in thirteen days), I think that from a technical perspective, this was my most difficult expedition. And even though the media showed two mountaineers smiling in the middle of winter, joking on extreme slopes like a sort of Starsky and Hutch of the Oberland, I haven't forgotten the psychological pressure we were under. Nor have I forgotten the sleepless nights when the danger of the next day would come to haunt us in advance. The direst of scenarios unfolded on the black screen of those nights. But if the actor didn't make changes to the screenplay, where would the pleasure be in performing?

NOTHING VENTURED, NOTHING GAINED

As the saying goes, "One cannot vouch for one's courage when one has never been in danger." Climbing generally offers the opportunity to test one's courage. Common mortals, sure of their bravery, try to climb without hastening the evidence of their own mortality. For in mountaineering, as in ice climbing and philately, there is always a way of reducing risk. Some mountaineers like to say that they "calculate risk." This expression is incorrect; it's a trap set by mathematicians to ensnare reason. There are many people who, from the bottom of their graves, show that risk cannot be calculated, that spending time in the mountains implies a calculation error, and that the evaluation of objective hazards is purely subjective. An editorial writer reminded us of René Daumal's definition: "Alpinism is the art of climbing mountains by confronting the greatest dangers with the greatest prudence." But some climbers subscribe to only the first part of the definition: They are fine with confronting the greatest dangers, but as for using the greatest prudence, not so much. Erhard Loretan clearly belonged to that category. He had barely discovered climbing when he threw himself into soloing extreme routes: aid routes rated ED. And when a piton failed, he abandoned aid climbing but not soloing! It's a form of original wisdom that may be specific to sixteen-year-olds: "What fascinates me about soloing is that I have no room for error; it's that feeling of playing with life," he said. From his first solo climbs on the faces of the Gastlosen, to the traverse of Annapurna, to Kangchenjunga, there is a constant: a thirst for risk. In speaking about his attempt to link the summits of Lhotse and Lhotse Shar, and the extreme commitment involved, Erhard dropped the remark, "In fact, that's exactly what I'm looking for: survival; the breaking point." Psychiatrists talk about a category of people who are aware of their life only when they come close to death.

In a safe and secure world, this thirst for risk comes as a shock and an affront to society. For ethnologists, it represents the vestiges of initiation rites: In our society, the prestige of adventurers is proportional to the tests that they have taken on. For a moment, they have seized public attention and gained respectability. Sociologists see an ordeal, or a rite calling on the judgment of God: A suspect must undergo a test that will determine his or her innocence (survival) or guilt (death). Mountaineers who venture into what they themselves call the death zone are taking aim at the next world. "If he survives," wrote David Le Breton, "the symbolic deal sealed with death adds to the ecstasy of being alive; it leads to the intoxicating feeling of being protected."[1] Psychologists have their own perception of daredevils. They think that certain negative emotions are able to create positive emotions. This is true of the fear that lies behind the feeling of euphoria. A study done in the 1960s on American parachutists identified this retroactive emotional effect. The researchers concluded, "This succession of fear and euphoria is what motivates recreational parachutists, mountaineers, race car drivers, and other risk takers to seek out the psychological impact produced by fear. In fact, this impact is the reason they love risk."[2]

Erhard Loretan didn't disagree that his adventures could be reduced to just his limbic system, which is the seat of human emotion. When he saw the situation as hopeless, he often relied on adrenaline rushes, which are the physiological manifestation of fear. "The more you risk, the greater the gain. For example, if I look at the expedition to Peru, the only thing I remember fifteen years later is Caras I and its impossible exit. I know that I was struggling on that section and that I was ecstatic on the summit." Lastly, there is a theory stating that "Everyone has a risk thermostat." These thermostats are set to different temperatures depending on the individual. "Each person tries to react to a new situation in such a way that the risk level corresponds to his or her personal thermostat," wrote Michael Thompson.[3] Neurologists mention an "anxiety trait" that is stronger or weaker depending on the test subjects.

Whether we're talking about thermostats or anxiety traits, we have to admit that risk was an essential component of Erhard Loretan's personality. He had only recently survived the 8000ers when he threw himself into snowboarding down impossible faces, skiing extreme couloirs, and paragliding on unpredictable thermals. Speaking about one of the friends he had lost, Erhard said, "Rubbing shoulders with death was his drug." Let's close with a saying since we started with one: "The traits we criticize in others are those we criticize in ourselves."

8

ALL YOU NEED IS A
LITTLE WILLPOWER

*"This first ascent, barely mentioned by the media, is worth more in
my eyes than a dozen 8000ers."*

—Reinhold Messner

AT THE TIME OF OUR climb, Everest was still 8848 meters. Six years
later, on September 29, 1992, Benoît Chamoux enabled a scientific
team to measure it precisely: A dumbfounded world learned that, for
years, Everest had laid a false claim to two of those meters. If we had
known this earlier, would we have stopped two meters lower? Who
knows. But on August 30, 1986, Jean Troillet and I were flushed
with pride at having conquered those 8848 meters that were actually
only 8846. Vanity of vanities; all is vanity.

At the very beginning of this expedition, there was Jean Troillet. He
had the Everest permit. He hoped to climb the north face alone. I
met Pierre Béghin at a mountain film festival in Annecy, France. Of
course I knew him by reputation. He was an engineer from Grenoble, France, with an impressive résumé: three 8000ers, including a
spectacular solo ascent of Kangchenjunga in 1983. He let me know

that he wanted to try something with me in the Himalaya. Jean Troillet invited us to join him. From then on, it was the story of the bullfrog that puffs up until it explodes. We were meant to be a team of three on Everest. Pierre Béghin then told us that he had commitments to sponsors. So he was required to allow a film crew to go with him, plus a doctor; and Pierre's wife and her son would come too. Given that herd of people, I suggested to Nicole Niquille that she come with us. In my entire life I have only been on two large-scale expeditions: to K2 and Everest. Both were horrid. Let's say you're trying to put together an eleven-piece puzzle and you have eleven puzzle pieces in your hand. If the eleven pieces come from two or three different puzzles, you can try to force them together all you want, or round off their corners, or cut off the parts that stick out, but you'll never fit them together into a single harmonious image. So we had Annie Béghin; her son, Olivier; Jean Afanassieff, the filmmaker; Marie Hiroz, the sound engineer; Alain Vagne, the doctor; Sandro Godio; Dominique Marchal; Pierre Béghin; Jean Troillet; Nicole Niquille; and me. Eleven people in total. Get the intruders out! I don't want to air my dirty laundry in public. Just know that we left for Nepal at the beginning of July and that on August 9, Nicole wrote to the *La Gruyère* newspaper, "The atmosphere has definitely changed; civilization has raised its ugly head in the group, sowing disorder and ill will in our peaceful haven. Self-interest, glory, and money use their tentacles to snuff out friendship, the joy of being in the mountains, and the desire for a team effort. . . . I am not trying to smear any expedition members. Everyone has their own motivation for participating in this kind of adventure. I am only venting my disillusionment about people I believed to be sane. I hope that the future will restore my faith in the values I thought were the bedrock of the mountaineering world." End of story.

July is one of the monsoon months in Nepal. The monsoon means that the earth begins to miss the time when everything was liquid. So it sends whole mountainsides, and the roads that were on them, back to their original state. On July 13 we left Nepal for China. Zhangmu, a remote little border post in the mountains, marked the beginning of China, the Chinese, and the Chinese way of doing things. It was the first time that an expedition had been there. We had to negotiate for hours with meticulous civil servants.

When a civil servant is also a customs officer, it's very hard to find the line between commendable zeal and lamentable idiocy. When we left the border station, which lay somewhere between China and Kafka, Sino–Swiss relations were forever compromised. We set off in a bus for Xegar, where we had to heave our two and a half tons of equipment into a truck that could drive for twenty hours, cross rivers with water up to its undercarriage, and hug the shoulder while holding onto the cargo. We went over a pass at 5200 meters before entering the Rongbuk Valley, which had led the first expeditions to Everest. The ground was slimy, the trucks got stuck repeatedly, and the men had to lend their muscle to help the reluctant engines. It was an ailing crew that arrived at base camp: We were at 5200 meters and, due to the vehicles, had ascended much too quickly. Nausea, headaches, insomnia, vertigo— every dashboard light on our depressurized bodies was blazing.

On July 21, the yak train arrived at base camp. We intended to set up an advanced base camp at the end of the moraine, at about 5500 meters. For the first foray, we prepared twelve loads of 120 pounds each. It was difficult to walk on the moraines; they looked smooth but in reality were very rough going. We had to set up a Tyrolean traverse in order to cross a raging torrent without being swept away. Yaks have many advantages over people, but they're very clumsy with ropes; since they couldn't use the Tyrolean, they had to walk uphill for an extra hour to find a fording point. As they crossed, they decided to reduce the salinity of the Indian Ocean by dissolving a few pounds of sugar in the café au lait–colored water. Our caravan was slow, and we had to constantly adjust the animals' loads. We arrived at advanced base camp at 7:00 p.m. The next two days were spent moving tons of rocks in order to make the camp more comfortable; we would be there for six weeks.

I had brought a paraglider along. Back in 1986, paragliding was in its infancy. In fact, a paraglider is an umbrella, but it's actually less practical because it doesn't have a handle. I had the somewhat crazy idea of descending from the summit of Everest through the air. On July 25, a few patches of blue appeared in the sky and I decided to take a break from the purely cerebral activities of reading and music to go on an acclimatization hike. I climbed to about 6000 meters; the camp would make a nice soft landing spot. As I unfolded my paraglider, the wind was whipping. Even better!

The fierce wind would make up for the lack of lift at these altitudes. I spent another hour and a half messing around with takeoff attempts; the wind crumpled the wing as soon as I launched it. Finally, a rainbow appeared and the wing filled with air. I took off! The only difference between flying and falling is how long the experience lasts: If you fall for a long time, that's flying; if you fly very briefly, it's a fall. Those who saw my flight unanimously termed it a fall. The doc confirmed that opinion when he examined me: "A serious ankle sprain, trauma to the heel, sharp blow to the tarsal bones, and damage to the calcaneum. Hopefully nothing's broken or cracked. Complete rest for eight to ten days, then you can try putting shoes on and see how it goes." My heart fell to my heels (pun intended).

I stayed at base camp for fifteen days while the others acclimatized on the nearby summits. Then one day I couldn't take it anymore! I felt that I absolutely had to try to walk. In sneakers, my foot hurt too much and I couldn't put weight on it. So I tried my mountaineering boots; the pain was bearable and I could walk. That same day, I went with Nicole to scout the route across the glacier. At midnight the next day, I geared up for two 6000- to 6500-meter summits. Two superb faces. At the top of the second peak, I hesitated to unpack the paraglider that I had lugged on my back. But then a virtue as old as humankind—the virtue that has allowed it to last for centuries—welled up in me. Timidly at first, but then it got hold of my senses: It was prudence (unless it was the following wind that had just come up?). Prudence made me give up on the paraglider.

The next day, the entire team headed for the Lho La, the col between Tibet and Nepal. As I was setting off down a slope, I fell into a hole and my ice ax cut into my arm. I had read somewhere that Trotsky died from an ice ax blow to the skull. I could now easily see why he wouldn't have survived the caress of the metal: Just above the elbow, I had a three-inch gash, and it was bleeding heavily. The expedition doctor, Alain Vagne, climbed up to me, applied a makeshift bandage, and took me down to Camp I at 5800 meters. The ax blade had transformed my arm into an anatomical model: You could see my artery pulsing in the middle of the peeled-back flesh. With no anesthesia, Alain put in two stitches to hold the edges of the wound together. It took us three hours to return to advanced camp. In the mess tent, now the operating room, he disinfected the injury site, sutured a torn vein, trimmed the tattered flesh, and closed the wound properly, applying a few subcutaneous sutures and eleven superficial stitches. My biceps and tendon weren't affected, but I had to wait a week before I could climb again. The weather stood by me in my inactivity: It snowed every day, as if to mitigate the burden of my convalescence.

On August 23, Nicole went back to Switzerland for the course that would anoint her as the country's first female mountain guide. At the foot of Everest, the monsoon should have been letting up. It was time for it to move on to other skies, but this year it thumbed its nose at the official schedule. Every day, it snowed eight to twelve inches. On the first nice day, we waited, dumbfounded. There would be four good-weather days in all—the only four nice days during that summer of 1986. On the second day, August 29, Pierre Béghin, Jean Troillet, and I climbed to the foot of the face. We crouched at the base of the wall, waiting for the downspouts above to stop vomiting their streams of snow. We planned to set off light, as experience had taught us: no tent, no sleeping bags; just a snow shovel to bury ourselves for the illusion of warmth on the mountain, and a bivy sack, a stove, and a few Ovo Sport bars as the only human fuel.

It was midnight when we started up the north face. A wall of darkness— that's the north face of Everest. We searched for the entrance to the labyrinth. What thread should we follow to flush out the sleeping Minotaur at the top of the world? After two or three attempts, we found the correct couloir. There was a huge amount of snow. At this altitude and these temperatures, it was impossible for it to have stabilized; at any time, it could sweep us down into the bergschrund. We floundered in knee-deep drifts, switching the lead every fifteen minutes. I had spent six weeks in base camp, and during that time I had broken bones, scraped my limbs, and climbed only two peaks to keep myself in shape. But when the moment came to attempt Everest, I felt like an Olympian. I think that the elevation of base camp, 5500 meters, facilitates acclimatization. The three of us climbed in silence, each of us living his own internal adventure. Jean took the lead, then Pierre passed me. Their faces were haggard with effort; what thoughts hid behind them? I had no idea. What wordless thoughts drifted away on the steam of our breaths? I had no idea. Our pace was fast: We had climbed 6500 feet in ten hours.

At around 11:00 a.m., we were near the 8000-meter mark. Above us was the start of the Hornbein Couloir, named after the mountaineer who opened a new traverse on Everest. We decided to rest for a few hours. We dug a snow cave; the temperature was pleasant and I congratulated myself on having ordered a light SNC one-piece suit similar to what skiers wear. We settled into our pit, like wayward moles at the altitude where condors fly. Of course the pit wasn't roomy; in order to enjoy it, you would have to also enjoy elevators, spacecraft, submersibles, squash courts, and any activity that takes place in a tin can. Some of us—I won't name names—made themselves comfortable. Anderl Heckmair, who did the first ascent of the north face of the Eiger, was correct when he said that in a bivouac, some people have to suffer for the well-being of others. He was so correct that I left our pit to dig one just for myself. We tried to rest, halfway between heaven and earth. We didn't speak; we simply waited for the sun to burn the afternoon away. The gathering darkness drew us out of our lethargy. We got ready, which meant jettisoning anything that might slow us down during the final 3300 feet of climbing. All of our gear would have fit in a knight's belt pouch: a little food, a water bottle, a camera. In one hand, an ice ax; in the other, a telescoping ski pole.

We left our shelter at around 8:00 p.m.; we had been nestled just below the roof of the world, like a swallow's nest in the eaves. Right from the first few steps, I could feel that this eight-hour break had been a bad idea. I had hoped to start out refreshed for the final assault, and instead I felt wrung out. Bosses know that when their employees take overly long breaks, it hurts their productivity; I was finding that out for myself. But Jean Troillet felt good. In the language of competitive cyclists, he was just spinning along. We were continuing at the same pace when we heard shouting in the crystalline silence: "I'm going back to the snow cave!" Pierre Béghin was having a harder and harder time keeping up; his body was being overtaken by torpor. He preferred to put his chances off until the next day. We kept going, taking turns in the lead: The crusty snow was like a sponge soaking up energy.

At around midnight, the beams of our headlamps hit a black band. On every Himalayan expedition, I've always adapted to the terrain. I've never read anything, I've never studied topos, I've never consulted books, I've never memorized information. I know where the summit is and I know where the starting point is. After that, it's like life: I improvise. But while waiting for a burst of improvisational salvation, we were perplexed. Our headlamps searched for a weakness in this sixty- to seventy-degree rock band. Two points of light, like the two glowworms that we were, desperately clinging to a sequoia. The climbing looked abominable. I'll grant you this: If I had read a description of the route, I would have known that this abominable section is the crux of the Hornbein Couloir and is therefore described in every guidebook, that a fixed line runs down the middle of it, and that the route we were choosing in order to avoid it is far from recommended. In our ignorance, Jean and I headed toward the right, where the face seemed less menacing. We had just reached the right side of the couloir when a monstrous roar grew louder and louder: An avalanche had released, and it was sweeping down almost 10,000 feet of couloir. Not five minutes before, two mountaineers had been standing in the funnel that someone had just emptied; now the two mountaineers stared, dumbfounded, at the spot that was meant to mark the end of their journey. We were supposed to live out our last hour here, and just when the last grain of sand was about to fall through the hourglass, we were given a reprieve. We continued upward, convinced that we had pulled one over on destiny, and we came out on the great shoulder.

During that climb, however, something strange happened—something that I had never experienced before. It had been an hour or two since Pierre Béghin had split off from us, yet I was certain that we were being followed by a third person. I turned around frequently: There was no one. I continued walking, and the feeling of a presence behind me returned. Sometimes, when I was leading, I would wait for Jean to catch up, and then, instead of starting off again, I would scan the abyss, convinced that a third shape would soon emerge from the darkness. My brain knew full well that Pierre Béghin was several hundred feet below us, but my senses disagreed.

At around midnight, we were at 8400 meters. We had no photos of the face, so we didn't know exactly where to join the summit ridge; we were a bit lost. We decided to take a break for a few hours. We sat down on our packs and huddled together. In that darkness, animal warmth was too precious to be given away to the atmosphere. But the cold quickly recognized us as the only ambassadors of life, radiating our ninety-eight degrees Fahrenheit of warmth, and it enclosed us in its grip. We stayed there for three hours while our teeth chattered in rhythm. I cursed my stupidity: I had ordered a light climbing suit because I was going to Everest in summer and, as we know, it's warm in summer. I should have remembered that altitude couldn't care less about seasons. I came up with a proverb: Better a winter in Dar es Salaam than a summer at 8400 meters.

The moon rose and we saw where we were. We had more than 1300 feet to gain if we intended to stand on top of the world. After those three frigid hours, we brought some order to the manic movements of our lower jaws, squirted a little oil on our rusty joints, and set off again. That was the moment when we really started to struggle. The snow was so deep that we sank in up to our hips; progress was almost impossible. It would take us ten hours to overcome those final 1300 feet! One hundred and thirty feet per hour—that was the speed at which bipeds were clocked on that day, between 8400 meters and 8848 (8846) meters. One of us would drop his pack and dig a trench for thirty feet. Then he would come back down for the pack and pass the baton to the other, and so on. During this trenching work, we couldn't think that the slope might let loose, with us on it. And if that thought came to mind, we had to immediately dismiss it; that is a condition of perseverance. Finally, we arrived at the point where the west ridge and the north face merge. We continued like that for 160 feet, with our heads down as a sign of obstinacy. And then suddenly there was nothing above us but the sky. I felt a lump in my throat and tears in my eyes. It was 2:30 p.m. and I was on the summit of Everest, and the top of the world. Joy, tears of joy.

In the course of a lifetime, there are very rare moments when we feel complete—instants where, as humans, we want nothing except what we have. Happiness reigns in those few seconds of harmony. That was what I felt on the summit of Everest. We stayed there for an hour and a half, contemplating the world as its kings. It was the only time when neither Jean nor I was obsessed with the descent. We knew that there were no technical difficulties at all, that we would simply need to let ourselves slide down to safety. Jean took out a recording device to capture our slurred words and began to consider time: "We arrived on August 30, 1988, at 2:00 p.m . . . My impressions are inside me. . ." The context didn't favor a dissertation on the meaning of our quest. We said words that would have sounded hollow anywhere else: "A victory over ourselves . . . The 8000ers are crazy. Crazy!" We were surprised by what we had done: "Are you really there?" "Wait, I have to pinch myself . . . Yes, I'm really here!" It was one of those magical days in the Himalaya. The temperature was good—so good that I wasn't even cold in my lovely red ski suit. And above all, there was no wind; it was flat calm. We were close to the roaring 9000ers, and there was only the murmur of a zephyr. Unbelievable!

When Jean started seeing an electrical transformer on a cloud, I snapped out of my euphoria. I knew for sure that there was no electrical transformer near Everest; he was starting to hallucinate and we needed to go down. We descended to the top of the Hornbein Couloir and got ready to throw ourselves into the 9800 feet between us and advanced base camp. The angle of the Hornbein Couloir is about fifty degrees, which is good for glissading. We sat down in the snow and started off. It wasn't a dizzying descent, not Kitzbühel, but neither was it the dull plains of Waterloo. We simply had to control our speed with our ice axes, and if by chance we encountered an icy section, we had to use the tool as one would an alarm signal: firmly, without hesitating. At one point I was surprised by a sheet of exposed ice; I planted the ax with all my might and found myself hanging by my arm. Your life depends on this kind of reflex, because down below, the bergschrund is ready to eat you alive. Of course you also have to lift your feet; if you had the misfortune of catching a crampon point on the snow, it would launch you into a glide, and we would have accomplished the first skeleton descent of Everest.

We easily found a route through the rock band that had complicated our ascent. In three hours, we were at advanced camp, at 5800 meters. It had taken us forty-three hours roundtrip to climb Everest: thirty-nine hours up, then an hour on the summit, then three hours to descend. The adventure was complete. We were now at the foot of the face and somewhat stunned. Jean held forth with a drunken stream of deep thoughts. His mind was the screen for a psychedelic show, a pyrotechnic spectacle: He saw clowns coming out of crevasses, an American mailbag (!), majorettes, and big, strapping guys who were ten or twelve feet tall. And when he watched me ski down to base camp (he was on snowshoes), he saw several skiers instead . . .

That Everest climb is not a memory, it is a flash in my mind. The light style, the speed of the ascent, the refusal to use bottled oxygen, the state of grace that we experienced on the summit, all combined to make those forty-three hours an open parenthesis outside the bonds of time—an atemporal experience. I want to return to Everest, but I know that another success there would be a disappointment. I could never relive the experience we had in 1986. It was unique, and because of that, it's precious.

This meteoric ascent caused a stir in the mountaineering world, and in the medical world too. I know that some physiologists who specialize in high altitude admit that they can't understand that kind of pace and schedule. People asked me if we shot up with amphetamines. I answered, "No!" People told me that we had pushed the limits of medicine and that there was no scientific explanation for this kind of feat. I answered, "But it's simple. All you need is a little willpower."

JEAN TROILLET, THE ROPE PARTNER

Jean Troillet spoke softly, as do people who are sure of their inner strength. His shirt said "SOS." This was both a brand name and a joke at his own expense. A guide from Orsières, Jean had forty-eight years of life behind him, and life had often blended with survival. In 1984, he and Pierre-Alain Steiner attempted to escape from the west face of Annapurna by retreating to the north face. The retreat was a debacle: There were many falls, including one of 650 feet, and Jean fell up to his neck into a crevasse. Those fine feats were saluted by an avalanche that left the two comrades hanging by their ice axes, tensely perched on their crampons, with their faces powdered like a baby's behind. "A fabulous adventure," said Jean Troillet, demonstrating a very particular understanding of the word "fabulous." "Without the satisfaction of having conquered one's fear, certain climbs wouldn't be worth the effort," stated Sir Edmund Hillary, ironically. Jean Troillet loved these unlivable altitudes because they opened up unknown worlds within him. "When I fell on Annapurna, I was wearing electrodes that recorded my pulse. Nothing happened! My pulse didn't speed up when I fell. That's proof that, in the Himalaya, we're in an abnormal state. The brain lacks oxygen, and that relieves us of our fears, then causes us to forget our limits. The brain is the body."

After 1985 and the K2 expedition, Jean Troillet was Erhard Loretan's faithful companion. Because Erhard, like Charles de Gaulle and Che Guevara, didn't have friends, comrades, or partners; he had companions. Jean was the most faithful and valiant among them; he escorted Erhard on eight 8000ers. If the choice were between Pierre Richard and Gérard Depardieu, he would be Depardieu; if it were between Terence Hill and Bud Spencer, he would be Bud Spencer.

Alongside Erhard Loretan, who was five feet, six inches, it was easy to seem like a colossus. At five feet, eleven inches and 176 pounds, Jean Troillet brought a calm, physical strength to the rope team; it was a prerequisite for the adventure, and for its telling. What would d'Artagnan be without Porthos' girth? San Antonio without Bérurier's strong grip? Bob Morane without Bill Ballantine's muscle? Louis Lachenal without Lionel Terray's might?

Should we even use the word "rope team"? The two men were rarely joined by a rope—that link between two people that is so laden with meaning. During their Himalayan odyssey, they only took the rope out once, for a rock section on Cho Oyu. "A rope team," explained Jean Troillet, "doesn't mean that the mountaineers are linked by a rope; it means that they're walking together." Welcome to mountaineering in the age of virtual reality. With or without a nylon thread, the Loretan–Troillet rope team worked to perfection. Erhard coldly summed up their relationship: "Above 6000 meters, people become robots that are simply putting one foot in front of the other, and two machines always get along well." That was it for poetry. It ignores the fact that Erhard Loretan and Jean Troillet were the greatest rope team in Himalayan climbing. Pierre Béghin, who was with them on Everest, saw them as "by far the best Himalayan climbers at the present time." Their achievements include new routes on Cho Oyu and Shishapangma, a first winter ascent on Dhaulagiri, new attempts on K2 and Makalu, and astoundingly fast times on all of their climbs (their forty-three-hour ascent of Everest is merely the best-known). No other rope team had a similar list of accomplishments, no other rope team had lasted so long, and no other rope team had survived ten years in the Himalaya, with its risks and its storms (both weather-related and human).

Expeditions sour human relationships, or at least complicate them. Jean said that Erhard "is not always easy to live with in base camp." Erhard said of Jean, "Likewise." Ten years spent in motion and in silence. People who climbed with them spoke of their surprise: Everything united these two climbers, except words. "We really got along well," acknowledged Jean Troillet. "Especially when it came to the fast style and the spirit of the climb. We could make decisions without speaking, and that's an incredible advantage." Their comments made it seem that telepathy was their way of expressing themselves and that intuition was their way of reasoning.

Jean and Erhard shared the same fatalism. When they spoke of a danger they had miraculously escaped, they both used the same phrase: "It wasn't our time." And anyone who made the mistake of mentioning luck, or the role that it might have played in preserving a life momentarily under threat, would be immediately contradicted: "It's not luck," Jean retorted. "It was written that we should continue to climb 8000ers together and that we should continue to live." Continue in order to progress through this life, which sometimes seems like a walk through the Stations of the Cross, with Calvary at the end: "Human beings must be tested in order to improve, and to grow as people." Making little distinction between mountaineering and stoicism, Jean Troillet commented, "It's not that we want to become philosophers, but we become philosophers by living through extreme risk and by shedding tears when our friends have died." The mountains didn't always treat Jean gently, however. They took away Pierre-Alain Steiner, whom he thought of as a brother. But Troillet refuted this vision of a predatory environment: "The mountains aren't cruel. Mountains don't kill; men get themselves killed in the mountains."

Kangchenjunga marked the end of the story. Jean and Erhard were certainly going to go their separate ways. Jean was tired of endlessly ascending and dreamed of a blue, horizontal world. With the sailor Laurent Bourgnon, he was planning escapades on all of the world's oceans. Erhard would continue without Jean—without the man who, for many years at those deserted altitudes, had been his only companion.

| 9 |

My Vacation in Slippers on Trango Tower

"What is the essence of adventure? It's being thrown into the unknown and not knowing how you're going to get out."

—Voytek Kurtyka

Imagine a granite cathedral, with a forest of bell towers rising to 6257 meters, and 4000-foot-high organ pipes. And to better appreciate its proportions, two men strolling around the nave. On the way to Concordia, at the heart of the Karakoram, the traveler progressively discovers a breathtaking massif: the Trango Towers. In this boulevard that leads to some of the world's highest peaks, toward a world of ice, snow, and whiteness, the Trango Towers are a testament to the survival of rock in its blackness. This alignment of spires and these layers upon layers of faces are reminiscent of the Andes of Patagonia, and you don't have to be particularly observant to recognize Cerro Torre's twin in one case and Fitz Roy's likeness in another.

In June 1988, I was with Voytek Kurtyka at the foot of Trango Tower (also known as Nameless Tower), 6257 meters, to attempt the fourth ascent of this granite obelisk—the most beautiful I had ever seen—and the first ascent of the east face. We were planning to do a route whose path was no more complex than a plumb line: first a 3300-foot ice couloir, then a 4000-foot pillar. The idea had sprung from Voytek Kurtyka's mind. This Polish climber hadn't waited for me before muscling in on the greatest Himalayan climbers of the time. Of course he had some fine accomplishments on the 8000ers (first ascent of the east face of Dhaulagiri, new routes on Hidden Peak and Gasherbrum II, traverse of Broad Peak), but he was best known for a glorious feat on Gasherbrum IV. In 1985, he conquered the impressive west face of that 7925-meter pyramid. And as he and Robert Schauer were preparing to head up to the summit, they were cut off by a storm and went four days without eating and three days without drinking. When he descended from Gasherbrum IV, Voytek had become a living legend. That is the outcome that mortals reserve for those who have cheated death. In 1988, Voytek was forty-one. He had fallen in love with Trango Tower a few years before, but he had been rejected; his first attempt, with two Japanese climbers, had ended after two pitches. When I first made his acquaintance, in Kathmandu, he was coming back from that unfortunate expedition and he consoled himself by telling me about the adventures that those granite curtains held in store. I was seduced by the beauty of his project.

For me, our expedition to Trango Tower marked the end of a dark period. In the fall of 1986, Pierre-Alain Steiner died before my eyes during our expedition to Cho Oyu; at the beginning of 1987, I broke two vertebrae during an attempt to enchain thirteen north faces; in the spring, I broke two other vertebrae in a paragliding accident; and in the spring of 1988, Jean Troillet broke a leg on the approach trek to Makalu. In fact, it wasn't so much the approach march that gave him problems, but the approach flight. In Nepal, treks rarely follow rivers, they usually leapfrog across valleys. At one point on the way to Makalu, you have to descend 3300 feet and then immediately regain them. The Cartesian mind recoils at that kind of gratuitous effort. So we had brought along our paragliders in order to cross that steep gap with the flap of a wing. I could see that Jean was not very enthusiastic about the idea of this aerial shortcut, so I decided to set the example. I inflated my paraglider and it promptly got shredded in the nearby trees.

Jean had no choice but to go out on point. I helped him get ready. The wind died; it was impossible to launch. And then, courageously, he took advantage of a gust to take off. I saw him go, crossing the valley majestically like the albatross in the poem, only to crash pitifully into a wall like the fall guy in a joke. A wall—the only wall in the district! Result: a broken leg. I sold off all of our expedition food and returned to Kathmandu, where I then worked as a carpenter for an entire month. I told Voytek that I was available, and we decided to meet in Islamabad. On June 1, he met me in the Pakistani capital.

We would be setting off as a team of two for Trango Tower. Jean Troillet's absence saddened us, but it wasn't going to stop us. The time when a three-man rope team was considered the pinnacle of safety had disappeared with the arrival of Mummery one hundred years before. And climbing as a pair would make our style of ascent more efficient.

The Trango Tower story wouldn't be complete without the obligatory mention of "administration." It's a classic element of expedition tales, where one sees the mountaineer dreaming of blue skies, then beating his or her head against the wall of bureaucracy and civil servants. Islamabad is a city born of the right-angled imaginations of urban planners, and there I spent almost twenty days waiting for my invisible man: an improbable liaison officer. During that time, the expedition supplies were sitting in a warehouse where it was 109 degrees Fahrenheit in the shade. Our carabiners, pitons, and ropes did fine in that kind of temperature, but the chocolate, salami, and cheese were melting into an amorphous mixture. Let the record show that I was the inventor of pyramid-shaped salami. But isn't Switzerland a country of diplomats? And I'm Swiss, so I'm a diplomat. We had finally reached an agreement, and on June 14 we left Islamabad. On June 20, after six days of walking, escorted by twenty-seven porters, we reached base camp, at 4000 meters. I assure you that it's harder to battle human stupidity than to do battle with mountains. Mountains, after all, have holds.

The weather was outstanding, which is unusual in that massif. On the 22nd, we did a short reconnaissance to drop off a few supplies in that huge rock maze. Leading up from this enormous talus field was an ice couloir that gave access to the tower—"our" tower. When we got back to base camp, we examined the face with powerful binoculars. We discovered a crack on the left side of the pyramid; there was a flaw in Trango Tower's armor. The next day, we prepared the gear for the climb: more than 260 pounds, including 1300 feet of rope, that we would have to haul up the face. We were planning to make two trips. Some quick math gave us sixty-five pounds per head, sixty-five pounds per beast of burden. We tried in vain to pare down our gear and food; there was nothing we could eliminate. Every ounce had a purpose. I was a little worried: How would my spine, weakened by two accidents, hold up to this load?

I must add a few words so that you know how this climb finally played out, and so that you don't lose the thread of the story, while we are busy ascending our own ropes. Our plan was to set up three camps and to descend back to one of them each night. Camp I would be at 5000 meters, to begin the attack on Trango Tower; Camp II would be at 5300 meters, on a band of snow that separated the obelisk from its base; and Camp III would be on a ledge at 5800 meters. Every morning, when we set off again from a camp, we would ascend the ropes to get back up to the previous day's high point. Is that clear?

At around half past midnight on Friday, June 24, Voytek and I left camp. We absolutely had to get to the base of the wall before the sun came up. The couloir that led to the tower was fairly exposed: Each day the sunlight set off rockfall in it. It took us seven hours to climb 3900 feet. I was reassured about my back's condition; I had no pain, except for the pain inherent in seven hours of forced marching under a sixty-five-pound load. What I mean is that I didn't feel any specific pain. I was overwhelmed with gratitude for our modern age, which—in exchange for a laundry list of annoyances (pollution, deforestation, the greenhouse effect, the atomic bomb, and so on)—provides such good doctors. At the top of the couloir, a thousand miles from any medical scanner, I thanked God for modern medicine!

The day was already long. Voytek negotiated for a two-hour break, and then we set up our bivouac on a snow ledge at 5000 meters. We planned to then equip the bottom section of the first pillar. We had been waiting for months for the moment when we could attack this monolith. From the instant our fingers touched the rock, our dream was coming true. Now the question was who would have the privilege of leading first. No one (especially not him) was motivated to give up his turn out of a spirit of sacrifice, so there was no other solution but heads or tails. I should have chosen heads. Voytek won the first pitch, 130 to 160 feet that we thought were IV to V+. Fortunately, we still had enough time to do a second pitch, and I set off free climbing on superb rock. At around 5:00 p.m., we were back at the bivouac. We sank luxuriously into our sleeping bags, and to celebrate this first contact with the rock, Voytek opened a can of caviar that he had exported from Poland. Say what you like, the Iron Curtain had its positive points! As for me, I confirmed my proletarian roots by hacking away at the salami and the garlic cheese.

The next day, we ascended the 330 feet of rope we had put up the day before, and we equipped an additional 660 feet, up to a snowy section. Until then, the climbing had alternated between free and aid. But there, Cinderella shook off her glass slipper and continued her dance in plastic boots and crampons, armed with two tools as anchors. The snow was bottomless; I was in up to my waist and I had to set down my pack in order to make progress. It took us more than an hour of work to cover the 330 feet that separated us from the second bastion of rock—the obelisk itself. We dropped off all of our gear and returned to the starting line to spend a second night. We had no trouble falling asleep; the sixteen hours of effort probably didn't hurt.

On June 26, I led another pitch (IV+ with one move of V) and we descended back to base camp. We didn't have enough food to go higher. In base camp, we could see from the faces of our liaison officer and our cook that our exploits meant nothing to them and that they had had enough. But we had to keep them there. It wasn't so much the human qualities of our liaison officer that we would miss, but rather our chef's culinary talents. Voytek agreed that we should give a positive review of those first few days on the mountain. Our line seemed good, although there were one or two enigmas in the middle of the face. But our pain wasn't over: 2300 feet of dead vertical still awaited us. For the moment, we savored these two or three rest days. We would set off fresh and enthusiastic for the final sprint, which should last ten to fifteen days—a sprint reserved for marathoners. During this interlude, Voytek showed himself to be a true professional: not wanting to compromise our future climbing plans, he chose base camp, with its ample space and guarantee of prompt attention, as the place to get a stiff neck.

On Saturday, July 2, we set off again for Trango Tower, each collapsing under the weight of a pack that contained everything we would need for fifteen days on the face. We began ascending the ropes to Camp II, at 5300 meters. Don't spiders ever get tired of climbing back up their webs? By around 3:00 p.m., we were at camp; we had 4300 feet of elevation gain in our arms, our legs, and our backs. That night, before I went to sleep, I passed a cordelette around my waist and clipped it to the rope that came down from the anchor. Of course the mountain looked solid, but one should never forget that a range like the Karakoram betrays the precarious balance of the earth's crust. To put it plainly, the platform might move!

On July 3, we resumed our ascent. We had decided to alternate days on lead. That allowed the second to dress warmly and to be bundled up in a down jacket as he kept track of the leader's progress. The rope that moves through the belayer's hands reveals everything about the leader's climbing: hesitations; bursts of speed; comfort or unease. Sometimes sudden slack in the line tells the belayer that the leader has just taken flight and that in a few split seconds, catching the fall will truly be in his hands. That day it was Voytek's turn to be "on the pointy end." He took a thirty-five-foot fall in the morning and another fall at the end of the day. His two attempts to escape gravity left him with a bashed elbow and thumb. That pair of incidents would affect him for the rest of our ascent. They reminded us of the need to climb as safely as possible. The massif was so remote and the face so committing that the smallest accident would take on catastrophic proportions. We weren't on the Eiger or the Matterhorn; we weren't messing around across from hotel balconies. We fixed the ropes and descended to the bivouac.

During those climbing days, we ate practically nothing. The "work" schedule spanned both bakery hours and mining hours. We got up at 4:00 a.m. and went to bed at around 8:00 p.m. So each night, two famished men arrived back at the bivouac, but our stomachs had been feeding on nervous tension all day and we ate very little. The menu doesn't take long to summarize: fondue with a lot of garlic (garlic is excellent for the arteries and the prostate, which will become important later in the story); bread; cheese; salami; and so on. And then night fell on our satisfied, crippled bodies. Our brains took advantage of our physical inactivity and came to life—thinking about the next day, calculating potential risks, programming reflexes of self-preservation. In short, we were ruminating. It would be my turn to lead, and I had noticed an overhanging pitch with a huge block wedged above it. Would it hold? The answer would be revealed the next day.

"Voy, be careful, I'm very uncomfortable," I said, while climbing a four-inch-wide crack. I had just realized that there was nowhere I could place any more protection, and my last piece was sixteen feet below me. I was on the sixth pitch and was looking at a thirty- to forty-foot fall, even if the protection held, which remained to be seen. I had to think fast, since strength fades quickly. In my situation, panic was a luxury I couldn't afford. Keep going, or downclimb? Either solution seemed risky. I glimpsed an escape: I could place a bolt. To do that, I would need a bolt, a hammer, and another hand, because both of mine were monopolized by the crack and being used exclusively to forestall my fall. Luckily, I was able to jam a knee in the crack and regain the use of my hands. Normally it would take five to fifteen minutes to get a good bolt in. Up there, I needed half an hour to catch my breath, hanging from that bit of metal. Higher up, things went better than I had expected: The wedged block looked as if it would hold, but I thought that I shouldn't push things, so I avoided hammering in a piton anywhere near it. At around 7:00 p.m. we went back down.

Half-asleep, I soon felt myself gasping for air; my space was closing in on me and everything felt narrower, as if I were sleeping in a coffin. Was I dreaming? I opened my eyes: There was snow everywhere. Small avalanches were sweeping down the wall and stopping on the first flat surface, which was our shelter. All of our gear was buried. We had to do something, and fast. Oh! There was a shoe . . . It would be great to find the other one. Good God, where was the shovel? Our fear increased; should we go down? No, given the steep slopes and the number of avalanches coming down them, we needed to stay anchored on our ledge and wait for the weather to improve. In those moments of crisis, when a situation seems to be getting the better of us, we begin to long for comfort and safety. But if we go on these undertakings because of wanderlust, why not try a beach in Brazil? Because, stuck on that ledge, we have a better sense of the fragility of life, and its beauty and value. Because in those months of deprivation, we are reacquainted with the pleasures of simplicity.

At around 10:00 a.m. the weather lifted, taking a good part of our uncertainty with it. We ascended the 650 feet of fixed ropes, and Voytek put up another pitch. It was snowing and getting dark, feeling like winter when we got back to our bivouac. During the night it began snowing again, and the feeling of suffocation was real. In the morning we had ten square feet of space for the two of us; the snow fell mercilessly. We had to get out of this mousetrap. Voytek was hesitant. He didn't know . . . Maybe. I left him to his prevarication and for half an hour I battled with the knots to prepare for our descent. When Alexander the Great was faced with a knot problem, he sliced through it with a sword; frankly, I couldn't blame him for that speedy solution. When I returned to the bivouac, my fingers numb, I found Voytek nestled in his sleeping bag. He placed an order for a drink. I don't know if my four-day beard and my rock-manicured fingers anointed me the sommelier, but Voytek wished to have something to drink—something hot, if possible. I explained to him that the breakfast buffet wasn't open just then, that today the house was serving only iced Isostar, and that it would be nice if he could make up his mind: Up or down? Finally, he agreed to descend.

By around 8:00 a.m., we had made it to the base of the great couloir— faster than three avalanches! At around 9:00, we flopped down in base camp. Here I must come back to the properties of garlic, because since the previous day Voytek had been decked out in a chastity belt: A locking carabiner had jammed shut and he could no longer take off his harness. That made it very hard for him to answer the call of nature, hence the reminder of garlic's benefits to the entire urinary tract. A saw and a pair of pliers freed my ropemate. This return to base camp gave us a three-day reprieve from the law of gravity. That law was burdening us; we were obsessed with falling, and we could not drop anything. The void surrounded us and inhaled anything we didn't hold onto. Losing a stove, a boot, or a crampon would be extremely serious. Everything that we handled had to first be attached to something, and that required our constant attention. Behind this fear of loss, of course, hid the fear that we ourselves might fall. If a piton pulled out, a rock came loose, our strength failed us, or we dropped our guard, then—like the stove or the boot—we would be swallowed by the void. The void was a black hole.

On July 9, we climbed the 3300-foot couloir for the third time. I was numb to this comedic repetition. I hoped that there would be no fourth attempt. We ascended the fixed ropes and passed the two bivouac spots, the first at 5:00 in the morning and the second at 8:00. Three hours later, we were at our high point. I continued up for one more pitch and found a ledge where a third bivouac would work. There wasn't much room; it was even a little cramped. A jumbo jet wouldn't land there, but we were at 5800 meters, two thirds of the way up a granite obelisk whose east face provided only a very few landing strips.

We would have to be satisfied with this balcony with a view of the Baltoro. We descended back to Camp II, having logged 5900 feet of altitude gain, including 2000 feet on Jumars.

On July 10, we forged on above the ledge. Voytek was leading, and he noticed a usable crack extending 500 feet up the rock. We could just get our fingers into it; climbing surely requires a pianist's fingers for a blacksmith's work. We were overjoyed to discover the crack, and suddenly it was as if the castle had lowered its drawbridge and announced its upcoming surrender; barring a storm, we should succeed! Voytek led two pitches that day. That evening, we began our first night at 5800 meters. In reality, there was space for only one person and the other slept with his feet hanging over the void. In those few square feet, we established the only truly communist state on the planet that respected the rules of ownership. For five nights, the collectivist system that we had freely accepted required that we alternate spots. One night in comfort, one night cramped—that was the rule.

From the third camp, we progressed at a rate of about two pitches, or 260 feet, per day. As the days wore on, the tension grew because the clouds seemed to be gathering. On July 11, I took the sharp end of the rope. I turned myself into a human pendulum, doing bigger and bigger swings in order to find a solution to our climb. If that had continued, I would have circled all the way around Trango Tower, and Voytek and I would have done the first spiral route in mountaineering. That kind of acrobatics required trust in the anchors that we had just placed; you have to tension sideways as far as possible on the rope, take a few running steps on the wall, and, above all, not look down between your legs at the 3000 feet of air below you! On July 12, Voytek took the lead. He free-climbed a large dihedral, then continued for another sixty-five feet. We stopped when it got dark. It was 8:00 p.m., and above us, beyond a large overhang, we could see the summit. That steep section might be the summit's last defense. We descended 1000 feet to return to the bivouac. We were overwhelmed by a sense of urgency; darkness had condemned us to motionlessness, while the clouds moved frenetically. They were gaining on us. We couldn't let ourselves be beaten so close to the finish line—not within a day of the summit!

Wednesday, July 13, was our fourteenth day on the face. We got up at 3:00 a.m., and I made coffee and muesli, as I did every morning. We filled our one-liter water bottles, and packed our bivy gear just in case. We attached our Jumars; a race against time was beginning. We ascended the ropes, our noses to the grindstone, and when we got to the end of the line, I took the lead because our system of taking turns gave me that honor. I had underestimated the challenge. The crack was difficult; where it wasn't clogged with ice, it was ice-rimed. After several feet, I found myself perched in my climbing shoes on a sheet of ice. What should I do? Ask Voytek to send up my crampons, or cut steps? I picked the second solution, continued up a crack system, and set up a good belay.

The ambiance was changing; we were above 6000 meters, ice was replacing rock, and I felt as if I were in my pajamas in a walk-in freezer. I put on my wind pants, my high-altitude jacket, my plastic boot shells, and my crampons, and I hauled my pack while Voytek ascended the ropes. Then I continued at top speed, dislodging two snow mushrooms, and came out on the summit slope. The air swirled from all directions, and I knew that I was close to the point where all of the cracks, dihedrals, and grooves that we had used during our fourteen days of climbing converged. There remained at most two ice pitches, which extended like a white carpet unfurled beneath our feet. Then, horror of horrors: A 100-foot rock bulge blocked our access to the summit. It was 3:00 p.m. and my arsenal consisted of three pitons hanging from my harness, and a handful of nuts. There must have been a moment when David faced Goliath and regretted having only a slingshot. I climbed the first sixty feet without too much difficulty, and then, forty feet from the goal, I got stuck. Voytek's voice floated up to me:

"Erhard, listen, we go down to take some equipment!"

Go back down for gear? That would cost us three hours and therefore, in our situation, an extra day. I stalled for time. "Just a minute, please."

Above me there was a piton, a relic from a previous Yugoslavian expedition. If I could get to it, I would be saved. I hammered in a pin behind a granite flake, threaded a cordelette through the eye of the piton, and stood up, at which point the entire flake broke off. The fruits of my ingenuity, the cordelette and the piton, hung sadly from the front points of my crampons. So I placed some sketchy nuts in an icy crack; it was time for DIY rather than technique, and for invention rather than repetition. It was time to activate the so-called springs of action—hope and fear.

"Be careful, Voy; I try."

To me, that meant that I was risking it all, staking my life on one or two nuts that didn't look like they were being held by much. I had just warned Voytek not to be surprised if he saw a human-like form sailing through the Baltoro sky. At least he had been warned. Then I made it up the crack! The last ten feet were ice, and completely vertical. I revived a great mountaineering tradition, whereby one ice ax can triumph over any difficulties. A half hour later, we were together on the summit of Trango Tower. Our eyes glowed with the pride of having climbed a superb line on a superb mountain.

If there hadn't been almost 4000 feet of rappelling to do, our celebrations would certainly have been longer. The first evening, we descended back to Camp III, and the next day we set off for Camp II. We divided the chores: I set up the rappel anchors, and Voytek checked to make sure that I had set them up correctly. Was the block stable? Shouldn't we double up the sling? Maybe it's this kind of questioning that allows us the hope of growing old as mountaineers. I did 330-foot rappels loaded down with two packs, one attached to my descender and one on my back. At one point, I found myself on an overhanging section of the face, and because of the length of the rope, I was a good ten feet from the wall. The Tower of Pisa isn't the only thing leaning, I thought. Fortunately, I was able to grab the anchor, otherwise I would have had to go back up the whole way on Jumars. The final couloir descent was difficult, because the seventy-five pounds I was carrying threw me around a lot; I had to resist with all my strength.

By 4:00 p.m. on July 14, we were both at base camp. It was raining, and I felt that we had gotten off the mountain at the right time. The cook asked me to repair his watch. After fourteen days of strangling rock, my fingers now had a crack at watch repair. Faced with the difficulty of the task, they wept from every pore, lamenting their loss of feeling; water oozed from my skin.

I loved this first ascent of the east face of Trango Tower because it didn't have the stressful aspect of an 8000er. Of course, the technical difficulty was far greater than on my Himalayan summits, but this time the altitude was hospitable and merciful. It was nothing like the death zone, which cannot be ventured into with impunity. This was a relaxed, chilled-out expedition—a vacation that I could have spent almost without taking off my (climbing) slippers. One night when we were sleeping on the wall, I had a nightmare: The police chased me and put me in prison. I think that there is no worse punishment for a person than being deprived of freedom, especially when that person is used to breathing under the open skies. Because climbing, even aid climbing, remains free.

WAS ERHARD LORETAN A PR...?

People say that Mozart never had trouble interpreting Richard Clayderman's scores. I admit that the comparison is what it is: Mozart was a mediocre climber, and Erhard Loretan's contributions to the world of music were modest, aside from a few improvisations for harmonica and solo vocals. But the point is that the concept of difficulty is relative and that one must take Erhard Loretan's assessments with a grain of salt.

A few examples of Erhard Loretan's ratings and comments. With regard to a fourteen-day climb on Trango Tower, on a route rated *Extrêmement Difficile*, with sections of A3 aid climbing (A5 being the hardest): "Technically, it's not harder than what we did in the Gastlosen. I have to say that after doing similar routes in the Gastlosen, we were totally prepared." About the south face of Shishapangma, 7200 feet of altitude gain with an average angle of fifty degrees: "It's walking; you do it with an ice ax in one hand and a ski pole in the other." He saw Cho Oyu as barely harder: "It's walking, with one or two rock sections." And when he was shown a mountaineering book in which a recognized author cites the two routes opened by the Loretan–Troillet–Kurtyka trio on Shishapangma and Cho Oyu as important milestones in Himalayan climbing, Loretan responded, "I'm going to tell you honestly—that's rubbish." As for the west pillar of Makalu, called the Walker Spur of the Himalaya, which includes sections rated VI and A2 above 7200 meters, Loretan reduced it to a rope-pulling exercise, or a biceps workout: "There are fixed ropes all over it! In 1991, when we climbed the west pillar, the Spaniards had just put up fixed ropes. I wouldn't say that you pull yourself up on them like a bastard, but it helps a lot, and it takes away from the accomplishment. Today, anyone who climbs the west pillar can no longer claim the distinction of having climbed grade V."

And the north face of Everest? That tremendous climb of the Hornbein Couloir, reported in the mountaineering literature as having slopes up to seventy degrees and some mixed sections rated IV? The Loretan–Troillet team climbed those 8500 feet in thirty-nine hours, without a rope and each holding a ski pole. Loretan explained the difficulty of the ascent by invoking the ease of the descent—"We did it on our asses."—and his skills as a snowboarder: "Personally, I snowboard down faces like the north face of Everest."

Let's leave the Himalaya to explore Alpine mythology. What did Erhard have to say about "the last problem in the Alps," the north face of the Eiger? "On a route like that, I'm really having fun!" During a winter ascent of the Eiger, he limited the use of the rope to a short section on the Ramp, and he dismissed the Hinterstoisser

Traverse as overrated in the literature—that infamous "point of no return" described by writers: "From there on, salvation lies over the summit," said the masters of suspense. "Today, you can retreat however you want; the Hinterstoisser Traverse is lined with fixed ropes," Erhard pointed out. In fact, right from his first confrontations with the monuments of mountaineering lore, Erhard showed irreverence. About the Cassin Traverse on the north face of Cima Ovest, he commented, with all the insolence of a nineteen-year-old, "You could ride a bike along that ledge."

Erhard Loretan reexamined myths and demystified legends. There was sacrilege in this, and some people were misled by the profaner. In Erhard's press book, you could find this highlighted item from an issue of *Alpirando* dated February 1991: "Sometimes we pump up an achievement, sometimes we minimize it in a dangerous way. For example, a well-known guide received a climbing application for Cho Oyu, a peak in Nepal that is slightly over 8000 meters, from a sixty-six-year-old man who had never been to any significant altitude but who had been swayed by Erhard Loretan's assessment that 'Cho Oyu is a walk.' The guide's reaction: 'Loretan is a pr . . .'" You can fill in the missing letters for yourself.

Erhard Loretan was one of those adventurers who makes any accomplishment sound mundane, in order to avoid being labeled a hero.

| 10 |

CHO OYU, A VICTORY
AND A NIGHTMARE

*"This cruel mountain, a merciless idol, does it deserve so much love
and so much hatred?"*

—René Desmaison

WE NEVER FORGET, WE ACCUMULATE more memories; we don't forget anything, we simply get used to our memories. I only need to
close my eyes in order to relive Pierre-Alain Steiner's death on Cho
Oyu. I can't forget those tragic hours, because they aren't memories;
they are trauma.

I knew Pierre-Alain well, because we had climbed Dhaulagiri
in winter together. That expedition was in early December 1985. A
little less than a year later, in September 1986, I was staying in Kathmandu. I was both euphoric and hungry for more. I had just climbed
the north face of Everest, and I was supposed to meet Marcel Rüedi
on October 15, to attempt the Everest–Lhotse traverse. Of course I
didn't know that, at that moment, Marcel was dying on Makalu. I
had six weeks ahead of me and I wanted to make the most of them.
I asked Nepal's Ministry of Tourism if they could find an available

summit for me, and they came up with Cho Oyu (8201 meters); a Korean expedition had just given up their permit for it. I really wanted to open up a new route on the west face. Wandering around the streets of Kathmandu, I ran into a friend from Gruyère, Christian Dupré, who was up for the adventure. A few evenings later, I returned to my hotel to discover that I had a telex from Pierre-Alain Steiner. He informed me that he was on his way and that he wanted to climb with me. I don't know how the Holy Spirit allowed him to find out my address and my plans, but his message was explicit: He was joining me. A tragedy is always a combination of unfortunate coincidences. Why did I have to have those six weeks free? Why did there have to be exactly one available peak permit? Why did Pierre-Alain have to find me? Later, I found out that Pierre-Alain could have gone to Yosemite with Michel Piola but decided on Cho Oyu instead. Luck is blind.

We set out as a lightweight expedition. On Sunday, October 19, Pierre-Alain, Christian, and I left base camp for a new route up the west face. At around 7300 meters a storm swept in. It was 1:00 in the morning and we were climbing unroped, when a diagonal rock band gave us pause. At that time of the year the face was bare; there was almost no ice on the rock, which raised the difficulty a notch. I told the two others, "We'll spend the night here, and then tomorrow, we'll see." We had to make do with a few grooves for a ledge, and the arctic temperatures were made even more brutal by the wind. The prospect of a night like that put off Christian; he went back down, leaving his sleeping bag for Pierre-Alain. It was a horrible night. The next morning, the situation was far from stellar: Pierre-Alain had altitude sickness. I had just come back from Everest and was well acclimatized. We decided to give up and descend back to base camp. At around 7:00 a.m., we began our descent. The first several hundred feet were steep, but then the slope eased off. I was walking about 300 feet ahead of Pierre-Alain, when I heard the characteristic sound of synthetic fabric sliding on ice. I turned around: Pierre-Alain was hurtling down the face at full speed. He went past me and I saw him sliding toward the cliff edge as if on a toboggan from hell. Then he disappeared into the abyss, plunging into eternity, I was sure. He must have fallen around 2600 feet.

It took me an hour to get down to him. I called to him, convinced that what was lying in front of me was now a lifeless body. The lifeless body answered me. I felt that it was the end of the world; we were at 6500 meters and Pierre-Alain was absolutely shattered. He had open fractures on his hip and his arm, and he was lying in a pool of blood. He was in shock, but he still asked me, "What the hell did I do? What the hell did I do?" He looked at me but didn't know who I was. What I'm about to admit is awful, but it's true: I didn't feel an ounce of joy when I heard Pierre-Alain answer me, because to me, the situation was hopeless and death had already exacted its horrible toll. It would take days to walk to Namche Bazaar, the nearest village, and Pierre-Alain needed to be rescued within minutes. What could I do to cheat despair? I put him in a sleeping bag and then slid him into a Gore-Tex bivy sack. Christian was waiting for us at advanced base camp, so I set off in that direction. When I arrived after two hours of walking, I asked him to climb up with some food and fuel. I continued on to base camp and arrived some ten hours later. There I found the cook and sent him to Namche Bazaar to get help—if possible a helicopter, but at least some Sherpas. He started out, and I waited for him at base camp.

When the cook came back two days later, he was alone. The helicopters couldn't fly, and the Sherpas were all busy with trekking season. The two of us climbed up to Pierre-Alain and Christian. Pierre-Alain was still alive; he had regained his senses and he was talking. He was also in pain. During the night we prepared him to be transported, but we didn't have a sled. So we dragged him across the glacier in the dark while he screamed; it was a scene of horror in the deepest night. Only his death eased our powerlessness. Because all of our efforts and worry had only had one goal: to mask the cruelty of our powerlessness. Pierre-Alain was twenty-six; we slid his body into a crevasse. A healthy person would have taken ten or twelve hours to reach base camp. How long would it have taken us to get Pierre-Alain there? Longer than his life expectancy. The helicopter arrived at base camp four days later; it was over.

For years, I've been reliving this tragedy in my head; now I think that maybe the solution would have been to head for Tibet and come back up with yaks. Maybe . . .

One day, the survivor must return to the world below and explain what happened up high, where there were no witnesses. The worst was not that we had tried, and failed, to save Pierre-Alain's life. The worst was confronting our critics. No one can imagine what it's like to watch a friend die, and to be powerless as someone's life slips away. The Himalaya aren't the Alps, where a helicopter can pick anyone up anywhere. In the Himalaya, at 6000 meters, on flat ground, there's nothing I can do to rescue an injured person. I know that if something serious happens to Jean Troillet on one of our expeditions, if he can't walk on his own, he's a dead man. And the next year, in 1987, when Jean and I set off for Shishapangma (8046 meters), I didn't have the courage to continue, because I was haunted by the nightmare on Cho Oyu. I sat down. Jean asked me what was happening and I answered, "I don't want to push your body into a crevasse." He understood, and we turned around. Alone, I can imagine the worst possible outcomes; there are no limits to my imagination. In a group, I refuse to think about accidents. Since the tragedy on Cho Oyu, I don't care what happens to me, but I'm wracked with worry about my companions.

I went back to Cho Oyu in 1990 with Jean Troillet and Voytek Kurtyka. This time we intended to begin our ascent from Tibet, for two reasons. First, we wanted to climb Shishapangma two weeks later. Second, if we needed help, the Tibetan side of Cho Oyu is easier to access. We planned to open a new route on the southwest face by climbing an 8200-foot couloir with a fifty- to sixty-degree slope and a few grade IV sections. We didn't anticipate anything extreme.

We flew out of Switzerland on August 15, and on August 28 we were at Cho Oyu base camp. Only three days before, we had been in Kathmandu, and now we were at 5700 meters. It's hard to acclimatize in an elevator. We had covered three-quarters of the distance by jeep, and we all had a headache. Jean seemed to be the most seriously affected. On Thursday, August 30, he was no longer identifiable as any race that exists on Earth. He was neither white, nor pink, nor black, nor yellow, nor red; he was green like a science fiction Martian. Without a doubt, he had altitude sickness. He had a hard time standing up, and walked with all the ease of a cybernaut. It took us nine hours to get down to the lower camp, as compared to six hours on the way up. We left Jean at that healing altitude; if he felt sick, he would have to take a jeep down to Zhangmu, 135 miles away and 6500 feet lower. Voytek and I went back up to base camp. On Wednesday, September 5, Jean rejoined us, looking a little thinner. But no one could accurately split the blame between the altitude and the local cuisine. In that region, a sumo wrestler would have become anorexic.

We spent the next few days waiting. I was reading a very interesting book: *A Bright Shining Lie*. We acclimatized on the standard route up by going up to 7000 meters; we took a few reconnaissance hikes toward the face and wagered guesses: It would take us three hours to get to the base, and twenty-seven hours to go from the base to the summit. It was a superb line, ideal for climbing in alpine style. We felt more and more motivated, until the day when it was time for action. On September 14, the three of us were at the foot of the southwest face. At 5:00 p.m. we were gathering our strength for the battle, when I saw Voytek dragging his heels. He was walking more and more slowly as we got closer to the wall. If his energy dropped any further, he would soon be walking backward. I joked with him in English (calling it schoolboy English would be an insult to my teachers):

"Don't you want to climb the face?"

"Oh! Probably not . . ."

"You're sure?"

"Yes."

Of course that threw a wet blanket over the team; a third of our members had just abandoned us at the decisive moment. But Jean looked motivated, so we set off. We crossed the glacier and I noticed that Jean wasn't looking in top shape, either. After an hour, he told me that he wasn't at all enthusiastic about this attempt. I didn't envision myself plowing like a bull up the 8200-foot face, and I gave up. I was crossing back over the couloir, when I heard a noise—or more correctly, a whirring sound. My brain quickly realized what it was. A rock was falling, and the couloir was its guide rail; and I was standing on the guide rail. I set off running and barely escaped the collision. We reached base camp with our ears nearly dragging, looking defeated.

The days passed monotonously. I was reading a very aggravating book: *A Bright Shining Lie*.

On Wednesday, September 19, the weather turned fair over Cho Oyu. At around 11:00 a.m., the three of us set off. Voytek seemed to have gotten over his attack of the blues, and he hit his stride, looking like Gene Kelly in *An American in Paris*. By 3:00 p.m. we were at the supply cache that we had left at about 6200 meters during our first attempt. We loaded up with technical gear—carabiners, pitons, nuts, and a rope—and we each took two ice axes and a ski pole. No bivy gear other than a Gore-Tex bivy sack. We could have fit the food in an eyeglasses case: four Ovo Sport and two Mars bars. In the end I didn't even exhaust that meager stash; when we got back, I still had half my rations left.

At around 6:00 p.m., Voytek took the lead and broke trail for two and a half hours. It's the kind of chore that overrides good sense; Voytek was convinced that after that much sweat, he must have broken 7000 meters. I didn't know what altitude we were at, but I was sure that we were lower than that. We kept going to a rock band; the night was pitch-black, so dark that the moon seemed afraid of getting lost in it. Everything was black. And in the darkness, our heightened sense of hearing heard the hiss of a monster; we couldn't see anything, but we knew that an avalanche had released. It was blind fear. A rush of powder snow flooded the couloir but didn't carry us away. Later, we sank in up to our waists on fifty-degree slopes. Then we had to deal with a section that was more intimidating than really difficult. I set up an anchor and waited while Jean and then Voytek, who were sixty feet below, climbed up to me. Voytek was no longer in a tap-dancing mood, and I did my best to keep up his spirits. He wanted to tie in to the rope, so Jean belayed him while I continued toward the big traverse that leads to the southwest ridge. I was sinking in up to my knees in the snow. At around 5:00 p.m. I came out onto the ridge. We were at 8100 meters and had been climbing for twenty-four hours. Voytek fell asleep as soon as he no longer needed to fight.

I set off again, following the ridge, but soon I encountered an obstacle: a layer of bottomless snow that was so mobile I could barely stay on top. I thought I would drown at 8150 meters; at least it would have been an original way to die. I had to break the snow crust ahead of me and heap it beneath my feet in order to progress a few inches. At that pace, erosion would have been faster; geologists will assure you that the summit would have been at my altitude within a few years. I called Jean to the rescue: I asked him to push me into the mass of snow—after that I would figure out how to get to firm ground. He catapulted me, and I kept thrashing until my feet were on something firmer. I slid into a little cave and threw the rope down to the two others. It had taken me two hours to gain 165 feet: a geologic pace, indeed. The summit was less than an hour away, but in our fatigued state, we decided to spend the night where we were. I wasn't happy about it, but the first light of day would illuminate the summit; it would be a photogenic atmosphere. We buried ourselves in our paper-thin bivy sacks and drank a few sips of revolting water, and the night passed, calm and uncomfortable.

We abandoned our bivouac at around 7:30 a.m., just before the cold really got hold of Jean. In an hour, we were on the big summit plateau. It had been four years since I had stood on the summit of an 8000er. During the descent, at Camp II, some Hungarian mountaineers offered us a beer, which the three of us celebrated with. We had just completed a new route in twenty-seven hours of actual climbing, and I dedicated it to Pierre-Alain Steiner, whose smile shone over that painfully beautiful mountain.

What is a communist country? It's a country where you dream as an individual and wake up collectively. On September 28, we were in Nyalam, Tibet. At 6:00 a.m. sharp, the occupying regime broadcasted its propaganda over decrepit speakers, and the Tibetans were asked to wake up on Chinese time. From Nyalam, we intended to gear up for Shishapangma base camp, which was only some thirty-five miles away. On Sunday, September 30, we set up our base camp on the carpet that nature provided at the foot of Shishapangma. A layer of moss gave the area the feel of having a warm lining, like a pair of long underwear. There were lakes and greenery, and every evening the 6500-foot south face of Shishapangma lit up in a pyrotechnic display; without a doubt it was one of the most beautiful places in the Himalaya. I had spotted this unclimbed face in 1987, and Jean and I were now planning to climb a strikingly simple line—the most direct line that had ever been climbed on an 8000er. I knew that we only needed two days of good weather to finish this first ascent.

On Tuesday, October 2, we climbed up the moraines, and at about 1:30 p.m. we were at the start of the route. We were carefully gearing up for this "speedy" ascent, when I realized, to my annoyance, that I had forgotten my pillow in the tent! That is to say, I had forgotten the neoprene overboots that I primarily used as a pillow, and also as protection against the snow and cold when I wasn't sleeping on them. I decided to take the risk of setting off without overboots, because my insulated climbing suit had gaiters. I swore to myself that I would turn around if my extremities were threatened by cold. We ate fondue; it had become a tradition for the three of us. We attributed all sorts of powers to this dish: It improved energy, vigor, and digestion, and maybe it even had a placebo effect on our morale and performance. Voytek Kurtyka is Polish, but he seemed to appreciate this Swiss dish. That's a revelation that will reassure any Swiss dairy farmers who are worried about European tariffs. At 6:00 p.m., with fondue stagnating in our stomachs, we set off for twenty-two hours of effort. Dieticians will say that ultimately we digested the ascent of Shishapangma faster than we did the 75 percent fat in the Vacherin cheese fondue.

We set off at nightfall, and at 10:00 p.m. we had already gained 3300 feet. Thirty-three hundred feet in four hours! I must admit that the going was easy. Any mountaineer who knows how to walk can do this route. Also, we hadn't brought any technical gear other than a rope, in case we had to cross a crevasse. I was as honed as a Gillette blade and felt in incredible shape. So much so that I climbed too high and had to come back down to correct my bearing. I passed Voytek (his cruising speed is different) and started up the final couloir. It would take hours to climb it. Those hours of effort are required to understand the full monotony of walking; there is nothing so much like a step on a white slope as another step on a white slope. The hours passed and the end of the couloir was not in sight. My feet seemed to be adapting to the lack of overboots, but the little finger on my right hand hurt. I tried hitting it, and it still caused me pain. Early in the morning, we came out at the notch. It was one of those magical moments where we felt that we were at the confluence of all the forces on Earth. On one side the sunshine and heat were imminent; we saw the triumph of life that began again each morning. On the other side was darkness, cold, and the empire of the shadows. We tried to melt a little snow, but the wind defeated us, buffeting and extinguishing the flame at every attempt. So we continued on. There were only two of us at the notch. It had been hours since we had seen Voytek, and we thought that he must have turned around. We set foot on the summit ridge and then only had to follow tracks leading to the summit. At 10:15 a.m., Jean joined me at the top of Shishapangma—or more correctly, on the middle summit, which is thirty-five feet lower than the main summit. It was very cold: too cold to take pictures, because the film would break. The cold penetrated through to our bones, and we decided that we wouldn't last that long up there. We gave up on the main summit after several feet; the traverse was too exposed.

On the descent, we heard someone shouting. It was Voytek, who was in the process of opening his own route on the south face of Shishapangma. He descended to where we were and explained that he had lost our tracks. He told us that he planned to continue to the summit. He's a bit like a tanker truck that, once it gets going, can go for miles on just its kinetic energy. We gave him the stove and wished him good luck, as he was still hours from the top.

The descent didn't allow any room for error; it was fairly steep, and the snow was balling up under our boots. At 4:00 p.m. we were back at the start of the route. It had taken us twenty-two hours roundtrip, but it took another six hours to cross the glacier. That was the point when my bodily needs, which had been squelched by the altitude, made themselves known: I was thirsty—a half liter of water for twenty-two hours of work isn't enough—and I was hungry. Thick fog blanketed the area and we almost walked past the tents. At 11:30 p.m., I cooked a huge plate of spaghetti and washed the dish and my gullet with a beer. My body was satisfied and rehydrated, and I was coming back to my senses: What had happened to Voytek? We scanned the face but saw no glimmers of light. Fatigue triumphed over worry, and we fell into a deep sleep.

Thursday, October 4, was a day of apprehension. We were constantly looking up at the face. I didn't want to believe that a mountaineer of Voytek's caliber had been defeated by that face. With every passing hour, I grew less certain of a happy outcome. Finally, pessimism injected me with its poison; tears fell on the scenes in my imagination. Jean assured me that at any moment Voytek would appear at the edge of the moraine. Pessimists are always correct, because everything in this world will end badly, it's just a question of time. On the morning of October 5, pessimism triumphed: no Voytek. We set off for the glacier at 9:00. I told myself that maybe he had descended via the north face; maybe he had followed some other climbers' tracks. For the moment, we could only watch the south face.

At 12:30 p.m., we came across our descent tracks, and there I was able to confirm that optimists are always correct when they see farther than the horizon and believe that the worst outcome is never certain and that only Satan has lost all hope, etc., etc.—because there were three sets of tracks, and one of them was an Adidas boot print, which wiped away all of our anguish and worry. Voytek had just walked there, wearing those Adidas boots that belonged only to him and that we loved.

In the afternoon, we found Voytek asleep at base camp. He had arrived forty hours after our initial return, nearly dead. He was having trouble talking and didn't recognize us. Later he told us that he had summited eight hours after we did and that he had fallen asleep twice on the descent. He hadn't eaten or drunk anything for two days. I've already mentioned that climbing an 8000er means putting one foot in the next world. Voytek's emaciated face and hollow eyes, his stupor and lethargy, all gave his story a sense of having come back from the grave.

DEFYING THE ODDS

"When I leave for an expedition, I try to have my affairs in order. When I shut the door of my house, I know there's a probability that I will never open it again." Erhard Loretan didn't believe in invincibility. He left that to heroes who are half-human and half-god. Above a certain level, mountaineering requires those who practice it to be Stoics. Is this actually indifference, or merely a pretense in the face of death? Who knows? "And truly, what when death comes remains?" asks the poet Paul Verlaine.

But the fact remains that extreme mountaineering, with its negation of the human condition and its quest for the impossible, raises the question of our relationship with death. And how many names disappeared from Erhard Loretan's story? Vincent, Peter, Jean-Claude, Marcel, Pierre-Alain, Stefan, Manu, Benoît, Pierre. And that is not an exhaustive list. When Erhard was on Makalu in 1991 and learned of Spanish climber Manu Badiola Otegi's death, he tried to help Manu's climbing partner Carlos Valles come to terms with the tragedy, and he later wrote in his journal, "Of course, it's hard for [Carlos]. Manu was a good friend and a father of two children. But everyone takes responsibility for his own risks, and we know that the chances of crossing over the line are very real during an expedition." Statistics prove the reality of these "chances," or rather the extent of this risk. In Kurt Diemberger's book about the tragic summer of 1986 on K2 (*The Endless Knot: K2, Mountain of Dreams and Destiny*), a note by Xavier Eguskitza tells us, "Of the twenty-seven mountaineers who reached the summit of K2 during 1986, seven died on the descent (as well as six others). Since then three more have also died: Michel Parmentier and Petr Bozik on Everest in the autumn of 1988, and Jerzy Kukuczka on the South Face of Lhotse in October, 1989." It's easy to do the math: Of the twenty-seven would-be ascensionists in 1986, sixteen were no longer alive three years later! We accept that one climber in thirty (or one in fifty, depending on the year) won't come back from an attempt on an 8000er. Reinhold Messner, who survived all fourteen 8000ers, wrote in one of his books that the risk of dying on an 8000er is 3.4 percent. Since he has been on twenty-nine expeditions, a mathematician can easily calculate that he had a 36.7 percent chance of returning alive from his Himalayan adventures. For Erhard Loretan, with eighteen expeditions to the 8000ers, his chances of surviving were 53.7 percent.

The statistics amplify Reinhold Messner's truism that "The best climber is the one who does great things at the highest level and survives."

But enough of these calculations that focus our minds on death. Does one Himalayan climber in thirty really die? As Tom Wolfe wrote in *The Right Stuff*, "The figures were averages, and averages applied to those with average stuff." And this "stuff," with all due respect, also applies to Himalayan climbers.

| II |

A One-Legged Man
on Makalu

*"And finally, when it's time to put on your crampons, sometimes in
the middle of the night and sometimes early in the morning, don't
forget that there's a right crampon and a left crampon!"*

—Gaston Rébuffat

MAKALU DOESN'T HAVE K2'S SLEEK elegance and flashy beauty; its
beauty is subtle and radiates its soul. The mountain glows from
within, and it somehow casts a shadow over its taller neighbors:
Everest, Lhotse, and Kangchenjunga. Every mountaineer has been
seduced by this strangely colored peak, this "magnificent mountain
with perfect architecture, a pyramid erected by nature," as Robert
Paragot and Yannick Seigneur described it. But at 8463 meters,
Makalu is no easy woman who can be conquered roughly or without consideration; it must be tamed through a gentle approach. In
the spring of 1988, Jean Troillet had clumsily botched a paraglider
landing and smacked against a wall, which forced us to retreat even
before getting to base camp. In the fall of 1988, we made it a little
farther: Jean Troillet and I were climbing the west pillar when the

wind turned us back at 7400 meters. In the fall of 1991 we were once again at the foot of this giant, who, it is said, sleeps six months per year.

We flew out of Switzerland on August 13. By leaving so early in the season, we hoped to be close on the heels of the monsoon. It had barely abated when we prepared to venture up the immense west face of Makalu. This 3000-meter wall is one of the "last great problems in the Himalaya," just as the "last great problems in the Alps" existed in the 1930s. The first part of the face has ice slopes and is fairly committing, but at around 7800 meters, the topography changes: The wall is blocked by a steep 1300-foot-high rock barrier that clearly requires technical skill. We therefore planned to bring etriers and all of the hardware needed for a very difficult mixed climb. Our intended new route went up the left side of the west pillar; Voytek Kurtyka and Alex MacIntyre had tried it and failed. The west face itself had been conquered in 1981 by Jerzy Kukuczka via a line that was fairly far from our project.

On August 28, the four of us—Sylvie, Annick, Jean, and I—met up at base camp, at 5300 meters. The altimeter had been damaged along the way, but the few bottles that we brought along to wash down the ordinary expedition rations were fine. True, a bottle gives only a vague indication of altitude, but can you drink an altimeter?

On Tuesday, September 10, it was snowing, but still we planned to cache some supplies at around 6500 meters. At about 7:00 in the morning, we were below the last large serac band. Above us was a rocky section. We stepped across a few unstable gullies, placed a few ice screws, and left all of our technical equipment there. It was a load: a portaledge, two sleeping bags, two sleeping pads, two ice axes, twenty pitons, twenty carabiners, a set of Friends, and so on. On "go day," we would only need to collect the gear. It's a proven strategy in the animal world; dogs find their bones, squirrels find their pinecones, and people find their checkbooks. Our cache was at about 6500 meters, near the start of the first rock bands. On the way back down to base camp, Jean was roughed up by a snow slide. He resisted the temptation of a quick descent, and extricated himself after several stressful feet.

The good weather seemed to be sticking around. That was our cue to get going. On Wednesday, September 18, at 6:00 p.m., we set off toward our cache, which was six hours of effort above us. At midnight, we were below the serac band. What is a serac band? It is a glacial formation created at a break in a slope, where the glacier cracks horizontally into a stack of blocks. The illustrious Tartarin of Tarascon, who preceded us into this hostile world, knew that ". . . the menacing line of immense and clustered seracs which the least shock would send down upon the travellers." This lengthy digression is meant to tell you that everything would have gone according to plan if the menacing line of seracs hadn't dropped by one story, completely burying our gear. Armed with a lone ice ax, we dug into the mountain. It was as if someone were asking us to move the Great Wall of China with a teaspoon. We scratched at the ice for two hours before facing reality: A free diver will never find the wreck of the *Titanic*. We left, and arrived at base camp at 5:30 a.m. On September 21, we set off again for the lost cache, this time with a shovel. We dug for more than six hours—an odd bunch of ditchdiggers in an odd spot in the world. It was the ice versus the tool, with the tool bending out of shape. At 1:00 p.m., after having run the gamut of possible theories about the disappearance of our gear (Atlantis, the Bermuda Triangle, the Loch Ness Monster, a yeti, a UFO), we headed back to base camp. That evening, the Spaniards brought us a Jumar, a few pitons, some overboots, and an ice ax. They invited us to join their expedition on the west pillar, and we were touched by their generosity.

Our hearts were divided between the commitment that the west face would require under these conditions, and the relative safety of the west pillar. We wondered about it for a few days and, finally, on Thursday, September 26, set off for the west face. I had woken up with a little nausea at 4:00 a.m., because the narcotic hadn't worn off. Six hours later, we took a break at the site of our cache. At around 2:00 p.m., we prepared our loads. We would have thirty-five pounds of technical gear on our backs: ice screws, Friends, 330 feet of nine-millimeter rope, 330 feet of Kevlar rope, thirty pitons. At 5:30, we resumed our ascent. Our pace was quick—after two hours we were already at the first rock band, almost halfway up the face. The conditions were good but not excellent; the rock was covered with a very thin layer of ice. Jean gave himself a fright by downclimbing a section that had led him to a dead end. At 5:00 a.m., we were both at the foot of the big dihedral, which is the crux of the face: 165 feet of very difficult rock climbing that would determine the outcome of our expedition in terms of success or failure. We were at the prediction stage, when Jean cried out in terror. He had just taken off his crampons and noticed that one of them was completely cracked. That model of crampon has a plastic plate in the middle; it had a crack running down its entire length. If the two parts were still holding, it was only because the cold had cemented them together. We shuddered retroactively: During the past twenty-four hours of climbing, how many times had we relied entirely on the front points of our crampons? I didn't dare to imagine the consequences a quick thaw would have had on Jean's well-being. Fortunately, there were holes along the edges of the crampon. We threaded a piece of cord through them to give these "crabs" the illusion of sticking together. The serious difficulties began just above us; they required sure-footedness, and we had a hard time imagining how a one-legged man would surmount them. We had no option but to descend, convinced this time that the west face of Makalu wanted nothing to do with us.

It's crazy how dependent we can be on an accessory. "Agile-footed Jean" was now concerned about where he placed his feet. Needless to say, he didn't have much faith in the cord that snaked under the sole of his boot. I placed gear in the trickiest sections and belayed Jean on the descent; it took six hours. At 7:30 p.m., we arrived at base camp. We were exhausted. The next day, Jean noticed that he had lost an overboot and what remained of his crampons. I examined the face with binoculars and located his gear just below our cache, at Camp I, at around 6300 meters. Jean took a night to rest and then set off to recover his equipment from up on the face. He came back seven hours later and I noted in my journal that when he returned, he was "in a foul mood." Cardiologists unanimously criticize the evils of a sedentary lifestyle, and here was Jean, complaining about a 3000-foot uphill stroll! I couldn't help philosophizing about humans being strange animals in that they prefer immediate comfort to future well-being.

Now, a break from philosophy: Plan B was the west pillar, where the Spaniards had so kindly invited us to join them. On Tuesday, October 1, I woke up a little after midnight. We left base camp at around 1:30 a.m. with minimal food, minimal equipment, and 165 feet of rope. I was a little woozy because my sleeping pill hadn't worn off. Could I summit Makalu while sleepwalking? I let Jean break trail, then I took over. At 7:00 a.m., we were at the foot of the perfectly straight couloir where in 1971 the French pulled off one of the finest Himalayan achievements. Let's be honest, the west pillar of Makalu is no longer what it once was: It is covered with fixed lines that allow you to avoid all of the technical passages. Today, a mountaineer who conquers the west pillar no longer has the honor of having climbed a grade V route; he needs a good Jumar and good trust in the fixed lines, which are "fixed" to varying degrees. But despite this depreciation of the climbing, the atmosphere is fantastic. It's certainly one of the most beautiful routes ever put up on an 8000er.

I ascended the fixed lines to Camp III, at 7400 meters, arriving at around 10:00 a.m. The wind was strong. Over the radio, Sylvie gave us an update on the Spanish team ahead of us. The afternoon passed, rocked by the rhythm of the stove. We made some drinks, and, to kill time, I read a novel from the *His Serene Highness* series (*The Macabre Tontons Macoute of Makalu* would be an original title!). At 3:00 p.m., one of the Spanish climbers, Juan, arrived in Camp III; he was too tired and was turning back.

We got ready at 5:00 p.m., predicting that we would catch up to the Spaniards a little before midnight. We now tackled the most interesting part of the pillar—a series of slabs, all fixed—before starting up a 130-foot dihedral where aluminum ladders made the climbing easier. A thirty-five-foot vertical wall then took us to the foot of the monolith that marked the end of the difficult section. At 8:30 p.m. I was at 7900 meters. There, the Spanish climbers, Carlos Valles and Manu Badiola Otegi, had set up their tent. They were asleep; I could hear them shivering through the thin nylon wall. They had no sleeping bags, only sleeping pads. I woke them up and they stared, wide-eyed, trying to make sense of what they were seeing. Manu asked me if I had come up by airplane. We agreed to leave at midnight. I looked for a spot to wait until the departure time, but found only a ledge to hold my meager mass. It was such a tiny space that I didn't dare to put both legs into the bivy sack, so I spent three and a half hours balanced on my sit bones.

We roped up at midnight. The darkness was thick, and if Thomas Edison hadn't invented the lightbulb, I think I would have invented it that night. The cold rising from the west face surrounded us. Contrary to what we had expected, the ridge was sharp. At the base of a bulge that sheltered us from the wind, we stopped to rest and wait for dawn. We had even planned to wait for the sun to hit us, but it took the leisurely route like a kid on the way to school, playing hooky behind the southeast ridge.

At 6:00 a.m. we started moving again, and as soon as we hauled ourselves up onto the ridge, the sun caught up with us. I'm sure that one day, this good old star will burn out, and when that happens, I hope that I'm somewhere other than on Makalu, where the normal air temperature is already cold. At 8200 meters, we reached the final difficult section on the route: a wall leading to some snow-covered slabs. The climbing was tricky. I continued upward while Jean fixed a rope for the Spaniards; they were behind us, but we had lost sight of them. Then I fell into a snow slab that was as rotten as an Italian government minister. I kept sinking in up to my stomach, but the traverse was short, and soon I found harder snow. I looked up and saw the summit. This time I was sure of it—we would get there. My throat swelled with emotion, and I felt like crying. At 10:00 a.m. I was on the summit of Makalu. After thirty-three hours of climbing, we had just made the fifth ascent of the west pillar. An hour later, there were three of us congratulating each other: Jean, Manu, and me. Carlos wasn't there. We waited, but when he didn't appear, I decided to descend with Jean. Manu stayed to wait for his friend. We planned to descend as far as Camp II so that the two Spanish climbers, who had been on the mountain for five days, could use Camp III. We had discouraged them from spending an additional night at Camp IV; the 7900 meters of altitude would deplete their bodies.

We picked up the pace, our steps a wild staccato. I felt good, and I was buoyed by the prospect of getting to base camp that night. At our second bivy spot I dropped off two canisters of fuel, in case Carlos and Manu didn't make Camp III. At the start of the fixed lines, we ran into Lhakpa, the Spanish climbers' Sherpa. He was waiting for them with food and drinks. He was kind enough to offer us some, and we told him that he would be waiting for another two or three hours. At around 2:00 p.m. we took advantage of Camp III to melt half a liter of water, then we kept descending the fixed lines. We were like Spiderman charging toward the plains. At the end of the ropes, we let gravity do most of the work: We slid on our backsides.

Our slide was uncontrolled, but under controlled conditions. In thirty minutes I was at the base of the couloir. I hurried along, because I wanted to be back at base camp before dark. I don't like to descend in the dark; I often feel as if it's haunted, as if there is someone ahead of or behind me—undoubtedly the angels glimpsed by poets. At 7:00 p.m., I was at base camp.

I was in the process of hydrating my desiccated frame with the liquid it craved, when the Spanish climbers' voices burst over the airwaves. Carlos was in Camp III and absolutely had to talk to me. I took the radio and heard these words from the "sleeping giant"—"Manu has fallen!" Carlos explained that on the rock section at 8200 meters, Manu had gotten to the end of the rope, slipped, and disappeared down the Chinese side of the mountain. He was probably on a plateau 2300 feet below. Carlos called on my experience; he was distraught and asked me what he should do. I told him about Pierre-Alain Steiner: his fall, the waiting, and our powerlessness. Manu had fallen 2300 feet, and we had to admit that there was nothing we could do for him. We would have to go back up to 8000 meters and downclimb the wall on the Chinese side to confirm that he had died. That much risk to identify a body?

Manu, who had two children, would not return from Makalu. No one survives a 2300-foot fall. I knew that, and yet, during the last days that I spent in camp, I couldn't stop myself from examining the west pillar with the spotting scope, looking for a silhouette to prove me wrong. But Manu didn't return. Our destinies had been intertwined for twelve hours filled with suffering and happiness, but then fate had separated us. Manu's death cast a shadow over our victory. I was convinced that without us, neither Carlos nor Manu would have reached the summit. Before we caught up to them, they were making practically no progress: 165 feet of elevation gain in the previous day! The altitude and the five days they had spent fixing the pillar had wiped them out. But at the same time, I was sure that we never would have been able to "conquer" Makalu without the enormous amount of work the Spanish climbers had done. Succeeding on the west pillar would have been unthinkable if we had had to fix the route ourselves. I'm not particularly proud of this expedition. Even though the Spaniards explicitly invited us, a part of me feels that we took advantage of their labor. It's the same remorse that haunts a cuckoo after it has squatted in a robin's nest.

ERHARD TALKS TO GOD...

Mountaineers are free spirits, like the migratory birds in the Jean Richepin poem:

> *Look at them pass by! They are the wild ones.*
> *They go where their desire wants, over mountains*
> *And woods, and seas, and winds, and far from slavery.*
> *The air they drink would make your lungs burst.*

So how can we explain mountaineers submitting so easily to the concept of destiny? If the art of tragedy consists of making peace with one's destiny, then mountaineers are tragic actors. Jean Troillet calmly said, "It was written that we should continue to climb 8000ers together. . . . When the call comes, we have to go." And each time Erhard Loretan felt the grim reaper's touch, he said afterward, "It wasn't our time!" They spoke as if all of that were predetermined: Life is a wire tensioned between the alpha and omega, and we are each free to play on our own wire; it is thin and, unfortunately, finite. Where did this fatalism come from? Erhard attributed it to his personal experiences. He remembered the time when one of his friends decided to do a seemingly safe ski ascent on climbing skins in the Prealps rather than tackling the terrifying north face of the Eiger. His friend never returned from Hochmatt, a harmless 6500-foot peak with a difficult approach. In the calamity that befell Nicole Niquille, he saw proof of a tragic and ironic destiny: One of Switzerland's greatest female mountaineers was struck down while picking mushrooms!

Moreover, Loretan only had to consider his own path. On the north face of Everest, he and Jean got lost and deviated from the normal line; at that very instant, an avalanche swept down the couloir they had been following a few moments before. The logical conclusion: "It wasn't our time!" Because Erhard's time had already been decided: "I'm sure; actually, I'm positive. We are free to make our own choices, but we are all headed toward a predetermined ending. This idea of destiny came to me suddenly, when I first experienced the deaths of friends, and then from all the times when, during my life as a mountaineer, I nearly crossed to the other side but didn't!" This certainty is very practical when, like most Himalayan climbers, one has to commit to exposed routes. "Exposed" is a term that—let's not forget—is used when risk exceeds reason: "The idea of destiny helps me during very committing undertakings. When you leave for a climb like the Lhotse traverse, it's reassuring to think that if it's not your time, you'll be fine, regardless of the danger. Maybe for a mountaineer, it's that kind of belief that makes you feel safe." But should we be talking about belief, or self-delusion?

Going back to Jean Troillet's words, however, if the mountaineer is called; if, as Erhard Loretan said, our time is predetermined, that raises a question: By whom? Who calls? Who decides the time? What is this powerful, or all-powerful, being? Maybe that being exists up there, very high up; like other mountaineers, Loretan mentioned a "presence" that he felt at those oxygen-deprived altitudes.

Twice—definitely on Everest but also on Makalu—he felt this "presence" with him. When he turned back, there was no one there, but he had the vivid sense of a third being in addition to Jean and him: "I could not convince myself that there were two of us, and only two. I don't know what to make of it. But up there, maybe we have a better understanding of our insignificance: We are nothing. The situation is beyond our control; someone else is in charge. All of a sudden, you have the sense that you're putting your destiny in the hands of this other being." God, since it's Him we're talking about, must therefore be at ease in the mountains, as is shown by the Sermon on the Mount. "Personally, I believe in God. If I had to practice a religion, I would choose Buddhism, for various reasons: first, it's a philosophy more than a religion; second, Buddhists are pacifists, so they're the only ones who haven't resorted to war to impose their beliefs; third, Buddhists are the only ones who say that we have to protect the environment." Erhard Loretan believed in an afterlife that might be reincarnation; perhaps some of his deceased friends had already returned to this world? "I have no proof, but I find the idea of reincarnation appealing."

A bit like Jacques Brel, who only prayed to God when he had a toothache, Erhard willingly confessed that he thought of God more readily on the slopes of an 8000er than in the cocoon of his chalet. Up high, when nature reduced him to a mere pinpoint and his frenetic heartbeat seemed to be counting down his final hours, Erhard would catch himself asking for divine grace: "I say to Him, 'Listen, not this time . . .' I have a sort of dialogue with God. Even if it's a one-way dialogue. Hah!"

| 12 |

A Grandiose and Crazy Dream

"The difficult we do immediately. The impossible takes a little longer."

—Fridtjof Nansen

First, we climbed the main summit of Lhotse via the standard route, then we started the traverse and made light work of the pinnacles blocking access to the two unclimbed middle summits, then we followed the mixed ridge that leads to Lhotse Shar, and then we only had to descend toward Chukhung on the southeast side. We fell into each other's arms. Jean Troillet and I had just completed the first Lhotse–Lhotse Shar traverse, the latest dream project of Himalayan climbers worldwide! What my finger had just accomplished in the photo of Lhotse—at a scale of 1:20,000—we now only had to accomplish in life size. To get an idea of what was in store for us, my imagination simply had to multiply the difficulties by 20,000. An unthinkable task.

In general, mountaineers don't like words that start with the prefix "un" and its cousins: unimaginable, undoable, unrealistic, unthinkable, impossible . . . And because climbers thrive on contrariness, you only need to describe something as impossible in order to motivate them to prove that statement wrong.

As a result of pushing that contrariness to the point of striking the word "impossible" from your vocabulary, there comes a time when, unavoidably, you end up on the Lhotse–Lhotse Shar traverse: A minimum of four days above 8000 meters, beginning at 8516 meters and ending at 8386 meters; almost a mile of pitfalls; obvious technical challenges; unpredictable cornices; and an overhanging gendarme. To me, this was the great challenge of the Himalaya. Until the late 1980s, mountaineers focused their ambitions exclusively on the south face of Lhotse, where Jerzy Kukuczka met his end and Tomo Česen found glory. When that face was conquered on April 24, 1990, people exclaimed that "the last great Himalayan problem" had been solved. This kind of phrase is so empty that it echoes forever. The last great problem? Of course, a face is striking to look at, and as long as a mirror hasn't been conquered, it reflects the world's failings back at it; but I had been obsessed with this traverse for years. It was a plunge into the unknown. No one had ever ventured beyond the main summit. However, I knew that this project was highly coveted; I didn't want a heavyweight expedition like the one to Kangchenjunga in 1989, when thirty-five Russian climbers stormed the summit, to defile my dream. A strange and powerful dream.

As with the Loch Ness Monster, we had only a few blurred and confusing photos that invited speculation. We had to guess about the line, and the joys that it had in store for us. The entire route description was written in the conditional tense: The central summit would require an ascent of 330 feet, primarily on ice; then we would have to climb three small pinnacles, or avoid them with a 165-foot rappel, in which case we would have to traverse back to the ridge on ledges . . . To this purely technical information we had to add a psychological component—the kind of thing that transforms a song by [the French crooner] Marcel Amont into a Stephen King novel: Once we had passed the main summit and committed to the traverse, our retreat would be cut off; there would be no escape. Our only return option would be to flee by going forward. During the months before our departure, I became engrossed in aerial photos of the ridge, and this contemplation alone gave me the creeps. My rational mind did what it could to prove that there was nothing unreasonable about this adventure, but my body turned a deaf ear to those arguments: "Whatever!" was the response from my sweaty skin and my thumping heart.

On Tuesday, August 16, 1995, Jean Troillet, Sylvie, Mireille, and I met at the Geneva airport; two journalists from Lausanne's *Le Matin* were also there. One of them, Olivier Kahn, would stay with us for the entire expedition. You can't allow a journalist to come along and then complain that they did their job: journalism. I will only say that with all the fuss that surrounded this expedition, you would have to be living in a cave to not know that two Swiss climbers were going to try to link the summits of Lhotse and Lhotse Shar. When we left Switzerland, we couldn't be sure of succeeding; you have to thrive on public humiliation to be willing to spread the word that widely about a potential failure.

During the approach march, which we reduced to three days (August 24–26) thanks to taking a helicopter from Kathmandu to Syangboche (3850 meters), we took a look in the direction of our project. After scanning the ridge and then the wall of the south face with a spotting scope, we breathed a sigh of relief; we had seen an emergency exit. Jean and I were nearly convinced that it would be possible to descend the south face, which is generally portrayed as a one-way chute. Of course, it wouldn't be a pleasurable stroll. We would have to pray that avalanches didn't follow us down into the abyss, but the plan wasn't in any way unrealistic. Besides, Pierre Béghin and Christophe Profit had bailed out that way, from high up in the central couloir. So we wouldn't have to give up all hope of retreat past the summit of Lhotse; salvation might not require being suspended between heaven and earth for four days.

Until September 4, we could maintain the illusion of a mountain that was far from civilization and that welcomed anyone who was fleeing from civilization. That day, a French expedition stomped into base camp and began dancing a jig under our awnings. Day by day, more expeditions (mostly commercial ones) arrived at this camp, which is used for both Everest and Lhotse. On September 22, we counted eighty-seven tents on this moraine at 5300 meters. But where are the snows of yesteryear?

On September 9, Sylvie and Mireille had to go back down to the villages, and we walked with them to Pheriche before returning to base camp. Now single, Jean and I got down to business on September 17, climbing through the infamous Khumbu Icefall—the gigantic icefall that leads to the Western Cwm—to Camp II, at 6400 meters. The Sherpas had fixed ladders and ropes on those 2300 feet of altitude gain; in exchange, they were collecting a toll of about $1,000 per person. Using our old bargaining methods, we were able to talk this modest tax down to $1,000 for the entire expedition. When we arrived at Camp II, we transferred the contents of our packs to a large dry bag and then descended. We got back to base camp at 3:00 in the morning. It had snowed during the entire eleven-hour reconnaissance trip. On the 22nd, we stretched our legs by climbing Khumbutse (6500 meters): four hours up and an hour down.

On Friday, September 23, we decided that the conditions were favorable for depositing the cache that we wanted to leave at 8000 meters. On the night of the 23rd, at about 12:45 a.m., we set out with loads of around twenty-seven pounds. Our packs contained all of the technical gear needed for the traverse. After a few minutes, I postholed into water; I was in up to my knees and maybe even deeper. A similar misadventure had befallen me in the Baltoro, and I had realized that a little liquid cooling is good for the human engine. At 5:00 a.m. I was at Camp II, where I decided to dry out my socks. I took my boots off, and in the blink of an eye, my socks were frozen solid. I got into my sleeping bag and, like a cold-blooded lizard, waited for the sun to hit me.

At around 5:00 p.m. we continued up toward Camp III, which we reached at 9:30. We poached some space in a tent and even a little fuel, which we burned to warm our feet. We rested until 2:00 a.m., then started off again. Daybreak snuck up on us as we were climbing the Yellow Band, a rock band that cuts across the Geneva Spur route. At around 9:00, we arrived at the spot we had picked for our cache. I was tired after breaking trail for seven hours. Based on our experiences on Makalu, we decided to trust rock rather than liquid, even solid liquid, when it came time to place the cache. We hammered a pin into a section of rock, attached a cordelette, and hung our dry bag. We agreed that we would push on to the south col, on the standard route up Everest. After walking for another hour, we were only a short distance from the col, but because there were no more tracks, we didn't go beyond the Geneva Spur. We must have been close to 8000 meters. At around 10:30 a.m. we turned back, sliding like maniacs on the seat of our pants toward base camp. We arrived at 6:00 p.m.

To me, base camp is often a form of torture, because being there means waiting. I was as taut as a guitar string; the tiniest vibration in the air amplified my tension. I'm always nervous on every expedition, but I had never been nervous like this. As I was closing my pack, I didn't feel an excited tension; I felt a kind of fear welling up in me that I had never felt before. Was this the feeling that marks a condemned person's walk to the gallows? But all I needed was to shoulder my pack, to feel a real and palpable weight on my shoulders, for the knot in my stomach to release. And besides, I told myself that if destiny truly didn't want me on the mountain, it would give me a sign. The days passed, and the sign never came.

On September 29, at 5:00 in the evening, we set off for Lhotse, after which we would begin the traverse toward Lhotse Shar. Four to six days for a journey to the limits of possibility. As I turned my back on base camp, I felt as if an airlock were closing behind me. When Yuri Gagarin heard the doors of the Vostok cabin lock, was he sure that he would see his loved ones again? I climbed the giant staircase of the icefall. At 8:30 p.m. I arrived at Camp II, at 6400 meters. Jean joined me and we crawled into one of the French expedition's tents. I set the alarm for 3:00 a.m., fell asleep easily, and woke up just before it rang. We resumed our ascent at about 4:00. I tucked in behind five Sherpas to go up the fixed lines. A little above the Yellow Band, I ran into a rope team that had just made an unsuccessful attempt on Lhotse. I continued in their tracks, which required me to do a long traverse to the right to get over to our cache. The snow was strange, and the trip back, with the large dry bag on my shoulder, took a long time. Like a good Christian, I left half the contents for Jean before continuing toward the tent of two climbers—a Canadian, Alex; and a Scot, Jeff—who had been there for two days. I was at 8000 meters, and it was noon. I went to meet Jean. Time was flying; it was already 2:00 p.m., and we would never be able to leave before 5:00 if we wanted to rest for a bit. We dug a hole to wait in for a few hours. But the wind had picked up, blowing half-mile-long snow clouds onto Everest. The snow was swirling in from all sides and landing in our hole; we had the unpleasant sensation of having chosen an hourglass as a bivy spot. We talked to Jeff and Alex, the only other tenants on the mountain, and all four of us agreed to leave at around 9:00 p.m.

This pause in the action allowed us to reflect on our attempt. Although the conditions were difficult, it was out of the question to give up on the traverse. But one question remained. Our packs weighed forty pounds; climbing with that kind of load in snow that can't hold weight would take too much energy. We decided on a light ascent, which would require us to climb from the snow hole to the summit of Lhotse twice. After barely seeing the sun all day, we enjoyed a blazing sunset. The cold was just waiting for that moment to pounce on us.

We got ready at approximately 9:00 p.m. At around 10:00, we left for the summit, which we estimated would take about ten hours to reach. The first few hours were kind to us; the hard snow didn't slow our progress too much. Jean followed me, and the two others were already far behind us. After four hours, we were halfway up the couloir that leads to the summit. It was bitter cold, the wind was fierce, snow was sloughing down the couloir, and we were walking against its flow. If whoever was following made the mistake of falling several feet behind the person breaking trail, he had to break trail all over again while feeling with his ski pole, because the blowing snow was blinding. We understood that the weather conditions were sapping our resistance, so we decided to hunker down in a hole and wait for daybreak. Alex caught up to us and dug a platform for himself; Jeff followed. His hands were almost frozen. We took turns rubbing them, trying to bring some life back into his white extremities. We waited for the sun to come up. I searched back through my "biting" memories but couldn't remember my hands and feet ever being so cold. Fortunately, we were wearing down jackets, which is the minimum for that kind of bitter cold.

When we started walking again, at around 7:00 a.m., everything was frozen; my ski goggles were unusable, so I took them off and immediately the snow started sticking to my eyes. My entire face was encased in a numbing layer of ice, and I could loosen my eyelids only with great difficulty. I had to stop to put on a face mask, but the mask caused condensation that immediately froze. We continued up the couloir. Jeff had turned back. Now there were only three of us confronting the elements, which were mistaken about the season; it felt like winter in the middle of September. Usually, you don't encounter those kinds of winds in the fall! With every step, we sank into the snow by a foot, and as we shakily progressed we tried to avoid wind slabs. It was every man for himself; as soon as the leader dropped back, someone else took his place. But now there were only two of us to take turns, because Alex had turned back as well. We kept going, because we had disconnected from every feeling except determination. The numbness that crept up our extremities toward our trunks; our hardened eyes; our heavy legs; our breaths, which were both absent and burning—this entire litany was propelled forward by determination.

At 9:10 a.m. we stood on the sharp summit of Lhotse; it was so cramped that more than two people couldn't have stood there. The wind was fierce, but we were above the swirling snow and for the first time in hours we could actually open our eyes without fear of being pelted with pepper flakes by the heavens. In those weather conditions, Everest's aura spread for miles. I kept going, maybe just to be sure, toward the spot where the traverse to Lhotse Shar would begin. I glanced at the summit; it seemed so close. I saw cornices the size of ski jumps, and turned my back on our dream, the folly of which was now completely apparent to me. It hadn't taken me more than a second to make the decision that I had been fearing.

Jean appointed me expedition photographer. I had the honor of capturing the moment: a photo of Everest, a photo of Lhotse Shar, a photo of Jean. And then we fled the summit, although the sunshine made it tempting to linger. We took full advantage of the thirty-degree slopes in the couloir. An hour later, we caught up to the Canadian-Scottish team. They were making slow progress and facing in on seemingly harmless sections. We passed them and they said nothing. We thought that silence meant that all was well, so we continued without worrying about them. Thanks to Jeff and Alex's tent, we knew when we had arrived at our snow-hole spot. We had to dig without a shovel, using our hands as excavators in the blown-in snow. We eventually dug out a few items that proved we were at the shipwreck location. At around noon, I radioed base camp and found out from Ruedi Homberger, a mountaineer and photographer from Graubünden, that Jeff and Alex had just called for a rescue. It seemed that they were in a dramatic situation. We made some tea, and I told base camp that we would handle it. When Jeff and Alex arrived at camp, we gave them something to drink. On the rest of the descent, Jean attended to them while I carried their packs. Jean, saint that he was, guided their steps. As the pack mule of the high peaks, I held 175 pounds on the rope. Thank God, the deep snow allowed me to anchor myself and I was able to hold onto this load, which was heavier than me. If I had let myself pick up speed, I would have taken off on a 6500-foot gliding flight. At Camp III there were two members of the Canadian–Scottish expedition and some Sherpas, and we were able to leave the two Lhotse strandees in their hands. However, Jeff's and Alex's toes weren't able to endure the cold of this peak and they later had to be amputated. At Camp II, the French offered us their hospitality again; we gratefully accepted.

The next day, we resumed our descent at around 8:00 a.m., while the wind barred all of the ascending climbers from making any attempt toward the summit. We crossed the icefall one more time, and at 11:00 we reached base camp. There was almost no one there; the journalist greeted me with these two words: "Too bad."

"Too bad." I couldn't say that he was wrong, but how could I explain to him that continuing along that ridge would have led to certain death, that my fingers and toes were tingling now that I could feel them again, that it's possible to love risk without being suicidal, and that this time, courage meant giving up. The winds would have buffeted us, the cornices would have betrayed us, and our strength would have failed. When you've removed a word from your vocabulary, sometimes the situation teaches you to spell that word again: i-m, im; p-o-s, pos; s-i, si; b-l-e; ble. Impossible? For us, under those conditions, yes. But tomorrow, maybe someone stronger would expand the concept of what was possible to include this Lhotse–Lhotse Shar traverse. Personally, I now knew that spring, when there's less snow, is better for this kind of project. I also knew that this traverse, which I had thought of as the apotheosis of a Himalayan climbing career and which had haunted my dreams and fed my ambitions, was no longer an immediate priority for me. The Kangchenjunga traverse or a new route on the west face of Makalu were more appealing, because they were more reasonable goals. As *The Song of Roland* says, "Folly isn't courage."

When I think back on the tension that gripped me before we set off for Lhotse, I feel that you have to take it as a sign—the sign from destiny that I was looking for. I had set the bar too high, and the fear that tormented me was proof of that. Maybe it is a manifestation of the self-preservation instinct.

TELL ME I'M DREAMING!

At the end of 1994, the Spanish magazine *Desnivel* celebrated its 100th edition. For the occasion, it had asked various climbers to contribute. Erhard Loretan wrote the following article, a somewhat disillusioned vision of mountaineering.

On every continent, the 1980s were marked by extraordinary accomplishments. In Europe, the trend of enchainments led to new routes being opened on simple and logical lines. In the Himalaya, all of the walls on the great peaks were climbed, the most recent being Tomo Česen's ascent of the south face of Lhotse. The spirit of mountaineering remained relatively pure, until an increasing number of mountaineers made media attention the motivation for their climbs.

Today, it must be said that mountaineering is on the decline and that it is entering the sad category of mass sports; it is losing its identity. The heroic era, when trust was a given, is long gone. I feel a bit uncomfortable seeing that mountaineers now have to provide proof of their accomplishments, while the justice system gives the accused the benefit of the doubt and it is up to the accuser to prove the suspect's guilt. Of course I'm thinking of the famous case of Tomo Česen, who was suspected of not having reached the summit of Lhotse. The names of the greats, synonymous with our dreams, have been replaced by mountaineering for the masses, with traffic jams on classic routes and gear being stolen from huts. Urban hell, including all its problems, has migrated to the mountains. Mountaineering has lost its sense of ethics, and thereby its spiritual dimension.

In the Alps, adventure with a capital A is practically impossible to find. In the Himalaya, there are more and more commercial expeditions. With a few exceptions, there is a total lack of imagination as to new routes. I've just returned from Lhotse, and I witnessed a circus erecting its big top at the foot of Everest. Jean Troillet and I laughed at these pseudo-mountaineers who have money but no skills. At the same time, this appalling spectacle made us feel tremendously sad. What a disappointment to set off on a fabulous expedition and then find oneself in the middle of an overpopulated base camp next to a generator running constantly for—it seemed—scientific use. Right now, a luxury hotel is being built at the foot of Everest on the Tibetan side, just next to the Rongbuk monastery. Under the pretext of helping the local population, it seems that anything is fair game to line one's own pockets. I ask you: How can one allow this kind of insult to the mountain? This would be a spectacular case for environmental organizations like Greenpeace or Mountain Wilderness. Fortunately, there are still places in the Himalaya where you can be alone to fight fairly against nature, far from all help and with no means of communication.

We have to stop this massacre and preserve these last playgrounds for future generations so that they too can experience great adventures.

Climbing Everest has become mundane. People will resort to any means to reach the summit; it's almost obscene. This fall for example, there was a sixty-year-old climber who paid for an escort of fifteen high-altitude Sherpas and a supply of fifty bottles of oxygen that he sucked on starting at Camp II, at 6500 meters. If we want to curb the pollution of these sites, there's a very simple solution: We only have to prohibit the use of oxygen and leave the mountain to those who are worthy of confronting it. The moon isn't accessible to everyone, and that's not so terrible. Without Sherpas, only 1 percent of expeditions would return victorious. These people do remarkable work, but no one notices. The Sherpas are in the process of forming a group to protect the Khumbu's interests, and I'm overjoyed at this attempt at a coalition.

I deplore the fact that the expedition system, with its royalties, favors the rich. Too many young people don't have the means to follow their dreams and bring their plans to reality. Few areas in this world are suitable for idealistic endeavors, and now one of them, the Himalaya, is exclusively for the wealthy. If you look carefully, there are still places on this planet that allow for the hatching of crazy projects, but we have to fight bitterly for them to come to fruition. This proves that there are still mountaineers who climb because it is their calling.

I willingly acknowledge that my words are selfish and idealistic, but we absolutely must keep mountaineering from going adrift. Until the beginning of the 1980s, I was proud to belong to the big family of mountaineering, yet today I almost feel ashamed. By nature I'm a fighter, an optimistic and positive person, but now, I would be happy if someone told me that I've been dreaming.

| 13 |

SETTING FOOT ON THE MOON

*"For someone who considers himself an adventurer,
solitude is an essential condition."*

—Walter Bonatti

TELEPHONES CAN BE AS STUBBORN as a homing missile. The two of us, Romolo Nottaris and I, were biding our time by the Strait of Magellan, where heaven and earth meet, when the ringing telephone interrupted the sound of the roaring fifties. The phone call informed Romolo that he absolutely had to return to Switzerland; business has its reasons.... Punta Arenas, in Chile, November 1994: I found myself alone, without a teammate, for a planned first ascent of Mount Epperly (4780 meters) in Antarctica. I hesitated for an instant; frankly, two people wouldn't have been too many for this expedition, and now I was going to try it solo? I had been thinking about doing an expedition in this style for a long time, and here I had only to seize the opportunity that had just landed in my lap: "If it doesn't bother you, I'll go alone," I said to Romolo. The question was a matter of basic good manners, because he was financing the bulk of this polar adventure, to the tune of 50,000 francs. Romolo, a guide from Ticino whom I had known since forever, agreed.

I waited in Punta Arenas for six days, then an airplane dropped me off at the Patriot Hills base, in Antarctica. Antarctica! In a world that shrinks a little more every day, where the unknown has retreated to hidden summits and to acres of forest, adventure has had to find remoteness. Antarctica, with its five and a half million square miles, has become the El Dorado and refuge of adventurers. There, they can find the only company their misanthropy allows them: solitude.

After an hour-and-a-half flight, the door of the Cessna opened into the solitude that I craved; the ten other passengers continued on toward Mount Vinson, the roof of Antarctica at 5240 meters. I was three miles from Mount Epperly, the peak Romolo and I had been coveting. Actually, we weren't the only ones with that idea. I knew that the competition was on, because I had heard that Doug Scott and Reinhold Messner had made this 2700-meter face one of their objectives. Scott, Messner . . . I didn't know anything about Sir Edward Whymper's intentions.

Once the engine noise had dissipated into the vastness and the silence had begun to whisper to me, I found myself immersed in a unique atmosphere. It was Wednesday, November 30, and I would be alone for about two weeks on this ice cap that is both the end and the beginning of the world. Due to the never-ending austral daylight, it was difficult to make a schedule and plan an attempt. What you put off until tomorrow you might as well put off for six months, and the proverb is entirely true here. I put up my tent and did not allow myself the luxury of reflecting; I didn't let myself be intimidated by the adversary, this enormous face that obscured my horizon. An hour later, I set off to attack those 8900 feet of ice and rock. I went very light, with just a few spare items in my pack. The lower part of the face was ice, and I quickly climbed 3900 feet in four hours. Suddenly the sky lowered to my level and I found myself enveloped in fog. I descended and arrived at my tent at around 11:00 in the morning. But the weather was strange. Antarctica is the turbine of the planet, and stability isn't a turbine's primary characteristic; I was in the fog and now the horizon was clear. In the summery temperatures (between five and minus four degrees Fahrenheit), I snatched a short nap. It was best to take advantage of this heat wave, because the mercury could easily change its mind and drop to minus fifty-eight.

After this first attempt, I understood that the conditions had nothing in common with the Himalaya. Over there, on a half liter of water per day I was as happy as a camel, as economical as a plate of lentils. Here, I needed a half liter per hour, so I knew that I would have to carry a stove. And in light of the face's size, I decided to take a bivy sack and a shovel. On Thursday, December 1, I set off again for Mount Epperly. From the foot of the face, I followed the great central couloir, which is primarily ice. I knew that the whole climb would not be like this, because the access to the summit plateau seemed blocked by a narrow rocky section. Too much anticipation leads to inaction, and I continued for another 650 feet. At that point, I had to admit that I had been correct: The exit was as nasty as it had appeared from below. The closer perspective didn't change the situation at all. Other than a few pins, I only had a sixty-five-foot five-millimeter rope with me. In fact, it was a clothesline that I had repurposed; I would be asking it to hold a few tons in addition to ordinary clothespins. I gained about 130 feet on some crumbling rock that was almost like sand. A few feet from the exit, I felt "bloody awkward," to borrow an expression from my youth. I tried many times, but each time I held back instead of committing. I searched in vain for a spot to hammer in a pin; the piton didn't like the sand, and the compact rock didn't like the piton. To add to the comedy of the situation and help me keep my cool, I was getting blasted with several pounds of snow in my face.

For an hour, I would take a single step forward only to immediately regret it and return to my starting point. Should I go down? I didn't see myself downclimbing what I had just climbed up. I told myself to be calm and deliberate and prepared a two-stage plan: first, get rid of the pack; second, see what happened. I looked around for a spot to hang my pack and finally hooked it on a small irregularity in the rock. I was afraid that the pack would fall and drag me with it, since I had tied myself to it in order to haul it up. Two or three times I tried to force my way up that section, but in vain. And the fourth time, without knowing how, I succeeded! I pulled up my pack. There were a few more difficulties, but the rock was solid, and an hour later I was on the summit of Mount Epperly. The face had cost me nine hours of effort.

It was midnight on December 1. The surroundings were fantastic; an unreal light flooded the landscape. It was grand! To think that I was the first human to set foot on this summit, that I had succeeded on a difficult route, and that it had taken a good dose of bravery to get there—it all blended into an intoxicating feeling. In the Himalaya, I had already conquered some unclimbed 6000-meter peaks, but I had never felt like this. I truly had the feeling of standing on the moon; I was opening the door to a new world.

The cold, however, is of this earth, and it brought me back to reality. I had to get down, but how? Given my sparse gear, the ascent route would be impractical to descend, and without a rope, the ridge would be impossible I hunted for an hour before finding another couloir, parallel to the one I had just climbed. It was the kind of terrain that can severely distort the population pyramid of a country or—in this case—a continent: For three hours, I wasn't able to hammer in a single piece of protection in this compact rock. I let myself slide, and when I felt speed overtaking me, I caught myself on whatever I could catch with my hand or my ice ax.

When I got back to my tent, the bad weather settled in. For three days I remained in contact with the people at Patriot Hills and the climbers on Vinson. On the fourth day, since I had no more radio contact with Mount Vinson, I deduced that the weather had lifted there and that they had left for the summit. I decided to join them via the four miles of flat open space that separated me from the attack. I took my tent, my stove, my down jacket, and a little food. Too little food, because the weather trapped me for two full days in Camp II, at 3800 meters. So I invented a diet that emphasized liquids over fats, proteins, and sugars. When the weather improved, I put on my skis and continued up the standard route. But 160 feet below the summit, skis proved less practical than feet, so I abandoned them (the skis, not the feet!) and kept going to the high point, at 5240 meters. Because the days were as long as a day without bread—and I knew what that comparison meant—I enchained with an ascent of Shin (4800 meters). Having left the tent at 9:00 a.m., I returned at 11:00 p.m.

At the end of this first polar experience, I could confirm that darkness hampers human activity. If it were up to me, I would abolish it.

When I came back from my expedition to Mount Epperly, I understood that Antarctica had renewed my ideas about mountaineering and, to use big words, adventure. Lhotse had left me disillusioned: Was it possible that we had corrupted the values of the mountains to that extent? In September 1994, there had been eighty-seven tents, including ours, at Everest base camp. Plus a generator running continuously in the name of sacrosanct science! And on the Tibetan side, a luxury hotel alongside a monastery! In Antarctica I had found what I was looking for: solitude, commitment, difficulty, and splendor.

After the conquest of Kangchenjunga, my fourteenth 8000er, I had only one desire—to return to the South Pole. Alas! It is incorrect to say that dreams are free; without the help of the Adia Interim corporation, I never would have raised the funds for my gear. The company agreed to finance a film about the first ascent of Mount Epperly. Télévision Suisse Romande would provide the editing and planned to show it on *Passe-moi les jumelles* [Pass Me the Binoculars], a program that breathed a bit of fresh air into the TV schedule. So the priority of this new expedition was to make a film about my adventure from the year before. Romolo Nottaris, a veteran cameraman, would be the director. He would be joined by Marco Zaffaroni on sound, and his friend Anna as the photographer.

On Wednesday, December 19, 1995, the Hercules landed at Patriot Hills. It had just added a thirteenth task to its list of twelve, as the Patriot Hills airstrip is considered one of the most difficult in the world. It's a windswept sheet of ice. The aircraft doesn't have skis, just normal wheels; when pilots have worn heart monitors, their pulses have been shown to rise to over 200 when they land there. Those kinds of tests have never been carried out on passengers. The staff are there, alongside the runway, to judge and give marks on the triple lutzes and double axels that the pilot may include in his or her free skate at any time. We transferred our gear to a Twin Otter, and at 8:30 p.m. we took off for Mount Epperly base camp. After dropping us off, the airplane left. No more sound. To the right, there was a glacier whose whiteness extended as far as the eye could see; to the left, 9800-foot walls that were both attractive and horrifying. It was there, in a desert that denies all life, down to lichen, that we would be spending three weeks. By the time we had set up our camp, at the same spot as the year before, it was 3:00 in the morning. We ate a plate of spaghetti and went to bed at 5:00. I wondered if these sojourns at the South Pole might not disrupt our body clocks.

We were there to make a film. It was a task that would take us two weeks, working ten to twelve hours per day. Every day, we set out at about 2:00 p.m. and didn't return until 3:00 a.m. At around midnight, the light was bewitching, but difficult to film in. The quality of the light was such that we had to film the scenes many times, changing the aperture. This was the price of a guaranteed good shot. In total, we recorded over three hours of usable footage; I don't claim that we had made *Gotterdammerung*, but I will say that in terms of length, we were getting close. Not every film director can say that. In addition, I can't resist speechifying about the difficulties of the filming, which—as the actress Sophie Marceau would say—was very difficult, very tedious, very demanding, and so on. The cold made Romolo's task more complicated, as he was working with mechanical film cameras. Instead of a motor, he had a crank and a spring. Our budget was limited, and sixteen-millimeter Bolex cameras remained the ideal solution for a small team. But changing the film spool was a delicate operation under those extreme conditions, and we would have to wait until we returned to Switzerland to check the quality of the footage. In the meantime, I could only hope that Romolo wasn't in the process of filming me with his electric drill, as Gaston Lagaffe did in a memorable gag in the comic strip. One day, I twisted my foot while filming a glissade scene. For the rest of my movie career, I decided, I would demand a double for all stunts. In actual fact, mountaineering doesn't lend itself to being filmed; repeating the same climbing sequence four times with bare hands is harmful to the body, and I nearly froze my fingers. I suggested to Romolo that we shoot the next film on a soundstage. He promised me that he would think about it.

After two weeks, the filming was done. Everyone took two or three days off. Anna, Romolo, and Marco left for Mount Vinson. I had an idea in the back of my mind, and it jumped out in front me, with all the power of its 2500 meters, every time I opened the tent. I had spotted it the year before, just next to Mount Epperly: a virgin summit with a superb face that—to me, at least—seemed more technical than Epperly's. The desire to have a go at it had been tormenting me for a year. While I was giving the impression of concentrating on the filming, the peak's attraction grew. At the end of the two weeks, the desire had become irresistible. I wanted to get close to the mystery of that wall; I wanted to recapture the unique, unforgettable feeling of being the first person to stand on a summit, to set foot on a corner of this earth. At the same time, I hadn't forgotten the fright of Mount Epperly and I knew that such happiness comes at the price of hours of fear. If I wanted the exultation that had been mine the year before, I would have to drag this all-consuming fear behind me like a ball and chain. I almost wished that the filming would go on forever or that bad weather would doom my project, but the time came when we heard the word "Cut!" and the horizon cleared. So I had no valid excuse, at least none that could override my introspection: I was in shape and the weather was good. I knew that if I yielded to the fuzzy temptation of staying in slippers—which, according to the most recognized historians, sometimes seized Alexander the Great—I would regret it for the rest of my life.

Action! I prepared my pack, bringing only some technical gear and a small stove. I planned to spend about twenty hours for the round-trip. I estimated that the face measured 2500 meters and that it was steeper than Mount Epperly. The ideal scenario, according to my calculations, would be to get to the start of the difficult section when the sun began warming the face. By "warming," I mean the moment when the temperature rises a tiny bit above absolute zero. I needed to leave at around 9:00 a.m., and it was now 1:00 p.m. My prevarication had cost me a day. So I had twenty-four additional hours of doubts where I could review everything that might await me on that kind of climb. From appendicitis to avalanches, from twisted ankles to hypothermia, it was a wide range.

Friday, December 29, 1995. I approached the wall on skis. I was in motion, so I was calm. Weird clouds hung over the area, but the weather was supposed to hold for another day. The wind off the wall was icy, and little by little, it paralyzed the muscles in my face. It wasn't too serious; I only had myself to talk to, and I can understand myself without enunciating. At the beginning, the snow was hard, and I was followed by the strange crunching of my crampons. Under my feet, the snow made an artificial sound. In an hour, I was at the first rock section. It posed no problems. Then the snow became deeper and I began to worry that the slabs would fracture. I tried to avoid them, which required some detours. In three hours, I had devoured 3300 feet of elevation. But I was suffering in the cold. I shouldn't have forgotten my overboots. They're a practical accessory when you want to mess around in Antarctica and you still have residual frostbite from Kangchenjunga. I strongly recommend that anyone who's nursing a frozen big toe avoid the South Pole.

I was going faster than planned, so the sun was having trouble catching up to me. For six hours I climbed in the cold shade. I continually wiggled my toes and loosened my boots, yet there was nothing to be done; the shade was an icy hell that was burning me. I felt the flames lick at my extremities. I climbed, but I couldn't shake one worry: What would I find higher up? Although one wall is not like another, I remembered all too well the exit on Mount Epperly—those seven feet that almost refused me point-blank. The sky was clear around me. At least that was already a plus. It was 4:00 p.m. when I came upon the crux of the ascent: The couloir narrowed and then died out on a small rock face covered with powder snow. I felt relieved, simply due to having identified my adversary. Remember, did [comic series hero] Michel Vaillant ever confront a tougher enemy than the "faceless pilot"? It wasn't going to be easy, but I knew what to expect. I increased my focus and committed to the first few sections of rock, then continued up to the vertical wall. I was freed from my worries; it thrilled me to be in motion. The rock was good, and I made fast progress with no protection. Alas, I was still ahead of the sun.

Soon I was caught in blowing snow, so I knew that the col was close. The face became vertical. I had to remove my gloves to get a better grip on the holds. The wind picked up and the snow got in everywhere; my eyelashes stuck together, making it hard to see, and my hands went stiff. You might ask, "Then what on earth were you doing there?" Good question, thanks for asking. My crampons scraped across the rock, hoping to hook onto a protuberance—anything that would support my weight. The engine was about to overheat, and suddenly my ice ax landed in good ice. I pulled myself up on it and found myself on a small ledge where I could stand flat on both feet, a rare luxury. Then suddenly it was Copacabana, the beach, warm sand . . . all because I had reached the sunlight.

From there, I could hear the wind sweeping over the col just above me. I knew that I hadn't yet won the match. I put on a face mask; my nose had definitely turned white. Another few hundred feet, and finally I came out on the col. It was extraordinary; I was across from Mount Epperly, and my memories came flooding back. Another magical moment awaited me, because the summit ridge proved quite gentle. The snow was hard and wind-scrubbed; the light was mystical. My shadow trailed behind me, playing leapfrog with the cornices. The moment was beyond description— one of those points in life when, surprisingly, I thought of myself in the third person. That only happens to me in two situations: When I'm the first person to reach a summit, and when I botch a pot of fondue, which is even more unusual.

> *"Six o'clock in the evening, 4600 meters. Loretan stands on the summit of this nameless peak, another one to add to the list of the 100 or so peaks he has already climbed. But his soul feels different; he is the first to set foot on this one. He is alone, lost somewhere near the celestial dome, in an environment that seems hostile but belongs to him. He feels at one with the mountain. Across the valley, Mount Epperly winks back at him. The spectacle of nature in all its unchanging glory is so splendid that he feels the urge to cry."*

End of passage in the third-person singular, which is the privilege of megalomaniacs and tyrants (who are often one and the same).

Speaking of which, why not name this orphaned summit after myself?

What did I learn from these experiences at the bottom of the world? That the kind of solitude I experienced during my first expedition, when I was my only company for two weeks, helps us understand how much attachment we have to the world, and to other people. Does a return to "heroic" mountaineering require a visit to the frozen continent, where an unnamed peak's only trace of human contact is an anonymous piton? After Lhotse's overpopulated base camp, after Kangchenjunga and the media circus, these two Antarctic expeditions healed my wounds and helped me reconcile with what is correctly termed "adventure."

FAME'S RANSOM

Erhard Loretan was blindsided by glory on Thursday, October 5, 1995, when he stepped onto the summit of Kangchenjunga, the end point of his "fourteenology." Until then, he had climbed the thirteen steps of that staircase in relative anonymity. Relative, because his other accomplishments had already made headlines. Oddly enough, the Himalaya contributed less to his reputation than did the Alps; the Swiss were particularly captivated by his two enchainments, and hundreds of articles were devoted to the Loretan–Georges team. This is possibly because the Swiss mountains speak to the Swiss heart. The mere mention of the Matterhorn or the Eiger makes the country's citizens feel knots in their calves and want to fight it out with the Hapsburgs; to a child of the Alps, the plains are a dismal place.

Certainly, the mountaineering press had seized on Loretan as a personality, and the Swiss Alpine Club journal, *Les Alpes*, had made him a regular in its stories. But his fame at that time was never proportional to his worth. When a French magazine decided to publish a list of the thirty greatest mountaineers at the time, it awarded Erhard Loretan . . . twenty-seventh place. This was in 1988, and Loretan had already completed nine 8000ers, including Everest via the Hornbein Couloir and Annapurna via its east ridge. Outside the Himalaya, he had also enchained the Valais Alps, and climbed *Les Portes du Chaos* on the Eiger in one day, to name a few. He told a journalist, "I don't like rankings, even less so when they have to do with mountains." So much for the so-called hierarchy.

And how much did he value the respect of contemptible people? Erhard was held in esteem by his peers, and the local media was friendly toward him; that was enough to make him happy. Legend has it that in the mountain huts, he was so modest that he hid anything that might reveal his identity—for example, an ice ax or a pair of crampons with his name on them. On Cho Oyu in 1990, he was doing a reconnaissance on the standard route and came upon a camp full of Spanish climbers. They started talking and then got to the point of introducing themselves. "One of them asked me my name," Loretan wrote in his journal, "and then they all wanted to shake hands with me. Bizarre!!!" He reacted like a movie star being asked for his autograph for the first time.

Erhard Loretan wasn't a fame seeker, but he didn't avoid it, either. When he found himself in the media spotlight, he adapted to it. He didn't remember refusing an interview; nor did he remember seeking one out. "Let's be honest," he said. "When a mountaineer dreams of summiting Everest, it's for two reasons: first, to climb a beautiful mountain, and second, for public recognition. Mountaineering has allowed me to climb the social ladder; I'm not totally unconcerned with that."

While he was battling on the slopes of Kangchenjunga, did Erhard imagine that fame was about to spin a tighter and tighter web around him? In France, in Switzerland, and elsewhere, the tragedy (in the classic sense of the word) involving Benoît Chamoux, with its unity of place, action, and time, fascinated the public. Jean Troillet and Erhard Loretan would now fully enter the media scene. "You just have to hit a slow news cycle, and then you're the champion," Erhard later commented. At the beginning of October 1995, the climbers on Kangchenjunga injected the news with a shot of talent. This drama needed a coryphaeus, a leader or two. Reinhold Messner and Kurt Diemberger were approached and gave their "authorized" opinions, and the machine raced out of control. The news media chose Erhard Loretan as one of its shooting stars; adored today, he would be shunned tomorrow. While the whirring presses printed their names, the airwaves broadcast their adventures, and the public seized on their story, Erhard and Jean thought that they were living a humdrum mountain life. But "humdrum" doesn't prevent drama: "If the media hadn't gotten involved, we would have landed back at the airport without being recognized. Outside the mountaineering community, no one would have talked about the third person to climb all fourteen 8000ers. But then Benoît Chamoux died, and everyone had something to say about it."

Erhard Loretan normally resisted any kind of public display, but now his name was all over the mass media. He rarely went a day without an interview, or an hour without a phone call. He expected a few hundred people at his talks, and got thousands. His income had come from a few loyal sponsors who paid him a few thousand Swiss francs per contract; suddenly he was offered a million francs to climb all fourteen 8000ers in a year. He felt dragged into a life that was no longer his own, and toward a personality that was no longer him. "I'm at the stage where people recognize me on the street; every day, someone asks me to sign a postcard. It's flattering to be recognized, but the price in terms of independence is too high. I enjoy cabinetmaking, and I don't even have the time to plane a piece of wood anymore. And yet I used to love my mountain career. These days I get up every morning with a knot in my stomach."

Those who've experienced it know that glory has a price: "Glory is but the brilliant mourning of happiness." Didn't George Brassens always say that the trumpets of fame are a most discordant din? "Refusing to hand over the ransom asked for fame. On my laurel sprig, I rest, sleeping like a dormouse."

| 14 |

THE THIRD MAN

"No one takes an interest in mountaineers unless they break their heads open, or a newspaper buys their story."

—H. W. Tilman

I WOULD BE LYING IF I said that the race to climb all fourteen 8000ers never mattered to me. It's true that for years I thought of it as media brouhaha. In order for news to resonate, the drum has to beat. For a long time, I refused to have my career summed up by a number between one and fourteen: Loretan, who has climbed nine 8000ers; Loretan, the man with eleven 8000ers. At one point I even said that the race to summit all fourteen would stop when Reinhold Messner finally did the last one. I was being honest, but I was wrong. On October 16, 1986, Messner became the first person to climb all fourteen. The race didn't end when the first person crossed the finish line, however; in the summer of 1987, Jerzy Kukuczka completed the grand slam via the west ridge of Shishapangma. At that time, I had done nine 8000ers. There was still one spot on the podium, and I had no interest in it whatsoever. After Everest, I spent a good part of 1988 on Trango Tower (6257 meters). I returned twice to K2 to attempt the west face, in 1989 and 1992. If I had been obsessed with the race to climb all fourteen, I would never have returned to a peak that I had already summited in 1985. But as I accumulated more and more 8000ers, I was gently won over by the idea. My brain couldn't resist the countdown that surrounded me. Everyone was asking me when I was going to do the remaining 8000ers so that I could be happy. Advertisers and torturers know how effective brainwashing is. After Makalu in 1991, I had two left, if you considered Shishapangma as complete. From then on, climbing all fourteen became a goal in and of itself. I failed on Kangchenjunga in 1993; in 1994, I added Lhotse to the list; in April 1995, I returned to Shishapangma and reached the main summit; and in the fall of 1995, I left for Kangchenjunga, secretly hoping to rid myself of this burden. I thought that after Kangchenjunga I would be free to do what I wanted, that I would have left most of my chains up on the mountain.

A few more words about Shishapangma. In 1990, Voytek Kurtyka, Jean Troillet, and I had done the first ascent of the south face in twenty-two hours roundtrip. We didn't reach the main summit because the traverse to it was too exposed. I never hid that. In an article in *Montagnes Magazine* in December 1990, this sentence appears: "Erhard specifies that they were not on the main summit but on the middle summit ([ten meters] lower) because of the many wind slabs on the traverse." In April 1995, I led a commercial expedition to Shishapangma, and I took the opportunity to do the summit in one day. On Friday, April 28, 1995, I left base camp at 3:30 p.m., and by noon on the 29th, I was on the main summit. By nightfall I was back at base camp. With that climb, I put a stop to the mountaineering historians who had been continually saying that my accomplishment was short by thirty-three feet, and I also erased the debt that might cloud my conscience one day; now if I wanted to claim all fourteen 8000ers, no one could contradict me.

When I was preparing to leave for Kangchenjunga, I couldn't imagine that, more than eight years after Kukuczka and nine years after Messner, there could be anyone on Earth, other than my brother and my mom, who would care about the third person to climb all of the 8000ers. Certain legacies remind us that we often underestimate the importance of our families, and I would never have believed that someone could die trying to become that third man.

I flew from Geneva on August 23, 1995. In addition to Jean Troillet, who was attempting his eighth 8000er, there was André Georges, who had climbed with me on the Alpine enchainments, and Pierre Izenda, a horticulturist from Thonon who was André Georges' client. I didn't exactly have good memories of Kangchenjunga; we had already attempted it in 1993 and the expedition had been a disaster. Every day, the porters wanted a little more money, and the approach-march budget had tripled by the time we arrived at base camp. Money problems won't kill you, but the same can't be said of dog bites. A day and a half before we arrived at base camp, a dog broke its chain and sank its fangs into my leg. I finished the march with a limp. We had barely arrived at base camp, when Jean and I came down with a terrible fever; fortunately, the fever went down while we did an acclimatization hike up to 6000 meters, but the next morning I was shivering and my temperature was 102 to 104 degrees Fahrenheit. For five days, I feared that the dog was rabid. We then had to walk down to a village to get our strength back, and when we returned, the snow had made our task more complicated. We had hoped to complete the traverse via the southwest ridge, but we finally opted for the standard route. After twelve hours of climbing, during which we gained 2300 feet with difficulty, we were forced to admit defeat. The 1993 Kangchenjunga expedition consumed two months of my life for no benefit whatsoever. It was the kind of fiasco you have to chalk up to experience, because that word has the advantage of smothering your regrets.

On August 31, 1995, I wrote in my journal, "The expedition is off to a good start, compared to 1993." That showed a keen sense of observation: The porters weren't making any wage demands, the dogs weren't breaking their chains, and the ones that were loose weren't sinking their teeth into my leg. Everything was going well. On September 1, we set up our base camp at the foot of the south side, at 5350 meters. We planned to climb via the standard route, then cut over to the southwest ridge to reach the summit.

Ten days later, on September 10, Benoît Chamoux arrived at base camp. It was the second time in a year that our destinies had intersected; the year before, we had both been on Lhotse, and this year we were meeting again on Kangchenjunga. In the meantime, Benoît Chamoux had added Makalu to his calling card. If my numbers were correct, we were therefore equal again,

with thirteen each. The decisive round would take place on the world's
third-highest peak. I wasn't going to play at "knights of the Himalaya," or
say that competition is for the mediocre, or bare my white doublet to the
enemy's bullets while crying "Honorable Frenchmen, shoot first!" I simply
thought that if Benoît Chamoux wanted to make history as the third person
to climb all fourteen 8000ers, he should have at it! Good for him. Personally,
my priority was the traverse of "Kanch." First we had to climb toward the
southwest col, at the foot of Yalung Kang, then we would continue to the
summit. By following that route, we would avoid any chance of a rivalry
with Benoît Chamoux. It wasn't until September 20, when the Italians told
me that the traverse was unthinkable because of the snow conditions, that I
fell back on the line to the main summit. At around that date, I also learned
that Benoît Chamoux was absolutely determined to beat me. Tents are never
very soundproof, and I didn't even need to eavesdrop to hear a conversation
between Chamoux and some journalists. At times I had the feeling that he
was sending his troops into battle; for example, on Sunday, September 24,
his Sherpas set off for Camp III (7300 meters) when the slopes were unstable. That evening, Benoît came to our camp to tell us that they had felt "a
little craving" for action and had succumbed to it. I listened to him but didn't
leave the tent. The atmosphere between the French expedition and ours was
never cordial; sometimes it was even icy. I did nothing to thaw it.

The competition was palpable; it hung in the air and made it difficult
to breathe. I've always found *Top Gun* pathetic. I detest competition where
victory results from a series of dirty tricks. Besides, since the conquest of the
Matterhorn, the mountains have clearly told us that they don't like competition: They feel that they have placed the bar high enough, without humans
adding a stopwatch. And I hate it when people run a generator day and
night. Kangchenjunga means "the five treasures of the high snow," and it can
surely do without the farting that characterizes our foul-smelling, backfiring
society.

On Saturday, September 16, we did a reconnaissance up to 7400 meters.
We were planning our attack for September 20, but a period of bad weather
delayed us. Twenty inches of snow fell on base camp. Although the weather
improved after September 29, everyone waited in camp until October 2;

it was as if no one wanted to be the hare for a pack of greyhounds. I had decided that we would leave on October 3. I felt strangely calm, surprising even myself. Unlike on previous expeditions, I took a certain pleasure in the waiting. I was sure that we would succeed. I thought that this attitude showed the first benefits of aging: a wisdom that justifies all the torments of being older (loss of flexibility, hardening of the arteries, softening of the cerebrum . . .).

October 3, 2:15 a.m. We left for what was intended to be the summit attempt. The Italians, led by Sergio Martini, had left the day before, but we planned on passing them and certainly felt strong enough to break trail to Camp III. At daybreak, I was at Camp I on the plateau. I didn't see anyone on the ice wall; everyone was still in bed. When I got to 6500 meters I met the Italians as they were leaving their camp. I let them have the honor of breaking trail, because there's nothing like it for warming up quickly. At 6800 meters I relieved them until Camp III, at 7300 meters. The snow was deep, and I was exhausted from plowing that furrow. We had established Camp III two weeks before; when I arrived there, the wind and snow had gotten the better of the tents. It took the skills of an archaeologist to expose the camp; I shoveled the wind-crusted snow for more than an hour. The inside of the tents looked like a mogul field. I had no doubt as to the benefits of acupressure, but if we wanted to get any rest, we would have to move the tents. One by one, people arrived and unloaded their gear. The wind was blowing fairly hard, so everyone took refuge in the tents. There were many people: five Italians, two Frenchmen and their four Sherpas, and we three Swiss climbers, because Pierre Ozenda had turned back at Camp I. That made for a village of ten tents, and everyone there yearned to reach the summit in the next few days. In the coziness of those tents, campaign plans were being laid. The Italians and the French intended to leave the next day at around 2:00 in the morning, whereas we remained faithful to our night owl ways with a 6:00 p.m. start time.

It was 1:00 p.m. by the time we could rest in our tents. We prepared something to drink, but had to force ourselves to swallow the repugnant liquid. André Georges was in rough shape and tried to regain his strength with some bottle oxygen. We left camp at 6:00 p.m. wearing snowshoes, but the wind slabs were so unstable that we soon put on our crampons. After two hours of walking, we were on the big plateau. It was slow going; we needed a speedboat with an outboard motor, and instead we had a sluggish diesel supertanker. André was flat-out exhausted and Jean was spent. I told them that at that pace, it would take us four days to summit! They nodded in agreement. I didn't feel capable of breaking trail all night, and we decided to go back to Camp III. There, no one had moved. The others planned to leave at around 2:00 a.m., and we thought that we would leave later on.

When we came out of the tents at 7:00 a.m., however, no one had left—not Benoît and not Sergio. The entire caravan rolled into action at around 7:00 a.m., and I immediately realized that the night at 7300 meters hadn't done me any good. There were more of us to break through the snow-drifts that blocked our way, but I still wasn't "in the mood." We all climbed together to Camp IV, at around 7800 meters, arriving before noon. There we took a break, which would cause an additional loss of energy. We slid into a hole below a serac band; we just had to stay near the edge of the hole in case the seracs toppled. We planned to stay there for only a few hours and then set off at around 10:00 p.m. André Georges wouldn't be going much higher; three hours after us, he arrived at Camp IV, completely cooked. At around 2:00 p.m., Benoît Chamoux asked us when we planned on leaving. He thought that at 10:00. it would be too cold, so we agreed to leave at 2:00 a.m. It would be easier to break trail as a larger group. We hunkered down into our bivy sacks.

October 5, 1:00 a.m. In the end André had decided that he wanted to come with us, even if it meant sucking on his oxygen bottle to mitigate the effects of altitude. I convinced him to turn back; I've often seen men in a comparable condition to his. They do all right descending under their own power, but if they continue toward the summit, they risk their lives a little more with every passing minute. He understood my point of view, and we separated at the bivouac at 2:00 a.m.

Everyone was there: the French, the Italians, and the Swiss. Two Sherpas from the Chamoux expedition had started out ahead of us. We soon caught up to them, and kept going. Jean and I broke trail, along with Sergio Martini, a veteran Himalayan climber who had summited ten 8000ers. The snow was deep and the going was tough. We soon realized that the French were leaving us to do all the thankless work of breaking trail. So Sergio, Jean, and I agreed that we would step aside and wait for Chamoux and Royer to catch up. It took them an incredibly long time to reach us, but not long at all to then step aside, returning us to the joy of breaking trail. I realized that we were limping across the giant south face of Kangchenjunga and that we were in danger of frostbite. Already, I knew that I was losing feeling in my fingers and toes. So the three of us decided to continue at our own pace, leaving the French to plod along. We were at about 8200 meters, and we still had 1000 feet of elevation to gain. No problem! The sun broke through and offered some sweet relief for our cold feet; we enjoyed it for the short time it lasted. Now we were headed toward the point where the couloir narrows, just below the col. Sergio was waiting lower down, at the start of the ramp that leads directly to the summit. He signaled to me, and I understood immediately: He thought that we were off route and that we would come up against the Red Tower, on the ridge. I gestured that he should follow us, but he didn't understand.

The wind blew, stronger and stronger; without it, Kangchenjunga wouldn't be Kangchenjunga. It was on this peak that a gust of wind nearly blew away a tent and its contents, which happened to be three men (Scott, Boardman, and Bettembourg)! We were nearing the col that separates Yalung Kang from the main summit, and we were frozen to the bone by the wind. The col is a doorway for the cyclone that blasts across the south face. As soon as we crossed the threshold, the north face felt like a haven where we could catch our breath. It was 11:00 a.m. and we were sheltered from the wind. The summit was still fairly far away; we could see the infamous Red Tower. We quickly dropped our plan for a complete traverse, as we would never survive that wind and those cornices.

No one had been there before us; the suspense was riveting. The tower was huge, and if I were to believe what Sergio had said, we wouldn't be able to negotiate it. He spoke from experience: Four years before, he had been defeated by that very tower. I had used the spotting scope to look at the route from base camp many times, and I was sure that we wouldn't have a hard time navigating around the tower. We just had to climb up to it, descend fifteen feet to the right, and then follow a ramp leading into a sloping couloir. When I got into the couloir, I hesitated: Should I continue traversing, or climb up the couloir? I used the radio to ask for some advice, but no useful information came back. However, I learned that a Sherpa on the Chamoux expedition had just taken a fall and that his body lay at the foot of the face. There was nothing we could do for him.

I also learned that Chamoux and Royer were continuing upward.

In the end, we climbed up the couloir and exited onto the ridge. We could make out the summit, but then we still had to skirt leftward around a pyramid and cross the final deep snow slopes before reaching the summit triangle. I found a weakness and, after a few climbing moves, hauled myself up onto the summit—my fourteenth 8000-meter peak. It was 2:45 p.m., and the circle was complete; it was a deep, strong feeling. A chapter was closing—unfortunately for Chamoux.

Jean and I took pictures of each other, then I photographed the traverse, and we started down a couloir. Not far below the Red Tower, we saw the French climbers on their way up; they were about 100 feet over from us. We waved to each other and kept going. They looked slow . . . very slow. It didn't seem possible that someone like Chamoux, whose reputation was based on speed, could be that slow. When you've done K2 in twenty-three hours, you shouldn't be two hours behind on Kangchenjunga.

On the descent to Camp IV, I thought that I should clean off my glasses, because I was having trouble seeing. A little later I had to face reality: The problem wasn't my glasses, it was my frostbitten eyes. Kangchenjunga had lived up to its reputation as a cold mountain; the Italians later assured us that with the windchill, it was minus eighty-one degrees Fahrenheit that day. At 5:30 p.m. we met up with Sergio Martini. He had given up for the day, and he continued down to Camp III with us. When we picked up our gear, I found out that Pierre Royer had just given up on his attempt. A little later, the radio announced that Benoît Chamoux had just turned around, only 160 feet below the summit. At 7:30, André Georges and Pierre Ozenda were waiting for us with some beer, the only drink that I could keep down. For three days, I had been drinking only a mouthful or two of water at a time. For the first time on an 8000er, I felt completely spent. Between Camp

IV and Camp III, I sat down fairly often. I knew why I was so tired: We had spent far too much time on the mountain. Jean felt good and wanted to continue to base camp that night. I decided to stay where I was until morning.

During the night, as if in a dream, I faintly heard Benoît Chamoux's voice. The radio informed us that at base camp there was no news of the two French climbers; they must have spent the night on the ridge. I pitied them. Sergio told me that he wanted to stay where we were for two days to wait for his countrymen and make another attempt on the summit. I continued down. Climbing up the traverse was awful as the radio convulsed with the worry and confusion that had suddenly taken over the mountain: There had been no news from Benoît Chamoux since 8:00 that morning, and Pierre Royer had disappeared. I realized that the French expedition was trying to organize a rescue. The team doctor, Marco, wanted to send Sherpas to Camp IV and even higher, but they refused to go if there were no fixed lines. Personally, I agreed with them. A Sherpa had already sacrificed himself for the glory of his "sahib," and the cost needed to end there. How many Senegalese snipers, and how many Zouaves, died for causes that were not their own—for their French colonizers? I reached base camp at around 2:00 p.m.

I treated my frostbite with baths and injections. While my feet were turning from one garish color to another, I was completely unaware of the hysteria that had taken over Europe. Kangchenjunga had just jumped from the mountaineering press to the mainstream news. The headlines came one after the other, and the story got away from us, its players. "Loretan and Chamoux become legends in Himalayan climbing," "Chamoux in peril in the Himalaya," "Hope fades for Benoît Chamoux and Pierre Royer." At base camp, there was no one to keep up the suspense with bombastic headlines. For us, the suspense had ended when Benoît Chamoux's radio went silent. How could they have survived more than three days at 8300 meters, when their pace was a sign of complete exhaustion rather than fatigue? How could they have survived for three nights without bivy equipment, in punishing temperatures? I've only gotten seriously frostbitten once in my life, and it was that year on Kanch. How could anyone imagine that they had descended via the vertical maze of the north face, when no expedition was on that side to help them? How could anyone think that there was a superman in base camp who could climb to 8300 meters and save Chamoux and Royer?

To all of us in base camp, Benoît Chamoux was dead on the morning of October 6, when he disappeared behind a boulder just below the west col, at 8300 meters. His last words were directed at Jean Troillet, who was guiding him by radio. "Thank you, Jean . . ." Two words of thanks, to close out the weeks of misguided rivalry. In base camp there was a journalist from Radio France who was reporting the events of the Chamoux expedition almost live. When I think back on it, I feel that if millions of listeners hadn't been following his stumbles and then his defeat as they happened, maybe Benoît Chamoux would have listened to his body instead of his pride. Maybe he would have turned back at the right time.

Later, I read that Benoît Chamoux enjoyed repeating Joe Simpson's description of mountaineering as "a fools' game." A fools' game? Maybe. So why give in to it? Because "It showed me the extent of my strength and the depth of my fragility. However much I despise it, I've learned to accept my precarious status as a mortal." That is a quote from Joe Simpson. I dedicate it to all of my companions in this game who aren't here to finish the round.

HAPPY THE MAN WHO, LIKE ERHARD . . .

Now that Erhard had finished his beautiful journey and conquered the fleece, he needed only to return, full of experience and reason, to live among his family for the rest of his days. If *The Odyssey* expresses humankind's two most basic aspirations— the adventure and the return—then Erhard Loretan was, at the end of his vertical odyssey, a man fulfilled. He had conquered a thousand perils and had returned, safe and sound, to the sweetness of the horizontal world. But Erhard wasn't like Walter Bonatti, who after an extraordinary achievement suddenly retired from the world he had occupied for fifteen years. He knew full well that Kangchenjunga was only the temporary end of his quest; he would try again and again to reach the inaccessible stars.

After the fourteenth check mark of his Himalayan adventure, Erhard Loretan wanted to expand his horizons, and sooner or later, Antarctica would become his new playground. First, he planned a solo, self-supported crossing of Antarctica, walking 1700 miles over four months and pulling a 440-pound sled up hill and down dale. In the daily newspaper *La Liberté*, he explained, "It will be long. Psychologically, I'll have to stick with it. The sled will be heavy. Everything is white. There will be technical sections with crevasses that can be miles long and many hundreds of feet deep." This adventure had been tried several times but never completed. It was planned for the fall of 1996, but the "pharaonic" costs of that kind of undertaking—$350,000—proved prohibitive, and it seemed that in 1996 Erhard Loretan would focus on a practice expedition: crossing the Southern Patagonian Ice Field over the course of a few weeks. "I've discovered Antarctica," he said. "I feel good there. There's this idea of solitude without the risks of high altitude; the psychological commitment is serious, but you're not going to 8000 meters."

When it came to mountaineering, Erhard wasn't planning to rest on his laurels. Voytek Kurtyka had kindly invited him on an attempt at the first successful traverse of Nanga Parbat via the Mazeno Ridge. Erhard intended to accept the offer in the near future: "I love ridges and the feeling of height when you're on them. And they're the least risky. There are cornices, but you can see them, whereas on the faces, everything's crashing down on your head." There was still the west face of K2, which Erhard had ventured up twice, in 1989 and 1992. Those two failures only rekindled his desire: "It's not the kind of project that you forget." But for the moment, his priority remained the west face of Makalu, where he and Jean Troillet had been rebuffed at the start of the most difficult section—160 feet of aid climbing at almost 8000 meters. "One hundred and sixty very hard feet, and after that it's OK. The ice chutes aren't easy but they're doable," he speculated. The west face of Makalu, which Andy Fanshawes and Stephen Venables saw as "the last great problem, with its smooth granite wall that starts at over 8000 meters. Many of the best climbers have reached the upper névé. But who can confront that kind of wall at that altitude?"[4]

It was a question that went along with Erhard Loretan's own concern: Now that Jean Troillet had given in to the sirens' song, who would go with him as he defied the mountains, and good sense?

By Way of a Postscript, Erhard *Humanum Est*

"Glory is the brilliant mourning of happiness."

—Madame de Staël

IN APRIL 2005, IN A café in Geneva, I met René Desmaison to talk about his most recent book, *Les Forces de la Montagne*, just published by Hoëbeke. Desmaison, a proponent of the heroic school of mountaineering, which considers hypothermia to be a natural state, referred to Patrick Berhault during our conversation. Berhault had died a year before on a trivial face on the Täschhorn while attempting an alpine traverse, and Desmaison said, "Look at Berhault; we all thought he was immortal."

I thought that Erhard Loretan was immortal, too—ever since I first saw him romping up and down mountains. At the age of about fifteen, I was rock climbing in the Gastlosen on a section that was, I thought, at the very limit of my abilities, and maybe even at the limit of the human race (4+ [5.7]), when I saw a human form running up the entire length of a couloir on Rüdigenspitze. The leader on my climb said, "You know who that is? It's Erhard Loretan!" I was able to put a name to the phantom whose exploits had previously flabbergasted us. It was 1979 and Erhard was twenty. He had already done first ascents of some hellish routes in the Waldeck, rated ED (*Extrêmement Difficile*). That was another world, a world forever inaccessible to the climber I was then (and always will be).

Then, on a hike on the Dent de Broc, I ran into Erhard. He was headed to the summit with a paraglider. That was in 1986, and Erhard asked me to move his car to the Broc swimming pool, because he was planning to take off from the north side. Paragliding was just beginning: fourteen cells that inflated like a sock . . . theoretically subtle, floating at random . . . God knows his own people. You have to imagine what the summit of the Dent de Broc looks like: a two-meter-wide ridge with a 200-meter drop below it. Erhard took off, meaning that he jumped; he thought he was paragliding, but it was actually base jumping. He often jumped from the Dent de Broc, and he disclosed the secret of a successful takeoff: "On the Dent de Broc, the paraglider has to be full of air before you jump." Silence, then, "OK, I've also jumped without it being completely full." Then laughter, like every time he had cheated death.

On a beautiful winter day around the same time, I found myself in the gondola that takes skiers to the summit of Mont Moléson. Erhard was next to me, with only one ski, and it was taller than he was. Our conversation:

"You've switched to a mono-ski?"

"Yeah, I bought it yesterday."

"Hey! Have you seen the tracks in the couloirs on Moléson?"

"Yeah, that was me."

To summarize: On his first day on a mono-ski, Erhard Loretan had shredded the east face of Moléson via couloirs of varying steepness.

After that, I wrote articles for *La Gruyère* and *La Liberté*, and then came the book *Les 8000 rugissants* in 1996. For hours, this man—who was thought of as reserved, who seemed to hide behind his bushy eyebrows—recounted to me his exploits and his adventures, his stunning successes and his crushing disappointments. He told me about the avalanches that had released under his feet; the pitons that had pulled out under his etriers; the approaching lightning strikes; his friends who had died—Vincent on Hochmatt, Jean-Claude on Mont Dolent, Pierre-Alain on Cho Oyu—the companions who start out with you and never come back; the "stiffs" (in his words) lined up along the way to the 8000ers. The wind slabs, the falling seracs, the falling rocks, and the falling humans. On Gasherbrum II in 1983, a cornice gave way beneath his feet; he had one foot on solid ground, in the world of the living, and the cornice fell without him. On Everest in 1986, halfway up the Hornbein Couloir, he deviated from the planned, predicted, and prescribed route, and just then a huge avalanche swept down the couloir. I remember Erhard's laughter when he recalled the avalanche: "What luck! Five minutes before that, we were still in the couloir!" It was the laughter of someone who had sold his soul to the devil and, at the last minute, had withdrawn his ante.

I think back on the vexation of the doctor who operated on Erhard twice at the Inselspital in Berne: two vertebrae broken at the foot of the Mönch, and two other vertebrae after a paragliding accident, for a total of four during the first few months of 1987. This doctor—a disciple of Aesculapius, and someone you would imagine as a thoughtful, level-headed practitioner respected by everyone—told Erhard, "If you keep this up, I'll put you in a cast from head to toe!"

So yes, given how long I had been listening to Erhard laugh about all the great tricks he had played on the mountains and on death, I thought that he was immortal. And he believed it somewhat as well. After the fourteen 8000ers, he told me, "I don't know what it would take for me to die in the mountains." Subtext: The mountains aren't imaginative enough to get me. Aside from a tsunami, they've already tried everything and I'm still here.

But on his fifty-second birthday, April 28, 2011, Erhard Loretan left on a guiding job, one of those "hut trips" he had long since ceased to enjoy. With his client, Xenia Minder, he planned to climb the Grünhorn, an insignificant, innocuous 4000-meter peak in the Bernese Alps. According to an investigation by journalist Charlie Buffet, the author of a biography of Erhard Loretan,[5] aspirant guide Marcel Schenk called for a rescue at 12:14 p.m. He had just noticed an ice ax below the ridge, on the northwest face, with more gear farther down, and he realized that there had recently been an accident. At around 5:00 p.m., the rescuers found Erhard Loretan's lifeless body; he had fallen 650 feet on this gentle, almost harmless 4000er in the Bernese Alps. Xenia Minder, later identified as Erhard's girlfriend, escaped with a broken arm and some scratches. Those used to climbing in the Bernese Oberland called the Grünhorn an easy peak. Those who knew Erhard's tightrope-walking ways didn't understand it. He and Xenia Minder had been roped together, with the rope tight between them; she had slipped, pulling him off. She described the fall to the *Le Temps* newspaper (October 10, 2011): "We had taken our skis off and were roped together, climbing the ridge that led to the summit. My left foot slipped on a thin layer of ice, which caused me to fall down the face. I somersaulted backward, and saw flashes of the rope extending, rock bands, and ice, and I prayed not to suffer too much before I died." There you have it; that is an ordinary death for a mountain guide. Dying in the course of one's duties. The Grünhorn succeeded where fourteen 8000ers had failed. Patrick Edlinger had in fact said to Jean-Michel Asselin, "Maybe all of us will die stupidly." In November 2012, Edlinger, the legendary spiderman, died at the bottom of the staircase in his house in La Palud-sur-Verdon, stupidly.

No, Erhard wasn't immortal. *Erhard humanum est.* Over time, I had forgotten that.

Between the fall of 1996, when *Les 8000 rugissants* was published, and April 28, 2011, the day of Erhard Loretan's death, many things happened. And when I leaf through the book again, I'm surprised by its tone: His enthusiasm amazes me; his lightheartedness throws me off. That's because gravity, so long defied in all its forms, finally invited itself into Erhard Loretan's life.

So yes, after his ascent of Kangchenjunga on October 5, 1995, Erhard did return to the mountains. He even attempted the traverse of the Mazeno Ridge on Nanga Parbat, first with Voytek Kurtyka (1997) and then with Jean Troillet (2000). Those two failures were almost guaranteed; it wasn't until July 2012 that Sandy Allan and Rick Allen's expedition traversed the eight miles of the Mazeno Ridge. Yes, in 2002, he climbed Pumori (7145 meters) via a new route on the north face; that same year, he set off for Jannu (7710 meters) with his then-girlfriend Chantal Oudin and a promising young climber named Ueli Steck, for an extraordinarily bold attempt on its 3000-meter north face. They turned back at 6800 meters. And yes, yes, the next spring, he returned to Jannu with Frédéric Roux, Stephan Siegrist, and Ueli Steck; the technical level of this expedition had rarely been equaled in the Himalaya, and they pushed to 3000 meters before falling back onto the northwest ridge and then retreating. "Being able to climb grade 8a [5.13b] on rock and grade 10 mixed routes isn't enough to succeed on a face like Jannu," admitted Erhard Loretan. He predicted that a "Russian-style" expedition would succeed—one that was heavily equipped and counter to his ideas about mountaineering (*La Liberté*, June 18, 2003). He didn't know how right he was: It was Alexander Odintsov's armada that sealed the first ascent of the north face the following year.

It's no secret that Erhard Loretan's life changed forever on December 24, 2001, when his seven-month-old son, Ewan, died of shaken baby syndrome. The night before, Erhard was at home in Crésuz, alone with his son, who began crying. Erhard went to the baby's cradle, grabbed him, and—he said later—shook him two or three times: a second or two. On February 11, 2003, the Gruyère criminal court sentenced Erhard Loretan to four months in prison with a two-year suspended sentence and a 1000-franc fine for negligent homicide.

For Erhard Loretan, that was his fall. The tragedy would follow him all the way to his obituaries: When he died on the Grünhorn almost ten years later, one evening paper reduced his life to a negligent homicide. The fourteen 8000ers were forgotten; they had made him famous, and after Ewan, they were his misfortune. Two years after Ewan's death, Erhard told me about the journalists who had laid siege to his chalet; the editor who sent him a bouquet of flowers with the usual condolence messages and immediately afterward asked for an exclusive interview; and the journalist who sought to disentangle the threads of a complicated love story and instead jumbled the facts, mixed up two tragedies, and ultimately stirred up pathos to a sickening degree. Fame is a pendulum, and its return swing should be feared. While reflecting on Erhard Loretan's fate, I remembered this quote from Madame de Staël: "Glory is the brilliant mourning of happiness." Celebrity is for better—and for worse, when the one mourning wants nothing more than anonymity.

Erhard had always had a penchant for solitude; he was a semi-sociable hermit. After Christmas 2001, this tendency increased: His home phone went unanswered, his cell phone went straight to voice mail, and the messages were never returned. One day, Erhard listed his paraglider for sale on the Gruyère paragliding club website. The ad included neither a phone number nor an email address, just his name. The message: I'll sell you my paraglider if you can find me. Not the most convincing of sales pitches.

When he was young, Erhard didn't want to provide topos of his routes; to him, they were secret and sacred. He didn't want anyone to add any fixed protection to his "hairball" new routes. Later, in interviews, he would express his ideas about the mountains and his loathing of everyone who tried to defile them. He didn't want safety chains on the Tour des Gastlosen, a hiking route intended for (lowly) walkers, and he gave his blessing to the activists who stripped the Vanil Noir hiking route, cutting the cable that secured the access to the summit. This is what he said in an interview in *La Liberté* (August 28, 2009): "I'll buy dinner for the guy who took down the cable! If you ask me, this is only the beginning of a huge movement: I talk to people in huts, I talk to mountaineers, and I see that there's a movement brewing. A radical movement that intends to rid the mountains of all these artificial things. The purists are going to take action." What's the explanation for this extremism? We have to understand that for Erhard Loretan, the mountains had become his last refuge, so any harm done to them was considered sacrilege. "The mountains always saved him," said Jean Troillet, who was with Erhard on eight 8000ers (*La Liberté*, April 30, 2011). The day after Erhard's death, *La Liberté* editor Louis Ruffieux wrote, "[The mountains] were his essential other place. He sought, and found, happiness in rocks, ice, frost and wind, in an endless quest for the heights—a quest that deprived him of oxygen but brought him closer to the stars, within the swing of an ice ax."

Erhard changed after the fateful Christmas of 2001, of course. He also went through the sorrow of losing his girlfriend in a climbing accident—a woman he loved and who had made him want to believe in the future.

In the last years of his life, Erhard Loretan went to Turkey to lead heli-skiing groups at the end of every winter. It was well-paid work for a guide who had bills to pay, but it went against my environmental beliefs and I thought it ran counter to Erhard's spirit. He was usually so pure and uncompromising, so particular about what he referred to as his ethics. He argued about it and acknowledged some of his contradictions, and in the course of the conversation, he told us about a fall that had almost killed him: "I fell in a couloir. I fell about 650 feet, and while I was falling, I thought, 'It wouldn't bother me at all to die here; I'd be happy for it all to be over.'" He had two years left to live.

What did he think as he tumbled down the northwest face of the Grünhorn in his final acrobatic performance? Was he happy that it was over? For the first time in ten years, did he feel the burden of guilt grow lighter, and finally disappear? Did he shed some of the remorse that haunted him? Did he believe, as Father Nicolas Buttet said in his homily, that Ewan was waiting for him? "Today, I see Ewan greeting you in heaven, eye to eye and smile to smile. A closeness that can finally come to life, forever. I hear him saying, 'Papa, I've always loved you! Come here! Now I'm going to teach you how to climb; together we'll climb onto God's shoulders!'" Maybe. I don't know, and I don't have the gift of communicating with the dead. Unfortunately, in cemeteries I hear only silence.

This much I know: I had the pleasure of writing Erhard Loretan's biography during his lighthearted days. I listened to him for hours, laughing at how he had cheated death at every turn and shuddering along with him at his fears. Seventeen years after this book was first published, I still hold onto the memory of having vicariously lived a heroic life. For that, Erhard, I can never thank you enough.

—*Jean Ammann*

How It All Began

LET'S CHALK IT UP TO altitude and Swiss apricot brandy, both of which are known to kill neurons. In Chapter 1 of this book, Erhard tells the story of his first climb, when he set off for the Dent de Broc via its west ridge. He said, "I've forgotten the details. I know that there were three of us; Michel (Guidotti) went first, I was in the middle, and Fred Sottas was third." When the first edition of this book was published, Carlo Gattoni, one of Erhard's close friends, had some doubts about this description. He remembered that he, not Fred Sottas, had climbed with Michel Guidotti and Erhard Loretan. But because he was modest and didn't want to lay claim to any of Erhard Loretan's fame, he said nothing.

Years later, however, when the second edition of this book was about to be published, Carlo checked with Michel Guidotti, who now lives in Saint-Gervais. Forty-three years later, here is the truth: On his first climb, Erhard Loretan was alone with Michel Guidotti. So that Erhard's mother, Renata, wouldn't be frightened, Michel had pretended that they were going mushroom picking. In reality, they climbed the Dent de Broc via its west ridge. And Carlo Gattoni was on Erhard's second trip, an ascent of the Dent de Broc via its south face, on a route rated *Difficile*, with a few sections of IV+ [5.7] and a bit of aid climbing. While looking through his slides, Carlo found two photos: The first shows Michel Guidotti, the master, the mentor, on the aid-climbing section; the second shows Erhard Loretan on the summit of the Dent de Broc, on a summer day in 1970. This young boy with his red socks and plaid shirt, an eleven-year-old who seems frightened by his own audacity, would become one of the best mountaineers in history. That's how it all began.

A Brief Climbing Glossary

aid climbing: Style of climbing where the climber ascends by putting body weight on protection placed in the rock, using etriers attached to pitons, bolts, nuts, camming devices, etc.

belay: Use the rope to limit the potential fall of a climber.

bolt: Small, permanent anchor fixed in compact rock.

exposed: Describes a no-fall section.

fix: Set fixed lines (ropes) and other equipment.

free climbing: Climbing in which protection is used only for safety and not as a means of ascent.

Friend: A brand of mechanical stopper that can be cammed, placed in a crack, then expanded when in place.

Jumar: A brand of self-locking ascender used to climb fixed lines/ropes.

liaison officer: Government employee who ensures that the expedition complies with the relevant ministry directives, follows the planned route, and adheres to environmental policies.

nail: A piton, in climbing jargon.

nut or **stopper:** A usually wedge-shaped or hexagonal piece of protection that is placed in cracks in the rock.

permit: Access to peaks in Pakistan, India, China, and Nepal requires a permit.

pin: A piton, in climbing jargon.

pitch: Distance that can be climbed in one rope length, usually 165 to 260 feet.

prusik: Self-locking hitch wrapped around the main rope so that it will hold body weight or a fall.

rappel: Rope maneuver that allows a climber to quickly descend a wall while controlling his or her speed.

Sirdar: Manager of the porters; the "steward" of an expedition.

topo: Description of a route, with a list of sections and key difficulties.

wind slab: Wind-blown snow layer that collects on slopes without adhering to the deeper layers of snow.

RATINGS CHART

The French rating system for rock climbs runs between 2 and 8c; the following chart shows the Yosemite Decimal System (YDS) equivalents.

Abbreviation	Difficulty	French Rating	YDS equivalent
F	Facile (easy)	2 to 3	5.4–5.5
AD	Assez Difficile (fairly difficult)	3 to 4–5.6	
D	Difficile (difficult)	4 to 5	5.6–5.8
TD	Très Difficile (very difficult)	5 to 6a	5.8–5.10a
ED	Extrêmement Difficile (extremely difficult)	6	5.10b
EXC	Exceptionnellement Difficile (exceptionally difficult)	6 and above	5.10b and above

Aid Climbing is rated according to the spacing and quality of the possible piton placement:

A1   easy piton placements
A2   difficult piton placements
A3   tricky or limited piton placements
A4   extremely difficult and labor-intensive piton placements
A5   exceptionally dangerous; pitons would not hold a fall

ERHARD LORETAN'S
MOUNTAINEERING
ACHIEVEMENTS

CHRONOLOGY

1980: Expedition to the Andes: First ascent of the south face of Pallcaraju (6247 meters), first ascent of the west ridge of Ranrapalca (6253 meters), first ascent of the south face of Caras (6025 meters), east face of Artesonraju (6025 meters), standard route on Huascaran (6770 meters).

1982: First expedition to the Himalaya-Karakoram. On June 10, Erhard Loretan (EL) became the first Swiss climber to summit Nanga Parbat (8125 meters). Diamir Face.

1983: Expedition to the Karakoram. Along with Marcel Rüedi and Jean-Claude Sonnenwyl, EL became the first person to climb three 8000ers on the same expedition: Gasherbrum II (8035 meters), Hidden Peak/Gasherbrum I (8068 meters), and Broad Peak (8047 meters) in fifteen days, from June 16 to June 30.

1984: Ascent of Manaslu (8163 meters) in the spring (April 30), and first ascent of the east ridge of Annapurna (8091 meters) in the fall (October 24): Four and a half miles above 7300 meters, four days of climbing, descent of the north face via an unknown route with almost no gear or food.

1985: Two attempts on the south face of K2 (8611 meters), then a three-day ascent of the Abruzzi ridge with Pierre Morand and Jean Troillet, July 6. On December 8, first winter ascent of the east face of Dhaulagiri, with Jean Troillet and Pierre-Alain Steiner. Also in 1985, EL climbed *Les Portes du Chaos* on the Eiger (ED+) in one day.

1986: EL climbed thirty-eight peaks in winter, including thirty above 4000 meters, enchained in nineteen days with André Georges. Everest expedition in August. EL and Jean Troillet successfully climbed the north face of Everest via the Hornbein Couloir in forty-three hours roundtrip—the first alpine-style ascent of that route—summiting on August 30. In October, dramatic attempt on Cho Oyu, ending in Pierre-Alain Steiner's death.

1987: On February 14, EL was caught in a snow slide while attempting to enchain thirteen north faces in the Bernese Oberland with André Georges. He fractured two vertebra and was nearly paralyzed.

1988: On July 13, EL and Voytek Kurtyka summited Trango Tower (6257 meters) after fourteen days of climbing on the east face (ED+).

1989: In January, EL enchained thirteen north faces in the Bernese Oberland with André Georges. Failed attempt on the west face of K2 with Voytek Kurtyka.

1990: On May 23, ascent of Denali (6194 meters). First ascent of the southwest face of Cho Oyu (8201 meters) on September 21, with Jean Troillet and Voytek Kurtyka. Twenty-three hours of climbing, bivouac at 8150 meters without specialized gear. Twelve days later, on October 3, new route on the south face of Shishapangma (8046 meters), also with Jean Troillet and Voytek Kurtyka.

1991: Attempt on the west face of Makalu (8463 meters). At the foot of the difficulties, EL and Jean Troillet abandoned the climb after a crampon broke. Ascent of the west pillar in thirty-three hours; summit reached on October 2.

1992: Return to K2: Another failed attempt on the west face.

1993: Attempt on Kangchenjunga (8568 meters), the world's third-highest peak. Health problems and bad weather led to failure.

1994: Attempt on the traverse from Lhotse (8516 meters) to Lhotse Shar (8386 meters), never tried before. On the summit of Lhotse on October 1,

Jean Troillet and EL abandoned their traverse attempt. At midnight on December 1, 1994, EL summited Mount Epperly (4780 meters) in Antarctica: First ascent, solo, of this peak, via an 8900-foot face.

1995: On October 5, EL summited Kangchenjunga (8586 meters), becoming the third person to climb all fourteen of the world's 8000-meter peaks. Jean Troillet reached the summit with him. On December 29, first ascent of a nameless peak in Antarctica (4600 meters). Maybe Mount Loretan?

THE FOURTEEN 8000ERS

Everest (8846 meters) First ascent: May 29, 1953, Edmund Hillary (New Zealand) and Tenzing Norgay (India). Erhard Loretan: August 30, 1986, with Jean Troillet (Switzerland), via the Hornbein Couloir on the north face; first alpine-style ascent.

K2 (8611 meters) First ascent: July 31, 1954, Achille Compagnoni and Lino Lacedelli (Italy). Erhard Loretan: July 6, 1985, with Pierre Morand, Jean Troillet (Switzerland), and Eric Escoffier (France), via the Abruzzi Spur (standard route).

Kangchenjunga (8586 meters) First ascent: May 25–26, 1955, George Band, Joe Brown, Tony Streather (Great Britain), and Norman Hardie (New Zealand). Erhard Loretan: October 5, 1995, with Jean Troillet (Switzerland), via the southwest face (standard route).

Lhotse (8516 meters) First ascent: May 8, 1956, Fritz Luchsinger and Ernst Reiss (Switzerland). Erhard Loretan: October 1, 1994, with Jean Troillet (Switzerland), via the west face (standard route).

Makalu (8463 meters) First ascent: May 15–17, 1955, Jean Couzy with Lionel Terray, Jean Franco, Guido Magnone, Jean Bouvier, Serge Coupé, Pierre Leroux, André Vialatte (France), and Gyalzen Sherpa Norbu (Nepal). Erhard Loretan: October 2, 1991, with Jean Troillet (Switzerland), via the west pillar.

Cho Oyu (8201 meters) First ascent: October 19, 1954, Herbert Tichy, Sepp Jöchler (Austria), and Pasang Dawa Lama (Nepal). Erhard Loretan: September 21, 1990, with Jean Troillet (Switzerland) and Voytek Kurtyka (Poland); first ascent of the southwest face.

Dhaulagiri (8167 meters) First ascent: May 23, 1960, Kurt Diemberger (Austria), Peter Diener (Germany), Ernst Forrer, Albin Schelbert, Michel Vaucher, Hugo Weber (Switzerland), Nawang Dorje, and Nyma Dorje (Nepal). Erhard Loretan: December 8, 1985, with Pierre-Alain Steiner and Jean Troillet (Switzerland); first winter ascent of the east face.

Manaslu (8163 meters) First ascent: May 11, 1956, Toshio Imanishi, Kiichiro Kato, Minoru Higeta (Japan), and Gyalzen Norbu (Nepal). Erhard Loretan: April 30, 1984, with Marcel Rüedi (Switzerland), via the northwest ridge (standard route).

Nanga Parbat (8125 meters) First ascent: July 3, 1953, Hermann Buhl (Austria). Erhard Loretan: June 10, 1982, with Norbert Joos (Switzerland), via the Diamir Face (standard route).

Annapurna (8091 meters) First ascent: June 3, 1950, Maurice Herzog and Louis Lachenal (France). Erhard Loretan: October 24, 1984, with Norbert Joos (Switzerland); first ascent of the east ridge, first traverse of Annapurna.

Hidden Peak, or Gasherbrum I (8068 meters) First ascent: July 14, 1958, Andrew Kauffmann and Pete Schoening (USA). Erhard Loretan: June 23, 1983, with Marcel Rüedi (Switzerland), variant via the north buttress.

Broad Peak (8047 meters) First ascent: June 9, 1957, Kurt Diemberger, Hermann Buhl, Markus Schmuck, and Fritz Wintersteller (Austria). Erhard Loretan: June 30, 1983, with Marcel Rüedi (Switzerland), via the west ridge (standard route).

Shishapangma (8046 meters) First ascent: May 2, 1964, ten members of a Sino-Tibetan expedition. Erhard Loretan: October 3, 1990, with Jean Troillet (Switzerland) and Voytek Kurtyka (Poland); new route on the south face (middle summit). Main summit: April 29, 1995.

Gasherbrum II (8035 meters) First ascent: July 7, 1956, Sepp Larch, Fritz Moravec, and Hans Willenpart (Austria). Erhard Loretan: June 16, 1983, with Marcel Rüedi and Jean-Claude Sonnenwyl (Switzerland), via the west ridge (standard route).

THIRTEEN NORTH FACES IN THIRTEEN DAYS: 36,610 FEET OF CLIMBING

Face	Height	Day Climbed	Date Climbed	Summary
Gross Fiescherhorn	4048 meters	Saturday	1/14/89	3900-foot face in 4 hours
Jungfrau	4158 meters	Sunday	1/15/89	1600-foot face in 5½ hours
Mönch	4099 meters	Monday	1/16/89	3100-foot face in 4½ hours
Eiger	3970 meters	Wednesday	1/18/89	5900-foot face in 10 hours
Ebnefluh	3962 meters	Thursday	1/19/89	2300-foot face in 2½ hours
Gletscherhorn	3983 meters	Friday	1/20/89	3600-foot face in 4½ hours
Breithorn	3785 meters	Saturday	1/21/89	2300-foot face in 2½ hours
Grosshorn	3754 meters	Saturday	1/21/89	3600-foot face in 4 hours
Morgenhorn	3627 meters	Monday	1/23/89	3900-foot face in 5½ hours
Blüemlisalphorn	3663 meters	Tuesday	1/24/89	1500-foot face in 2 hours
Weisse Frau	3650 meters	Tuesday	1/24/89	1150-foot face in 1 hour
Fründenhorn	3368 meters	Tuesday	1/24/89	1300-foot face in 2½ hours
Doldenhorn	3643 meters	Thursday	1/26/89	2300-foot face in 2 hours

NOTES

NOTES TO CHAPTER 7
1. David Le Breton, *Passions du risque* (Paris: Métailié, 1991).
2. *Les émotions* (Paris: Ed. Time-Life, 1995).
3. *Les plus belles ascensions dans le monde* (Paris: Arthaud, 1995).

NOTES TO CHAPTER 14
4. Andy Fanshawes and Stephen Venables, *L'Himalaya en style alpin* (Paris: Arthaud, 1996).

NOTES TO CHAPTER 15
5. Charlie Buffet, *Erhard Loretan: Une vie suspendue* (Chamonix: Guérin, 2013).

ABOUT THE COLLABORATION

Between January 1993 and April 1996, Jean and Erhard met regularly. These meetings resulted in dozens of hours of recorded conversations. Twenty or so of Erhard's personal journals, five binders of press articles, and a manuscript that Erhard wrote in Kangchenjunga base camp were added to this collection of raw material.

This vast amount of documentation provided an outline of Erhard Loretan's life, including his memories, emotions, and disappointments. From there, Jean Ammann brought Erhard's character to the page.

At the end of each chapter, Jean Ammann added a section that diverges from the chronological order of the account, in order to shed light on aspects of the story that are not otherwise directly addressed.

In the words of Jean Ammann, "To summarize and to conclude, let's say that Erhard and I divided the work between us—he climbed all of the 8000ers in the book, and I am responsible for all of the spelling and grammar mistakes and the awkward phrasings. That seems fair to me."

ABOUT THE AUTHORS

Erhard Loretan was born on April 28, 1959, and lived in Crésuz, Switzerland. By profession he was a cabinetmaker and mountain guide, but his greatest fame came as the third man to climb the fourteen 8000-meter peaks. He died on April 28, 2011, on the Grünhorn (4043 meters), in the Bernese Alps.

Jean Ammann was born in 1963 and is a journalist for *La Liberté*. He covered all of Erhard Loretan's adventures.

THE LEGENDS AND LORE SERIES honors the lives and adventures of mountaineers and is made possible in part through the generosity of donors. Mountaineers Books, a nonprofit publisher, further contributes to this investment through book sales from more than 600 titles on outdoor recreation, sustainable lifestyle, and conservation.

We would like to thank the following for their charitable support of Legends and Lore:

FOUNDERS CIRCLE
- Anonymous
- Tina Bullitt
- Tom and Kathy Hornbein
- Dianne Roberts and Jim Whittaker
- William Sumner
- Doug and Maggie Walker

SUPPORTERS
- Byron Capps
- Roger Johnson
- Joshua Randow
- Jolene Unsoeld

With special appreciation to Tom Hornbein, who donates to the series all royalties earned through the sale of his book, Everest: The West Ridge.

You can help us preserve and promote mountaineering literature by making a donation to the Legends and Lore series. For more information, benefits of sponsorship, or how you can support future work, please contact us at mbooks@mountaineersbooks.org or visit us online at www.mountaineersbooks.org.

**MOUNTAINEERS
BOOKS**

MOUNTAINEERS BOOKS is a leading publisher of mountaineering literature and guides—including our flagship title, *Mountaineering: The Freedom of the Hills*—as well as adventure narratives, natural history, and general outdoor recreation. Through our two imprints, Skipstone and Braided River, we also publish titles on sustainability and conservation. We are committed to supporting the environmental and educational goals of our organization by providing expert information on human-powered adventure, sustainable practices at home and on the trail, and preservation of wilderness.

The Mountaineers, founded in 1906, is a 501(c)(3) nonprofit outdoor recreation and conservation organization whose mission is to enrich lives and communities by helping people "explore, conserve, learn about, and enjoy the lands and waters of the Pacific Northwest and beyond." One of the largest such organizations in the United States, it sponsors classes and year-round outdoor activities throughout the Pacific Northwest, including climbing, hiking, backcountry skiing, snowshoeing, camping, kayaking, sailing, and more. The Mountaineers also supports its mission through its publishing division, Mountaineers Books, and promotes environmental education and citizen engagement. For more information, visit The Mountaineers Program Center, 7700 Sand Point Way NE, Seattle, WA 98115-3996; phone 206-521-6001; www.mountaineers.org; or email info@mountaineers.org.

Our publications are made possible through the generosity of donors and through sales of more than 600 titles on outdoor recreation, sustainable lifestyle, and conservation. To donate, purchase books, or learn more, visit us online:

MOUNTAINEERS BOOKS
1001 SW Klickitat Way, Suite 201 • Seattle, WA 98134
800-553-4453 • mbooks@mountaineersbooks.org • www.mountaineersbooks.org

LEGENDS AND LORE SERIES

The Legends and Lore series was created by Mountaineers Books in order to ensure that mountain literature will continue to be widely available to readers everywhere. From mountaineering classics to biographies of well-known climbers, and from renowned high-alpine adventures to lesser-known accomplishments, the series strives to bring mountaineering knowledge, history, and events to modern audiences in print and digital form.

Distinctive stories in the Legends and Lore series include:

Conquistadors of the Useless
From the Alps to Annapurna
by Lionel Terray
"The finest mountaineering narrative ever written."
–David Roberts

Freedom Climbers
The Golden Age of Polish Climbing
by Bernadette McDonald
"A brilliantly crafted tale of mountain and political adventure that reveals a golden era of Himalayan climbing that was as glorious as it was tragic."
–Sir Chris Bonington

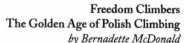

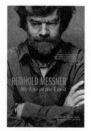

Reinhold Messner: My Life at the Limit
Interviewed by Thomas Hüetlin
A more thoughtful and conversational Messner emerges in this interview-format memoir of the world's premier mountaineer.

The Mountain of My Fear and
Deborah: A Wilderness Narrative
Two Mountaineering Classics
by David Roberts
"David Roberts has already written one excellent book, *The Mountain of My Fear*; *Deborah*, in my opinion, is even finer." –W.H. Auden

Sherpa
The Memoir of Ang Tharkay
by Ang Tharkay with Basil P. Norton
Never before published in English, *Sherpa* is a curious blend of innocence and insight, of adventure and hardship, offering a priceless glimpse into the lives of the local guides and porters of the Himalaya and Karakoram.

MOUNTAINEERS
BOOKS